D1038283

Hear

Margaret Roberts

speak on

		p.m.	
Thursday	11th Oct.	8.0	at Crayford County Girls' Secondary School, Iron Mill Lane.
Friday	12th Oct.	8.0	at St. Alban's Hall, Dartford.
Monday	15th Oct.	8.0	at Bedonwell Hill Junior County Primary School.
Tuesday	16th Oct.	8.0	at St. Paulinus Hall, Crayford.
Wednesday	17th Oct.	8.0	at St. Augustine's Infants County Primary School, Belvedere.
Thursday	18th Oct.	8.0	at North Heath County Secondary School, Brook Street, Erith.
Friday	19th Oct.	8.0	at Barnehurst Preparatory School, Barnehurst Road.
Monday	22nd Oct	7.45	at Electricity Showrooms, Erith.
Monday	22nd Oct.	8.0	at Crayford Town Hall.
Tuesday	23rd Oct.	8.0	at Maypole Junior and Infants School, Dartford.
Wednesday (Eve of Poll)	24th Oct.	7.45	at Belvedere Public Hall.
	24th Oct.	8.0	at St Paulinus Hall, Crayford.
	24th Oct.	8.15	at Dartford Girls' County Grammar School, Shepherds Lane.

Vote for MARGARET ROBERTS
THE CONSERVATIVE CANDIDATE

MAGGIE

The First Lady

MAGGIE

The First Lady

BRENDA
MADDOX

Hodder & Stoughton

First published in Great Britain in 2003
by Hodder and Stoughton
A division of Hodder Headline

A Hodder & Stoughton hardback

1 3 5 7 9 10 8 6 4 2

A CIP catalogue record for this title
is available from the British Library

ISBN 0 340 82545 6

Set in Monotype Sabon
Typeset by Rowland Phototypesetting Ltd,
Bury St Edmunds, Suffolk

Printed and bound in Great Britain by
Clays Ltd, St Ives plc

Hodder and Stoughton
A division of Hodder Headline
338 Euston Road
London NW1 3BH

For John

'I am not by nature either introspective or retrospective.'

Margaret Thatcher, *The Path to Power* (1995)

Contents

Acknowledgements

Many people helped me with this book. I am particularly indebted to Michael and Diana Honeybone for sharing their matchless knowledge of Grantham and for walking me over the terrain. Hilary Hillier of the University of Nottingham helped with her rare expertise on the accents of the East Midlands.

The political biographer John Campbell, with one half of his comprehensive political biography of Margaret Thatcher completed and the second half under way, generously helped with private conversations, insights and information. Mark Hollingsworth, biographer of Mark Thatcher and Lord Tim Bell, was also generous with his store of information on the Thatcher finances.

Brook Lapping, in spite of the pressure of preparing four television programmes on *Maggie*, gave much assistance – not only with transcripts of extensive interviews but with background research and advice. My special thanks go to Anne Lapping, Sarah Gowers, Jane Bonham Carter, Anna Ewart-James, Ben Watt and Victoria Stable.

I am grateful to my publishers, Hodder and Stoughton, and especially to Rupert Lancaster, Juliet Brightmore, Karen Geary and Hugo Wilkinson, for their patience and energy in working against a shifting television deadline, and to Celia Levett for copy-editing. My admirable literary agents at A. P. Watt and Co. have seen me through many books, from the first to this latest; my thanks go once more to Caradoc King, also to Martha Lishawa and Rinku Pattni.

As always, my family have been patient and encouraging. Bronwen and Bruno Maddox provided acute comments on subject and style. My husband John, ever a source of wisdom and love, turned out to have useful undergraduate recollections of Margaret Roberts in the Oxford chemistry laboratory.

I would like to thank HarperCollins for permission to quote from Margaret Thatcher's *The Path to Power* and *The Downing Street Years*, Weidenfeld and Nicolson for permission to quote from Alan Clark's *Diaries*, and *Private Eye*.

The following have been most helpful with books, correspondence, interviews and hospitality: Bruce Arnold, Howard Bailes, Sir Edward du Cann, Georgina Ferry, Dr Garret FitzGerald, Professor Warwick Gould, Pauline Cowan Harrison, Hazel Bishop Hofman, Mark Hollingsworth, Anthony Howard, Dick Leonard, Andrew Lownie, Lord Marlesford, Pamela Mason, Bernard McGinley, David McKittrick, His Excellency Daithi O'Ceallaigh and Mrs O'Ceallaigh, Jane Peel, Anthony Sampson, Tom Stacey, June Wood, Sir Peregrine Worsthorne and Gila Reinstein of the Yale University Office of Public Affairs.

Picture acknowledgements

Advertising Archives/Topham Picturepoint/photo Selwyn Tait: 21. Camera Press: 1, 8, 15, 26, 27, 42. Srdja Djukanovic: 4, 24, 35, 36. Stanley Franklin/NI Syndication: 29. Local Studies Collection, Grantham Library, Lincolnshire County Council, Education and Cultural Services Directorate: 2, 5. Courtesy Michael Honeybone: 2. Hulton Archive/Getty Images: 7, 11, 14, 19, 22. Peter Jordan/Network Photographers: 32, 37. Barry Lewis/Network Photographers: 44. Mirrorpix: 28. News Group Newspapers Ltd/NI Syndication: 43. PA Photos: 20, 25, 30, 31, 34. Popperfoto: 18, 23. Private Collections: 3, 17. Rex Features: 33, 38, 39, 40, 41. Topham Picturepoint: 9, 13. Courtesy Nellie Towers: 6, 12. UPI: 16. Waldegrave Films, Twickenham: 10.

Author's Note

This book is based largely on interviews undertaken for the Brook Lapping television series, *Maggie: The First Lady*.

The following list names Brook Lapping interviews that have been used in the preparation of this book. Quotations unsupported by a note or textual reference come from this source. Those from my own interviews and other sources are indicated by a numbered endnote.

Sir Antony Acland
Lord (Robert) Armstrong
John Banks
Lord (Tim) Bell
Revd Bowlby
Terry Bradley
Lord (Edwin) Bramall
President George Bush Snr
Lord (Robin) Butler
Lord (Peter) Carrington
Kenneth Clarke MP
Cynthia Crawford
Eric Deakins
Lord (William) Deedes
Jacques Delors
Margaret Denis King
Sir Edward du Cann
Tessa Gaisman
John Hedger
Madeline Hellaby

Lord (Geoffrey) Howe
Kim Howells MP
Lord (Douglas) Hurd
Sir Bernard Ingham
Richard Ingrams
Rachel Kinchin-Smith
Neil Kinnock
Lord (Nigel) Lawson
Sir Henry Leach
Paddi Lilley
Patricia Nicholson Madge
Colinne Martyn
Pamela Mason
Richard Miles
Gerald Necklen
Mary Necklen
Denis Oliver
Lord (Cecil) Parkinson
Matthew Parris
Sir Chris Patten

Amanda Ponsonby

Lord (Charles) Powell

Lord (James) Prior

Lord (William) Rees-Mogg

Mary Robinson

Terry Shelbourne

Lady Anne Shelton

Stephen Sherbourne

Dennis Signy

Hilary Skaar

Sir Dudley Smith

Lord Norman Tebbit

John Tiplady

Ken Tisdell

Nellie Towers

Christine Upton

Lord (Bernard) Weatherill

Alan Wells

John Whittingdale MP

Margaret Goodrich Wickstead

Baroness Shirley Williams

Lord (David) Wolfson

June Wood

Petronella Wyatt

Introduction

At the start of 2002 when I was finishing a biography of the DNA
scientist Rosalind Franklin, the opportunity presented itself of
writing a book to accompany the television series *Maggie* being
made for ITV by Brook Lapping. The intention was to look
at the woman rather than the politician. Indeed, 'The Personal
Story of a Public Life' was the original subtitle of the series. I
undertook the project from admiration, curiosity and nostalgia.

My admiration is for Brook Lapping's elegant television
documentaries. Their cool, intelligent approach to recent history
is combined with the ability to persuade major figures and
unexpected minor players to think back aloud before the camera.
For *Maggie: The First Lady*, transmitted in March 2003, the
range of those interviewed was remarkable. It stretched from
former US Presidents George Bush Snr and European Council
President Jacques Delors to Margaret Thatcher's leading cabinet
ministers; from her fashion adviser and her driver to close
personal friends from all stages of her life.

My book, like the series, concentrates on the personal turning
points, rather than the political events, of Thatcher's life. My
principal source has been the lengthy interviews conducted by
Brook Lapping, full of far more material than could be squeezed
on to the small screen. A list of those whose interviews I drew
appears on pp. xiii–iv.

Curiosity is my response to the enigma of Margaret Roberts
Thatcher and the great changes wrought since 1979 in Britain,
my adopted country. How did she become Britain's first woman
prime minister when her contemporaries picked Shirley Williams
or Barbara Castle as far more likely? Did she achieve Lady

Macbeth's wish – 'unsex me' – or did she deploy the so-called feminine wiles when called upon to do a man's job, such as sending men to their deaths? Did she really end socialism and the Cold War? And if she changed Britain so radically, why has it not achieved anything like constitutional reform or even an elected second chamber?

The recovered memories are of rich years of my life. The governments of Heath, Wilson, Callaghan and Thatcher co-incided with the raising of my young family in Roehampton in south-west London. Thinking back to Edward Heath's three-day week in 1974, with its sudden black-outs to save electricity, I see our mischievous four-year-old son racing through the house, flipping off light switches and shouting, 'Power cut!' Retracing the steps leading to the creation of British Telecom in 1982 is equally evocative. I recall how, as an American infuriated by the crossed lines and dead silences of an antiquated nationalised telephone service, I used to argue with the General Post Office, then in charge. The GPO haughtily assured me that there was no foreseeable possibility of ever getting an itemised, let alone a monthly, telephone bill. And why would anyone want one? I also remember the Winter of Discontent, with its constant strikes and uncollected rubbish. Realising then (well before I got a British passport) that Britain had become so much my home that I would never leave, I confessed to a fellow American, 'I don't see how anybody can say Britain is not run by the trade unions.'

Part of the good fortune I had in those years was to work on *The Economist* – the oh-so-highly regarded weekly newspaper (as it insists on calling itself). To be on its staff guaranteed not only sharp and versatile colleagues but also an entrée to anyone in public life as long as you did not expect them to remember your name. *The Economist* still carries no bylines. 'You're the American lady, aren't you?' Jim Prior, then Secretary of State for Northern Ireland, said to me. The wide-ranging brief and small staff of the paper allowed anybody to write about anything. I ventured into subjects as disparate as telecommunications and Ireland. When Mrs Thatcher came to power, I had the satisfaction of delivering my anonymous pronouncements on her efforts in both these fields.

When I rejoined *The Economist* after a period away, I shared an office with Anne Lapping. The reasoning behind this placement was that as I was inheriting from her the subject of local government, she would pass her knowledge on to me. The fact that we might also use our shared space at 25 St James's Street, SW1, to talk about our children and what we would cook for dinner was immaterial.

In March 1979, just before the general election that she was expected to win, Margaret Thatcher, Leader of the Opposition, came to lunch at *The Economist*. Such occasions, as on many newspapers, are competitive performances in which the staff vie with each other to ask the sharpest question. For my part, still struggling to master the difference between the Association of County Councils and the Association of Metropolitan Authorities, I sat mute while the about-to-become prime minister sounded off. 'Rhodesia is the only democracy I've got in Africa' was the magisterial phrase that has stuck in my mind.

With time running out, I knew I had to say something. Stutteringly I interjected: 'Are you really going to abolish the rates?' The blue radar swung towards me and fixed me in its beam. She began to recite the inequities of the existing rating system. Then, remembering where she was, she modestly interposed: 'But I needn't tell *you* about the Rate Support Grant!'

Mercifully the lunch soon ended. Back in our office, the telephone rang. It was Norman St John Stevas, a contributor to *The Economist* as well as a Conservative MP and shadow minister for education and the arts. 'How did she do?' he enquired about the lady he had not yet christened 'The Leaderene'. Anne Lapping gave the verdict: 'Fine, but shoes and handbag too new. They looked as if she was trying too hard.'

Margaret Thatcher tried hard, perhaps too hard, over the length of her career, yet she succeeded in becoming what many believe has been the most influential prime minister of the second half of the twentieth century. In the end she stayed too long and her enemies toppled her. Even they, however, admired her farewell speech as prime minister when she interrupted herself to declare, 'I am *enjoying* this.'

To my surprise, I have enjoyed writing her life through the perspective offered by Brook Lapping: the personal woman under the public veneer. I have enjoyed also answering the inevitable question: what relation does Margaret Thatcher have to the other people about whom you've written biographies?

Plenty. It should come as no surprise that the lives of people who live in the same country in the same century are seldom totally unrelated. D. H. Lawrence was born in the East Midlands, twenty miles west of Grantham, Mrs Thatcher's birthplace. He too enjoyed the beach holidays at Skegness, and Methodist hymns, and, in his own way, came to terms with the Midlands accent and dialect. When writing a life of W. B. Yeats, I was well aware that he was not only a poet but a Senator in the Irish Free State. Like Thatcher he tried to halt the antagonism between Ireland's North and South and he too lost friends to the Irish Republican Army's armed struggle, which can seem a terrible beauty to those engaged in it.

Rosalind Franklin, subject of my most recent biography, was born just five years earlier than Margaret Roberts and chose to study chemistry at a time when, even more than now, science was an unlikely field for young women to enter. As undergraduates, both were isolated by long hours in the laboratory from much of the social scene at their respective universities, Cambridge and Oxford. Both looked to the eminent woman scientist Dorothy Hodgkin for guidance. Both too found their first jobs in applying their science to industrial processes.

That said, Margaret Roberts Thatcher may resemble most of all Nora Barnacle Joyce, the subject of my first full-length biography. Denis Thatcher may have little in common with James Joyce – apart from recognising the force of his wife's personality, freeing her from drudgery, giving her his name, introducing her to a sophisticated and less reproving world, and providing steadfast love, loyalty and finance throughout their decades together.

For my part, I would not be unhappy if what follows were thought of as a 'wife of' book. It is the personal story of a public figure and a marriage is at the heart of it.

Brenda Maddox
February 2003

I

'Methodist means method'[1]
(1925–1939)

Iron ladies are not born but made. The four-year-old smiling coquettishly at the photographer in 1929 gives no hint of the prime minister to come. On second glance, the future is all there, pre-programmed as if by some genetic Saatchi and Saatchi. The big hair, artfully arranged at some cost to the sitter's patience; the knowing, slanted smile; the shrewd eyes; the assertive upright posture. Little Margaret Roberts was photogenic and possessed what the camera loves: symmetrical features, good cheekbones, a large head and an instinct for the photo opportunity. Political careers can be made with less, but these assets help – especially a woman of the mid-twentieth century.

The little girl is prettier and sharper than her eight-year-old sister Muriel, who sits beside her. She knows that heads will turn to look at her and that, in her white frock bordered with lace triangles, she is wearing the nicer dress.

Muriel was always there, not least on the long walk to and from school in their early years in Grantham, a market town in the East Midlands county of Lincolnshire. Four times a day the elder led the younger over more than a mile between their home in the northern part of the town and their primary school on Huntingtower Road, near the centre and the railway station. There was a primary school much nearer her home, but it was a Church of England institution. As staunch Methodists, Alfred and Beatrice Roberts stayed well clear of the bells and smells of

I

Anglicanism. They sent their girls to the Huntingtower Road School, a council school, which was new, with modern buildings and a reputation for good teachers. Its facilities, however, did not include a lunch room, and its pupils had to go home at midday. Trudging her four miles a day, little Margaret Roberts learned early that principles must be paid for.

Home was a three-storey brick house and corner shop at 1 North Parade in a Grantham district called Little Gonerby. Alfred Roberts was a grocer – no, better than that: 'a purveyor of quality provisions', with three shop assistants and a sub-post office under his roof. On the birth certificate for his second daughter, born on 13 October 1925, he described himself as 'Grocer (Master)'. Two years earlier he had acquired a second shop across the road from the Huntingtower school. (Sometimes in her schooldays Margaret may occasionally have eaten her lunch there.) Two shops? No small boast for a tradesman.

To the heavy lorries rumbling along the A1, Grantham was simply a conduit between London and Scotland, as it was for the main line of the Great Northern Railway which ran through the town, with a branch to Nottingham, twenty miles to the west. Industry lined the tracks: gasworks, leather works, brickworks, boiler works, ironworks, and on the banks of the Grantham Canal a workhouse. The big manufacturers were in the southern part of the town, where Ruston and Hornsby made locomotives and steam engines, Aveling-Barford steamrollers and tractors. London was 110 miles away but might have been a thousand.

Glimpses of a grander world shone through the 'Help Wanted' columns in the national newspapers. (The Robertses took the *Daily Telegraph*.) Under 'Domestic Situations Required', myriad specialities were sought and offered: 'Between-maids', 'Scullery maids', 'Laundrymaids', 'Cook-housekeepers', 'Chauffeurs' and 'Menservants'. Some job-seekers prefaced their advertisements with boasts such as 'Lady Emmott highly recommends', 'Mrs Harold Balfour can thoroughly recommend excellent Head Housemaid'.[2]

Grantham, like many English towns of the day, was a world of its own, as stratified as a sedimentary rock face. While there were no very rich families, no 'top hat' street of wealthy homes, each family knew its station. The working class laboured with black and greasy hands. As tradespeople, the Robertses were well above them, in the lower middle class. Higher were the professionals – doctors, clergymen, teachers and salaried white-collar workers, who lived in large houses with libraries and gardens. No one could say – or seemed even to want to say – that theirs was a classless society.

There was a local Big House, three miles to the north-east in the Lincolnshire countryside. The architectural historian Nikolaus Pevsner called Belton House 'perhaps the most satisfying' among the later-seventeenth-century houses in England. Set in splendid isolation in a beautiful park dotted with grazing deer and ancient oaks, Belton House was the seat of the Brownlow family and a succession of Lords Brownlow with a strong sense of *noblesse oblige*.

'Lord Brownlow was very kind to people in those days,' one of Margaret Roberts's contemporaries recalls. Nellie Towers remained grateful for a party Lord Brownlow gave for the schoolchildren. 'In the 1930s, there was quite a lot of unemployment, people were hard up. We went for buns and lemonade.' Better still, 'Twice a year, men that were out of work could go and collect wood from trees that had been taken down for them. They could go for a whole week and do that.'

Growing up during the Great Depression, Margaret Roberts was well aware of mass unemployment. On her way to school, she surveyed the dole queues with a strong sense of 'them' and 'us'. What impressed her was how neatly turned out the indigent children always seemed to be. She knew (or heard at home) the reason why. 'Their parents were determined', she explains in her memoirs, 'to make the sacrifices necessary for them.' The evidence of her own eyes told her that self-reliance and independence could pull people through and that, rich or poor, parents shared common values. None would neglect their children.

Some of the children from the lower social orders, however, did not feel much sympathy with the Robertses. 'They were better off,' says Mary Robinson, one of Margaret's contemporaries. 'We lived in rented accommodation. My dad had the dole, and my mother had to go out to work at times, and it was very, very hard. When my dad died, there was only the ten-shilling widow's pension, which was not enough. I had to have police shoes. You went to the police station and you filled in a form, and you went to a posh shop and you got a pair of boots – shoes – and you took them up to the police and they were nicked in the tongue, and the girls at school knew that you'd had police shoes.'

Terry Bradley, a schoolboy at the time, saw the Robertses as 'business people'. 'We were working people. We had a job to struggle to live . . . And I used to think that she considered [us] below her. They had a good living, and we didn't. Simple as that. Our attitude to all business people then was – you had to keep your place. Grantham was then run by what we used to call "the forty thieves".'

(A sardonic view of the cut-throat world of Grantham small business in the 1930s can be found in Oliver Anderson's novel *Rotten Borough*. Published in 1937, it was reissued in 1974 with the subtitle, 'The Real Story of Mrs Thatcher's Grantham'.)

Both of Margaret's parents, Alfred and Beatrice Roberts, had been born under Queen Victoria in modest circumstances and made their way up by their own efforts. Alfred's father, Benjamin, was a shoemaker in Ringstead, near Oundle in Northamptonshire, the rural county to the south. The family had come from Wales generations earlier. Beatrice's father, Daniel Stephenson, was a railway worker who finished his career as a cloakroom attendant at the Grantham railway station. Her mother, Phoebe Cust, worked as a factory machinist before marriage.

The moment around 1904 when Alfred Roberts had to leave school at thirteen with a good, if untrained, mind may have been when Margaret Roberts's future course was set. As a father, with his frustration, and determination that what had been unused in himself would be developed in his bright daughter, he dedicated himself to her advancement. 'He was anxious', Margaret told one of her first biographers, Patricia Murray, 'that I should have every educational opportunity possible.'[3]

Had his family been able to afford to educate him, Alfred would have been a teacher. Instead, he observed secondary education from behind the counter of the tuck shop at the boys' public school, Oundle. In succeeding years, he held various grocery jobs until 1913, when he landed the managership of a grocery store, Clifford's, on London Road, Grantham, at fourteen shillings a week. In Grantham, almost certainly through Methodist church activities, he made the acquaintance of Beatrice Stephenson, a dark-eyed, attractive, plump and serious young woman. A dressmaker, four years his senior, she had her own business and was a musician and Sunday school teacher as well. Their courtship coincided with the outbreak of the First World War. Six times Alfred tried to enlist, only to be rejected because of his poor eyesight. (His younger brother Edward succeeded, and was killed.)

In May 1917, with the war still on, he and Beatrice married at the Wesley Chapel, Spittlegate, at the southern end of town. As the better-known of the pair, as organist and Sunday school teacher, it was she who made the headline on the social page of the *Grantham Journal*: 'Wesleyan Teacher's Marriage'. Alfred was described as a teacher and secretary at the Finkin Street Chapel, and the event reported as 'a very pretty but quietly celebrated wedding'.[4] For their honeymoon, the couple went to Skegness – 'Skeggie' – the Lincolnshire seaside resort that is Grantham's Brighton.

For the next two years they lived with Beatrice's parents on South Parade until their savings were sufficient for them to take out a mortgage and, a social climb in itself, move from South Parade to the other end of town, to North Parade, where they bought the house and shop at Number 1.

After a sensible interval, their first child, Muriel, was born in 1921. In 1923 Alfred acquired the Huntingtower Road shop; two years later a neighbour returned home and announced to her daughter, 'Beattie's got another little girl.'

Margaret Hilda Roberts was born at home. For the next seventeen years the centre of her world was the four rooms above the shop on North Parade. (Downstairs the shop had an extra room at the back reserved for clients and salesmen.) The family lived on the top two floors, where they had to walk through a bedroom to get to the sitting room and downstairs and out the back to use the toilet. Hot water was available if heated in a copper boiler. Traffic noise was constant. There was not a speck of dirt in the place – every surface was clean and polished. The dominant features were the table and the sewing machine. It was a sensible home for sensible people.

With their second daughter, the Robertses had completed their family. There was no wasteful trying for a boy. In 1925 Alfred expanded the North Parade shop to take in the two houses adjacent. As an increasingly prominent tradesman, he was a member of the Grantham Chamber of Trade and a Rotarian (the Rotary motto: 'Service before Self'). In 1927 he became a town councillor. He was an independent – that is, he was not a member of either the local Labour or Conservative parties. He was a liberal on education, yet had decidedly conservative views on commerce. He favoured, for example, private companies taking over many of the jobs done by the council. Until his fellow councillors elected him alderman, he represented St Wulfram's ward.

Its churches were as stratified as the rest of Grantham. The beautiful thirteenth-century Anglican church of St Wulfram's was at the top, socially and physically. With one of the tallest spires in England, rising from the centre of town to dominate the landscape, it was, and remains, the town's symbol. When the sixth Lord Brownlow left office as Mayor of Grantham in 1935, the town council gave him a green enamel box with a view of the church on its lid.

The Robertses were Wesleyan Methodists. The church they attended was also near the town centre, the handsome Finkin Street Chapel, built in 1840. With its allegiance to John Wesley, a Lincolnshire man, it was the most Anglican among Grantham's Methodist churches, more spacious and ceremonial than either the Primitive Methodist chapel behind the Roberts house, the Free Methodist Chapel or the Wesley Chapel in Spittlegate, where Alfred and Beatrice were married. Finkin Street, with beautiful curved pews of polished mahogany, held a thousand when full – which on Sundays it always was. The children's Sunday school alone filled one side of the upstairs. Its acoustics were splendid. Standing in its high pulpit, with eye contact with the balcony, anyone might feel blessed with the gift of tongues. Alfred Roberts certainly was. On this stage, as lay preacher, as in the council chamber, Alfred Roberts acquired a local reputation as an orator. With his commanding height, wavy pale blond hair, upright bearing and extremely pale colouring, he radiated sincerity and authority.

And, as they walked into church, pride in his young daughter. The congregation at Finkin Street could see that she was Daddy's girl as they entered hand in hand. 'She was', Mary Robinson says, 'very much like him to look at except that her hair was darker. He thought the world of her.' Of course, Robinson allowed, Alfred probably thought a lot of both of his girls. 'But Margaret was more outgoing and I think she was brighter.'

A Sunday school teacher at Finkin Street cherishes the memory of the day when Muriel Roberts brought her little sister Margaret, then about three, with her. 'That brightened up that Sunday,' says Nellie Towers. 'She had got such a personality and said quite quaint things. She was streets ahead of the others. She was very bright. She was a real chatterbox. At the end of the class, I thought to myself, She will be a schoolmistress one of these days.'

Growing up, Margaret Roberts went to church every Sunday, not once but three or four times. Morning Sunday school came first. Then with her parents she would go to morning service at eleven, return home for lunch and go back to church at two-thirty for more Sunday school. At six o'clock, once again with her parents, she would attend evening service. She loved the hymns: the glories of Methodism such as 'Immortal, Invisible, God Only Wise' and 'Guide Me O Thou Great Jehovah'.

Sunday, too, was the chance to wear best clothes. The Roberts girls were always beautifully turned out – 'in tailored coats, hats and gloves and all – always very prim and proper. They stood out compared to the rest' – and the congregation knew the reason why. The careful details like matching trim, piping and edging were Beatrice's handiwork.

After church the Robertses went to friends' homes or the friends came to theirs. Having people in to tea or supper and keeping a good table, looking after them well, was a family tradition. All through the week there were events, sewing meeting on Wednesdays, youth club on Fridays. Their life revolved around the church.

In any event, church was a welcome relief from the tedium of Sunday. The Robertses were strict Sabbatarians. When Margaret asked her parents whether she could go out for a walk with a friend on a Sunday evening, the answer was no. Board games were not allowed. Nor Sunday newspapers. The only permitted activities were cooking and doing the shop's accounts. Sunday was hardly a day of rest. The only real respite was early closing on Thursday. As she once poignantly told an interviewer, 'My parents used to look forward to it all week.'[5]

A different kind of Sunday observance could be seen from the front rooms of the Roberts home on North Parade. Facing them was an imposing neo-classical building that the Robertses never dreamed of entering: St Mary's Catholic Church. Margaret would watch the Catholic girls in their pretty white first-communion dresses with bright ribbons. She had pretty dresses too, thanks to her mother, but these could be worn only for special occasions like the annual League of Pity party, not for going to chapel. Such sensual indulgence was frowned on at Finkin Street. Her autobiography recalls, 'If you wore a ribboned dress an older chapel-goer would shake his head and warn against "the first step to Rome".'

She was never alone. Weekdays or weekends, the whole family – father, mother, two girls and Beatrice's mother, who came to live with them – took four meals a day together (although one usually had to be absent from the table to mind the shop). They all worked together as well. They never relaxed. Idleness was the only sin readily available to them and they took a puritanical pleasure in thrusting it away. There was work for all in the shop. With its sub-post office handling savings and pension payments, the place was always full of people until seven o'clock on Friday, eight o'clock on Saturday. Margaret's task when she was old enough was to weigh out the tea, sugar and biscuits and pour them into one- and two-pound bags. Everything, from biscuits to soap flakes, was bought in bulk, and all her life she retained an ability to curl paper into a serviceable cone.

The Robertses were as non-Co-op as they were non-Catholic. There were several Co-operative stores in Grantham, favoured by a working-class clientele, like Mary Robinson's family, which looked forward to the dividend: 'after so long you got your Divi, which was quite helpful for poorer people'. The Robinsons went into the Roberts shop only for stamps. 'Better-off people than us went in there.' Everything seemed expensive, like the Huntley & Palmer's biscuits, 'better biscuits than the Co-op which was at the bottom of the street – in these clear cases so that you could see what they were like, but you had not enough money to buy'. Other customers remember from their youth that the place 'was very nice to enter', that it was 'like most shops in those days stocked, absolutely packed to the gunnels', that it offered a variety of cheeses. The ordinary grocery would have only one type. There were bales of goods stacked outside and huge sides of bacon hung in the back of the shop. A recurring image in local memories is that of Mr Roberts in his white coat, slicing the bacon.

Margaret, daughter of the shop, would remember all her life the aromas of coffee, cheese and bacon; bacon, a comforting link with her past, would remain a staple of her family diet for the rest of her life.

Grandmother Stephenson, Beatrice's mother, who lived with them until her death when Margaret was ten, reinforced the parental sententiousness with her own Victorian dose. They escaped her disapproval of music-halls only on summer holidays to Skegness where, living in self-catering accommodation, after exercising in the public gardens they would go to a music-hall and join in the singing. These escapades took place without Alfred Roberts. He took his holidays on his own: a week a year at Skegness to play bowls. As he and his wife were always on call, they could not be away from the shop at the same time.

When her grandmother died in 1935, Margaret was bundled away to stay with friends until the funeral was over and all her grandmother's belongings had been packed away. Even if she had attended, it is unlikely she would have seen extravagant expressions of grief. However, she and her mother would visit Phoebe Stephenson's grave on early-closing day.

It was in many ways a joyless life. In her own words, she was 'brought up very, very seriously. We weren't allowed to go out to very much entertainment. To go out to a film was a very great treat – a very great treat.'[6]

Only when her grandmother had gone did the family allow itself the luxury of a radio – the wireless. The day the Robertses got their first, Margaret ran all the way home from school to listen. Her favourite programmes were *Monday Night at Seven*, *Saturday Night Music Hall*, *The Brains Trust* and *ITMA*.

What she did very much enjoy were aphorisms and proverbs – plain truths, plainly put: 'Cleanliness is next to godliness' and

'If a thing's worth doing, it's worth doing well'.[7] She liked their confidence and conciseness even if sometimes she did not get the point. Why, she wondered as a child, say 'Look before you leap'? Wouldn't it be better to say 'Look before you cross'?[8] (Telling this joke on herself in her memoirs, she observes with uncharacteristic self-deprecation, 'I already had a logical and indeed somewhat literal mind – perhaps I have not changed much in this regard.')[9]

'We were Methodists and Methodist means method,' Margaret Thatcher told an early biographer, Patricia Murray. 'We were taught what was right and wrong in very considerable detail.'[10]

So were many people of that, and earlier, eras, but few retained so literally the strictures of childhood into adult life. The brand of Methodism Alfred Roberts followed was tailored for the self-made man. It promoted personal salvation, damned the evils of alcohol and saw the world in black and white. Alfred Roberts, as seen by John Campbell, in the first volume of his meticulous biography of Margaret Thatcher, 'made no distinction between commercial, political and religious values. Shopkeeper, local politician and lay preacher, he conducted his business on ethical principles and preached business principles in politics.'[11] In other words, for the Roberts family religion was not so much a matter of seeking salvation through diligence as a way of demonstrating that they had achieved it: if you want proof, look around you.

Alfred Roberts was Margaret's mentor and inspiration. 'To know Margaret,' said her sister Muriel, in a rare interview, 'you had to know him.'[12] As Margaret herself was fond of saying, 'My father constantly drummed into me, from a very early age, "You make up your own mind. You do not do something or want to do something because your friends are doing it."' Her mother reaffirmed this: 'Your father always sticks to his principles.' (Appropriate for the father of the woman whose celebrated boast was 'The lady's not for turning'.)

The echoes of paternal teaching were so loud during her prime ministership that the historian Peter Hennessy remarked that Britain was being governed by Alderman Roberts from beyond the grave.[13]

A brilliant perception – but only half the truth. Beatrice Stephenson is remembered only as quiet, gentle and unobtrusive. She combined marriage and work with efficiency and skill, but also with a self-effacement that kept her out of the history books. Yet those who believe a later remark of Margaret Thatcher's, about her difficulty after the age of fifteen in communicating with her mother, are blinding themselves to the permanent signals of a loud internal maternal voice. There is a right way and a wrong way to do everything and mine is right.

Her own memoirs sound a more grateful note. She says she learned from her mother that a household should run like clockwork, with polished furniture and daily and weekly cleaning supplemented by an annual spring clean 'to get to all those parts which other cleaning could not reach'. Also, 'She showed me how to iron a man's shirt in the correct way and to press embroidery without damaging it.'[14]

The Robertses slept between ironed sheets – ironed by Beatrice with a heavy iron heated on the grate in the times when she was not serving in the shop, making her daughters' tailored coats or preparing food. 'My mother was an excellent cook and a highly organized one. Twice a week she had her big bake – bread, pastry, cakes and pies – and she always made extra to give away. On Sunday mornings, by the time we all got downstairs at about eight, the first batch of cakes would already be out of the oven. She was a very, very capable woman.'[15] Those were the views of Margaret Thatcher, looking back over half a century.

Another obvious, if unquoted, motherly teaching was 'Never go out of the house looking less than your absolute best'. Beatrice Roberts taught her daughters the skills with which to maintain this standard – how to turn a hem, to curl straight hair, to brighten up a much-worn dress. There was no circumstance so severe that a little deft handiwork could not improve appearance.

From father and mother in unison, she learned that waste and extravagance were great evils. All birthday money had to go into savings. 'My goodness me,' she said in a television interview, using the kind of girlish expletive she allowed herself, 'you never buy anything you can't afford to buy. Never.'[16] From the past she drew out a memory of going with her mother to buy some new covers for the settee – 'a great event' – and wanting something that was 'rather lovely, light, with flowers'. But it was rejected as 'not serviceable'. 'How I longed for the time when I could buy things that weren't serviceable.'[17]

Margaret soon found her own strengths. She could read before she started school and was top of her class at the Huntingtower Road School. Between church and school, she was early in acquiring a liking for the sound of her own voice, and she seems to have been good at performing. At the age of ten she won a prize for reciting poetry in a competition in Grantham curiously called by its Welsh name, an eisteddfod. Her selections were the sonorous and sentimental 'Moonlit Apples' by John Drinkwater and 'The Travellers' by Walter de la Mare.

When she won, her deputy headmistress, Winifred Wright, congratulated her. 'You were lucky, Margaret.' Margaret's retort has acquired almost biblical resonance: 'I was not lucky. I deserved it.'

Surprisingly, perhaps, not public speaking but piano-playing was her main avenue of advancement. The family loved music and belonged to a chamber music society. They also liked to sing, sometimes with friends, around the piano, 'The Lost Chord', 'The Holy City' and selections from Gilbert and Sullivan as well as other sing-along favourites.

From the age of five Margaret learned the piano. Taught at first by her mother at home, she played on an instrument made by Alfred's great-uncle, John Roberts, in Northampton. (He also made church organs and, on one of his niece's rare visits, let her play on one in his barn.) She sang too, and with the church choir performed Handel's *Messiah* and other staples of the oratorio repertoire.

As her skill as a pianist grew, Margaret displayed an assertiveness that annoyed some of her contemporaries. Several recall an incident when she was cast as an angel in a nativity play and was required to sing a solo. The piano for the performance was behind the curtains, propped against a wall. When Margaret got up to sing, she moved over to the piano. Let the accompanist do the playing, the director advised her; otherwise, her voice would not be heard. 'I shall play for myself,' she insisted. 'All right, Margaret,' he conceded, 'for tonight. But on the night, Wilfred will play for you.' But on the night of the actual performance, Margaret, as before, played for herself.

Her ability as a pianist was complimented by the *Grantham Journal*, which described her as displaying 'a great deal of ease and facility'.[18] But, Nellie Towers recalls, she had 'these mannerisms, you know, throwing herself about the piano'.

Nonetheless, the girl was 'really good' – so good that Towers asked Beatrice Roberts, 'Do you think she'll be a concert pianist?'

'Oh no,' the proud mother said. 'We've got – she's got – higher aspirations than that.'

2

Getting out of Grantham
(1939–1943)

It was possible to rise above Grantham. Proof stood in the form of the statue in front of the colourful neo-Byzantine Guildhall honouring Grantham's then most famous inhabitant, Sir Isaac Newton (1642–1727), who offered the first theory of gravity after an experience in his apple orchard in a village seven miles away.

Through the poems of Kipling, taught at school, Margaret Roberts became conscious of a wider world. Kipling offered, she said, 'glimpses into the romantic possibilities of life outside Grantham'.[1] His words also awakened her to the facts of empire, such as that her country held 'Dominion over palm and pine' while 'Far-call'd our navies melt away'.[2] Kipling became her favourite poet and, upon his death in 1936, when she was eleven, she precociously asked for a book of his poetry as a Christmas present.

Her admiration for the patriotic poet was matched by *The Times*, which eulogised him as 'the plain Englishman of genius'.[3] In its extensive coverage, *The Times* iterated several times what Margaret came to believe in her heart: that the English were that ill-defined entity, a race. It called Kipling 'the most typical representative of his race' and, while acknowledging his imperfections and limitations, judged nonetheless that his work was composed 'at a crucial period in the history of his race'.[4]

Chapter 2

What the Roberts family did not admire in 1936 were the Jarrow marchers – the line of protesting unemployed who passed through Grantham on their way to Westminster. Alfred Roberts held that such unfortunates should find ways to help themselves. With his belief in thrift, cleanliness and living within your means, he refused to give them charity.

Margaret's first civic memory was of the Silver Jubilee of King George and Queen Mary in 1935. Grantham was festooned with blue and yellow streamers. As part of the celebrations, the town's schoolchildren were organised to form the letters of 'Grantham', and Margaret was assigned to the letter 'M'.

At ten she entered a good grammar school: Kesteven and Grantham Girls' School. Kesteven (local pronunciation usually stresses the first syllable: *Kes*-teven) was included in the name to indicate that the school served the outlying areas as well as Grantham itself. About a mile from the Roberts home on North Parade, it was built in 1910 on a hillside in a residential district of town where the villas of local well-to-do businessmen could overlook the neighbouring countryside. As before, Margaret returned home for lunch – an extra two miles a day to avoid the expense of school meals. On the walk back to school after lunch the grocer's daughter munched a bar of chocolate and her friends remember her generously sharing it.

KGGS was a mixed-entry school – that is, it took both fee-paying and scholarship pupils – which made for a varied social blend. About a quarter of its 350 girls were there on scholarship; the rest were daughters of landowners, farmers and churchmen. Madeline Edwards (later Hellaby), who was there at the same time as Margaret, explains, 'If a girl was clever and got the scholarship, it wouldn't matter what her background was, she would come. A lot of them did extremely well. Some of them went on to university with a very ordinary kind of background. And some that were fairly high class were not very clever and didn't.'

Margaret Roberts fitted both categories. She sat for, and won, a scholarship, yet her father paid the fees of £65 a year. He saw the scholarship as a kind of insurance; if anything happened to him, Margaret would be able to continue at the school.

Once again she was considered to hold an advantage over girls less well off. Mary Robinson could not have attended the school even with a scholarship because of the cost of the uniform. Margaret, in Mary's memory, 'had no worries like that. The Robertses were a different class.' What was uniform about the KGGS summer uniform was the designated fabric – Halls Saxby gingham. This could be made into any pattern of frock that the girl or her mother liked, providing that there were no frills or bows. Winter uniform was a gym tunic and blouse.

The High School girls considered themselves superior to the boys from the Boys' Central School, a technically oriented secondary school nearby. The 'Central' boys were well aware of this. One of them, Terry Bradley, who knew Margaret Roberts from seeing her at the shop, says, 'We thought they [the KGGS girls] had a right to belong on the footpath, walking home, and we used to pass them, of course. Actually, we used to run in the gutter.' The attitude was 'They were High School girls and we were Central School boys, and never the twain shall meet'.

KGGS sincerely hoped not. Its girls were not allowed to mix with the local boys. Even so, the school saw itself as a liberal establishment and prided itself on having only five rules whose severity may be judged by the ban on sitting on the grass unless 'the white paper was on the netting'. The logic was clear. The ground was usually wet. If it had not rained for a time and the headmistress decided the grass was dry enough, she would pin a note on to the netting that enclosed the tennis courts, thereby lifting the ban. Other rules were that the KGGS girls had to wear blazers and panama hats, and were not to leave the school grounds without their hat.

Margaret greatly admired the headmistress, Miss Williams, who had been at KGGS since the founding of the school in 1910. For prize-giving days Miss Williams wore beautiful tailored silk outfits and impressed the young Miss Roberts with her elegance. With elegance went common sense. Her advice stuck in her most distinguished pupil's memory: 'Never aspire to a cheap fur coat when a well-tailored wool coat would be a better buy.'[5]

At her primary school on Huntingtower Road, Margaret had come head of the class every year. At KGGS she was also a good student but for some unexplained reason was placed in the second stream during her first year. Soon she was raised to the first stream and stayed at or near the top; school reports praised her diligence, thoroughness, logicality and clear expression.

Her looks were pleasant, her complexion smooth, her hair light brown and straight until, eventually, she had it permed. She joined the hockey team and she made new friends. One from an outlying district, the village of Corby Glen, who was to remain close all her life, was Margaret Goodrich, the daughter of the vicar. He was a scholarly man and his vicarage had a room lined with books. Margaret Roberts loved to browse through it.

From her father Margaret had already acquired a respect, if not a love, for learning. Alfred Roberts had the zeal of the autodidact. He was a heavy user of the Grantham Public Library next to the town hall, and the head librarian said he was the most well-read man in the town. He guided his brighter daughter's reading. She hadn't read Walt Whitman? He encouraged her to try and Whitman became a favourite. He introduced her to the English classics – the Brontës, Jane Austen and Dickens, of whose work she liked *A Tale of Two Cities* best. He would take out two books a week – a biography or political book for himself, the other a novel for his wife. Soon Margaret took over this ritual of small-town life. She went 'every single Saturday, and the librarian knew I would come'.[6, 7] She also accompanied her father to hear staff from University College, Nottingham lecture on current and international affairs.

In October 1941, when she reached sixteen and entered the lower sixth form, she began to focus on science. Chemistry was

her best subject and she got on well with her chemistry teacher,
a Miss Kay. She was impressed, as everyone was, to find that
Britain had survived the German air raids largely because of
new British discoveries in radar. It was clear, she wrote with
hindsight, that 'a whole new scientific world was opening up. I
wanted to be part of it. Moreover, as I knew I would have
to earn my own living, this seemed an exciting way to do so.'[8]
At that time she also developed the capacity (abandoned in later
life) for going for long walks on her own – going out of town
by Manthorpe Road and returning by the Great North Road,
and also up Hall's Hill.

Her years at KGGS coincided with her father's rise in local
government. In 1936 he became chairman of the Borough
Finance and Ratings Committee. The local newspaper described
him as Grantham's Chancellor of the Exchequer. He was a
governor of KGGS as well as of the King's School, Grantham,
a sixteenth-century school for boys (where Newton learned Latin
and Greek and began his mathematical studies), as well as trustee
of ten other churches in Lincolnshire. In 1936 he became president of the Rotary Club and stood proudly with Lord Brownlow
at his side for the photograph at the annual dinner. Beatrice can
also be seen farther along at the head table. As a consequence
of his position, Margaret had the privilege of watching Remem-
brance Day parades from a window of the Guildhall.

Alfred Roberts now took his daughter to political meetings
as well as to church. Her first taste of campaigning came in 1935
when, in the general election, she worked for the Conservatives.
Although her father was locally identified as a Liberal, by her
own recollection 'I was always a "true-blue" Conservative by
both instinct and upbringing.' Her job was to act as a runner
between polling stations and Conservative committee rooms.

There were other new horizons. At the age of twelve Margaret
first saw London. She went to stay in Hampstead with family
friends, a Wesleyan minister named Skinner and his wife. Among

the treats they gave their young visitor was a trip to Lewisham to see Sigmund Romberg's *The Desert Song* playing at the Catford Theatre. She stayed a week, was dazzled and did not want to go home to the provinces. The crowds, the bright lights, the great buildings left a memory so vivid that in her memoirs she curiously breaks into French and quotes Talleyrand to describe her first taste of 'la douceur de la vie'.[9] There *was* a world outside Grantham and she wanted to get into it. For the time being, however, she had to console herself with the sheet music of *The Desert Song*, which she bought and took home to play on the piano over and over, 'perhaps too often'.

Awed as she was by the capital city, she is unlikely to have been uncomfortable about her clothes. Her mother, a professional seamstress, still made most of what she and her sister wore, mainly from Vogue and Butterick's patterns. 'In the sales in Grantham and Nottingham we could get the best-quality fabrics at reduced prices,' she recalls, 'and were, by Grantham standards, rather fashionable.'[10] They never had the luxury of a dress bought 'off the peg' until Muriel went to train as a physiotherapist in Birmingham.[11]

Muriel was a bit on the heavy side, like her mother, and is remembered by her former Sunday school teacher Nellie Towers as 'very reserved, like her mother. A lot of people said she was as clever as Margaret but she was a different personality altogether. She would just say "hello" in the street. Margaret would say "Hello, Nellie", so patronising. Like I was the little girl.'

But Margaret learned a lot from her sister, especially after Muriel left home. 'Muriel soon found her way around the big city shops and my knowledge of makeup really began when she started to give me the odd glamorous thing for Christmas such as a powder compact,' she confessed to Patricia Murray. 'It all stemmed from there.'[12] ('It' presumably meant a dependence on the compact, the lipstick and the powder puff.)

Another vision of glamour came when Margaret became

entranced by Hollywood movies. Once she began going to Grantham's cinemas, James Stewart took his place with Rudyard Kipling as a formative political influence. Stewart shone in *Mr Smith Goes to Washington*, released in 1939, a cinema classic in which the honest (and handsome) small-town man becomes Washington's youngest Senator and exposes corruption in high places.

Margaret's voice was becoming as fashionable as her clothes. There were elocution lessons offered at the grammar school for those interested in public speaking or who had heavy country accents, and Alfred Roberts encouraged her to take them.

When he became chairman of the governors of KGGS, he would preside over the school's annual Speech Day. Despite his reputation as an orator, some of the girls made cruel sport of an oddity of his pronunciation. He pronounced 'ew' as 'oo'. Every year, one of them recalls, 'some of the girls anticipated with horrid, though well-suppressed glee' his annual comment that, as he looked around the hall, he could see a 'foo noo poopils' sitting at the front. Old Girls of the school from that period would do imitations of it.[13]

The odd vowel sounds were probably regional, derived from his Northamptonshire youth. The accents of Lincolnshire and adjacent counties differ. Research done at the University of Nottingham has shown that on the Northamptonshire edge of Cambridgeshire the local pronunciation of 'few' is always 'foo'.[14] 'Linguistic insecurity is common in the Midlands,' says Hilary Hillier, an accent expert at Nottingham University. 'Sounding too rural or regional can hold you back. In any event, anybody who takes elocution lessons as a child is being nudged towards social mobility. The unspoken message is that you will stay where you are unless you change your voice.'[15]

Among the myriad accents in Britain, those of the Midlands are not universally admired or even understood, particularly when they incorporate idiosyncratic vocabulary and grammar.

D. H. Lawrence, born in a village near Nottingham, advised a girlfriend who wanted to be a writer to use slang sparingly: 'a little is all most folks can bear'.[16]

The question, therefore, presents itself: was Councillor Roberts oblivious to this small defect or aware of it and thus determined to get rid of any local blemish in his clever daughter's speech? In any case, if Margaret Roberts Thatcher's life can be seen as one constant effort to remake herself, her voice was where she began. As she explained to Margaret Goodrich, 'One simply must talk properly.'

Her confident new tones, like her pianistic mannerisms, drew some ridicule from her peers. But she did not attempt to hide her voice on the occasions when the head of the school arranged for lectures by visiting speakers. The subjects varied, but a question period always followed. 'When they were to do with current events or that sort of thing,' Madeline Edwards remembers, 'you could bet your life that when it came to questions Margaret Roberts would jump up on her hind legs and ask very penetrating questions. We would look at each other and say, "Oh, she's at it again."'

A similar scene stuck in Margaret Goodrich's memory. 'A famous lecturer came, a writer of spy stories, and after his talk opened up for questions. Margaret Roberts stood up and said, "Does the speaker think such and such a thing?" in the third person – the most sort of almost parliamentary way. People would say, "Oh, look at her again, look at Margaret Roberts again."'

Another quieter but politically useful skill Margaret acquired during her Grantham education was penmanship. She learned to write rapidly, with many underlinings and no crossings-out in a confident flowing hand, a skill that was to stand her in good stead in the years to come when she would dash off handwritten personal letters, sometimes by the hundreds.

*

In 1938 the Robertses took into their home a beautiful Austrian-Jewish girl, Edith Muhlbauer. She was Muriel's penfriend, whose father in Vienna had asked whether the Roberts family would help her get to England. Tall, sophisticated and well-dressed, Edith told them what it was like to live as a Jew under an anti-Semitic regime. It gave them a personal glimpse of the Nazis' nastiness – something Alfred Roberts had already begun to suspect when Hitler banned the Rotary Club in Germany.

War broke out when Margaret was thirteen. Alfred Roberts was one of those in charge of Grantham's ARP – air-raid precautions. She and her mother went out to buy yards of black-out cloth. Following the Battle of Britain in September 1940, Grantham was badly hit. With its heavy industry, nearby airbases and the British Manufacturing and Research Company – known locally as 'Marco's' – which made munitions, it was a tempting target for the Luftwaffe. The north–south rail link also invited disruption. At one stage Grantham suffered more bombs per head than any other city in the country.

Margaret and her father would get the atlas out and follow the progress of the war. As they listened to Winston Churchill on the wireless, they knew that, with the right leader, there was almost nothing the British people could not do. Margaret was moved, too, by the local preacher, who uttered another of the phrases that would guide her life: it was 'always the few who saved the many'.[17]

As a girl Margaret had disagreed with her father on his rigid insistence that Grantham's parks and places of entertainment should be shut on Sunday. He finally abandoned this principle after American airmen began to be stationed around the town. (They flew from the local airfield for the Arnhem invasion.) The town grew quite rowdy at weekends as the Allies jostled for the local girls. Alderman Roberts saw that it was clearly better to have the cinemas, sports fields and parks open on Sunday than to leave the soldiers to their own devices.

At KGGS there was no bomb shelter. When a raid came, the

girls went to the cloakroom and sat under the coats hung on pegs – pretty futile protection against a direct hit. At home, Margaret sometimes had to dive under the kitchen table to do her homework. Under these conditions, in 1942, with the war at its darkest hour, she set her sights on Oxford.

She proposed to read chemistry. It was not unusual for KGGS girls to go to Oxford or Cambridge, but neither was it easy. Latin was required but the school did not teach it (an example of how girls at that time were often not offered the same quality of education as available to boys).

She developed a close friend in Margaret Goodrich, through the hockey team, then through the lower sixth. They did chemistry together and also biology, where they dissected the same fish, worms and frogs. Goodrich noticed that her hard-working friend despised anybody who didn't apply herself. They were both set on Oxford. As Goodrich reconstructs it, Margaret Roberts 'was determined to go if she could and her father was determined for her – that's important – and so she did work very hard'.

She was clearly very keen to leave Grantham and progress to Oxford. In 1943 she sat and obtained the Higher School Certificate (in chemistry, biology and French), and already held offers from Nottingham and Bedford College, London. But Oxford was her goal. As Margaret Goodrich sees it:

Her father wanted her to do it too, you see. Anything he could do to help her, he did. Her father used to come to my village as a Methodist local preacher. My father was the vicar of this place, Corby Glen, and they had a lot in common. They talked a lot about their daughters, I'm quite sure. He asked my father if he would be prepared to coach Margaret for the general paper, which, in those days, you had to pass and involved questions of all sorts, like the difference between plants and animals or what did Plato think about this or that. All sorts of things that a small grammar school had no opportunity of teaching. So Margaret used to come out to Corby Vicarage on the bus and have a go with my father.

And they got on very well indeed. 'I should have hated to be coached by my father,' Goodrich says. 'But she got on famously, and used to come out with a string bag full of goodies from the shop.' She herself went to tea at the Roberts home, however, only once.

At KGGS a new headmistress, Miss Dorothy Gillies, a brisk Scot, had replaced Miss Williams, who had retired at last. As Goodrich remembered, 'We needed both of us to get Latin because that school didn't teach any Latin or Greek.' But, as Margaret Roberts was the younger of the two, Miss Gillies advised her to wait, stay on at school for another year, get her Latin and try her Oxford entrance then. At that, Goodrich said, 'she was extremely angry. That was one of the first times I've ever seen her angry. She said to Miss Gillies, "You are thwarting my ambition."'[18]

Accounts of this much-described conflict differ as to the extent to which Miss Gillies helped or hindered Margaret Roberts's mastery of the Latin language. Goodrich says that as Miss Gillies herself was a classical scholar 'she coached us in our Latin. I can remember learning my Virgil by heart, and getting my O level quite easily . . .' Margaret Thatcher, in her memoirs, says that Miss Gillies arranged for lessons at the King's School, coached her herself and lent her own books, including a textbook written by her father. Others say Miss Gillies refused to help with the Latin challenge and that father and daughter combined forces to overcome the obstacles in her path and that he paid for her Latin coaching.

The reason for her not wishing to remain another year at school was a sound one. True, she was only seventeen and ordinarily could afford to wait a year. However, in wartime, women were called up for national service at the age of twenty. If she were not to start university until she was eighteen, then she could not expect to fit in the three-year course and would be allowed only a two-year 'wartime degree'.

In the event, Margaret did travel to Oxford to sit for the Somerville scholarship on a cold December day in 1942. It was a tough examination, not only in Latin. Another provincial girl, Pamela Mason, shudders at the memory. 'The English essay particularly was agonising – three hours on one subject. I hit lucky and I got "Chance" and it just happened that I could work in Shakespeare and Hardy. As she was a scientist, I guess it was all the more difficult for them in the general paper.'

The end result was that Margaret Goodrich was offered an Oxford place for the autumn of 1943 while Margaret Roberts narrowly missed out on the Somerville scholarship she was seeking, but was put on the waiting list and promised a place at the college for October 1944.

There was no alternative in September 1943 but to return to KGGS. With Madeline Edwards, Margaret Roberts was made joint head girl. The two were not close. (Edwards, who had been her partner in science laboratory work, found her 'quite nice looking, well covered but not fat and with no sense of humour at all'.) Suddenly, out of the blue, just before her eighteenth birthday, a telegram arrived from Somerville to say that someone had dropped out and that, as she was first on the waiting list, the place was hers. 'So,' as Edwards remembers it, 'she upped sticks and went to Oxford, having been head girl for not much more than three weeks.'

Her ambition was thwarted no longer. She had certainly earned her place, but this time luck played its part as well.

3
Crystal-clear Conservative
(1943–1947)

When Margaret Roberts went up to Oxford in 1943, the university was far from its peacetime self. There were fewer male students. The city was dark and silent. There were no bells, no traffic, no lights at night. Food rationing presented a new challenge to the colleges' chefs; students were allowed two ounces of butter a week. In the bath, they were permitted only five inches of water – no hardship for Margaret, for whom a fixed bathtub was a luxury.

The standard Oxford degree course runs for three years. With only nine terms to get in, get on and get out, there is little time for changing personality or course of study. Margaret went in as a scientist and a preacher and as such she came out. The one alteration was that her allegiance shifted from Methodism to Conservatism.

But not right away. At the start she joined the Wesley Memorial Church's Students' Fellowship and found, as in Grantham, a warm social life. Rather than spending her weekends partying, she went with the society to give sermons in Methodist chapels in the environs of Oxford. She joined the Bach Choir. With all student organisations touting for members, it was not long before she found her way to the Oxford University Conservative Association (OUCA) and discovered her undergraduate identity. It was conversion by total immersion; in OUCA she found certainties matching the moral truths she had brought from home.

At the outset she experienced loneliness for the first time. Apart from her heady week in London and holidays at Skegness, she had never been out of Grantham. The monumentality of the buildings awed her. Her solitude was reinforced by long hours in the chemistry labs. When she was free she took long walks across Christ Church Meadow and along the Cherwell.

Her school friend from KGGS, Margaret Goodrich, had already been at Oxford for a year. When the vicar of Corby Glen visited his daughter, he ventured that it would be nice to look up Margaret Roberts and see how she was getting on. The pair sought her out in her room in Penrose, an unattractive modern block, and found her rather homesick, toasting teacakes. Margaret Goodrich recalls, 'She was thrilled to see my father and we had a nice afternoon.'

Being a science student was isolating in itself. To an arts student, the scientists spent their days in the labs while the rest of them went to lectures and classes with the object of producing an essay every week. The discipline was quite different. 'After you'd sat up most of the night writing your essay,' recalls Pamela Mason, one of Margaret's contemporaries at Somerville, 'you felt you deserved two or three days off, so the whole cycle would repeat itself again.' The arts students, moreover, seemed to go out more in the evening. They had to be back in college at 11.15 p.m. 'So you came in, and looked round to see which of your friends still had their light on. If you knew they weren't doing an essay, you'd go and knock on the door and say what about a cup of cocoa, and that led to all-night sessions. I wouldn't have dreamed of knocking on Margaret Roberts's door. She went to bed at night which many of us did not do.' One night around midnight, when the merriment grew loud, she emerged from her room and bellowed, 'Some people are trying to get some sleep here!'

Margaret Roberts did have some difficulty making friends. In hall she 'sat on the table nearest the high table' and her voice was shrill and loud. Ruth Clayton, a fellow Somervillian, said, 'We all tried to keep away from the sound'. To fellow science students, she did not seem a dedicated scientist, although she undoubtedly worked hard.[1]

Her first question to a fellow Somervillian and fellow chemistry student, Pauline Cowan (later Harrison), was 'Will you join the Conservative Association?'[2] Politically, Cowan was inclined quite the other way and told her so. So too was their tutor, the eminent crystallographer Dorothy Hodgkin. Margaret was conspicuous for her Conservatism.

Many of the women at Somerville, certainly Janet Vaughan, their principal from 1945, were left of centre and supported the Beveridge plan – the comprehensive welfare scheme advocated in a report in 1942 by the economist William (Lord) Beveridge, which was felt to offer much hope for post-war Britain. They did not take kindly to Margaret's proselytising at breakfast. 'Welfare is wrong!' she would announce.[3] For such opinions, Vaughan (later Dame Janet) excluded her from Somerville weekend social occasions. 'We used to entertain a great deal at weekends, but she didn't get invited. She had nothing to contribute, you see.'[4]

At the end of her first year, as part of a civil defence firewatching exercise, Margaret was thrown together with an Essex girl who later became known as the writer Nina Bawden. Over the shrouded head of a third girl who was treating a cold by inhaling friar's balsam under a towel, the two young women argued fiercely about politics in strong language. Bawden, an enthusiastic member of the Labour Club, was shocked to hear that Margaret had joined the Conservatives. She argued that people like themselves – lower-middle-class grammar-school girls, on state scholarships, lucky to get to Oxford at all – would be 'despicable' (her word) if they used their good fortune to join the ranks of the privileged.[5] Far from deferring to 'top people', their duty was to make sure that post-war English society would be more generous and open. Besides, Bawden added, the Labour Club was more fun.

Margaret smiled (in Bawden's reconstruction of their contretemps). *Of course* the Labour Club was for the moment more *fashionable*. But she herself was not playing at politics. She meant to get into Parliament and there was more chance of being noticed in the Conservative Club, if only because the other members were so stodgy. From under the towel the friend emerged to say, 'You lost that round, Nina.'[6]

The first declaration of Margaret's political ambitions is usually placed at a later date, at a party at the vicarage in Corby Glen. But she was dead serious about Conservative politics. It was one of the opportunities that the great university offered and she was not going to waste it.

She did not seem to receive many invitations to tea – a great event in the student's first year. The ritual, as Pamela Mason remembers it, was 'If you'd been out the previous evening to some club and somebody'd asked you your name and college, then a note would appear in your pigeon-hole with an invitation to tea'. No one recalled seeing many notes in the Roberts pigeon-hole.

To Mason she exuded an air of knowing where she was going – 'That's possibly hindsight' – yet she manifested 'a seriousness which I for one, and many of us probably, didn't admire particularly. It was all that we were not. One had to live for many years to get as serious as that.'

Her seriousness and her political convictions made a strong impression. Hazel Bishop (later Hofman), who was in Margaret's year reading history and who had done summer farm work at Corby Glen, was introduced at tea by Margaret Goodrich. Bishop found herself in the presence of someone 'brown-haired, plumpish, with a voice that she had worked on and used with great care'.[7] Their encounter was unlike that at other tea parties where the girls chatted on about their boyfriends – 'a bit daft and let their hair down'. She recognised instantly that 'you would never do that with Margaret Roberts. She never seemed young.'

Pamela Mason also remembers 'a plump, bonny girl, quite well covered. She had brown hair and brown eyes – she gave a brown impression.' Mature for her years, she seemed 'more like a woman of forty than a girl of eighteen'.

The Somerville photograph of the 1943 first-year students confirms this description. Margaret Roberts is in the back row, with flat waved hair darker than blonde, a broad forehead, full cheeks and a squarish figure: indistinguishable in face, form or clothing from the rest.

At Oxford she did not have a serious boyfriend, possibly because eligible men were in short supply. It was impolite to ask the young male undergraduates why they were there. Did they have flat feet, poor eyesight or some other disability? A few of the men had won exemption from service because they were studying science, engineering or medicine – a few of the exempt having been selected by a committee headed by C. P. Snow as 'scientists of the future'.

Women students were supposed to do four hours a week of war work. A fellow Somervillian who did canteen duty at the Clarendon Hotel was appalled at the amount of food the American GIs left on their plates. Margaret Roberts served one or two nights a week at the services' canteen in Carfax where American airmen mixed with British soldiers. She found it fun: 'hot, sticky and very hard on the feet'.[8]

Few of the girls, according to Bawden, had had sexual experience before university, but many were willing to try. Margaret appears not to have succumbed to temptation. In her memoirs she concedes that she experimented with wine and smoking but decided to spend the money on *The Times* instead.

In any event, the Somerville girls were warned by their dean to avoid the over-eager GIs who could be seen pawing girls in public places like Carfax. The British hostility to the 'oversexed, over-paid and over here' American troops grew so intense that the US Office of War Information dispatched the anthropologist Margaret Mead to see what was going wrong. In 1944 this expert on the courtship customs of the South Pacific came up with the answer. In a pamphlet, 'The American Troops and the British: An Examination of Their Relationship', Mead diagnosed that there was a cultural misunderstanding about the meaning of a date. English girls had been raised to expect the boys to impose restraints, while Americans expected the girls to call a halt. In consequence, things were getting out of hand and each side thought the other immoral.[9]

In the summer of 1944, at the end of her first Oxford year, Margaret returned to Grantham and taught chemistry at the Boys' Central School – the school whose boys once scurried out of the KGGS girls' way on the footpath. The desperate shortage of men led to the wartime novelty of hiring women to teach boys.

If she had been short of admiration at Oxford, she had it now. Terry Shelbourne recalls her coming into the classroom and being introduced as the new science teacher. 'She was extremely pretty. All the boys, as twelve-year-old boys are, were agog. We did have one or two lady teachers but they were older people. We liked her because she was pretty.' Also 'she was nice. In those days where the men teachers would square us up, and corporal punishment was still much in, there was nothing like that. She was just a lovely young lady.'

Female company was a rarity. Central's headmaster frowned on boys having girlfriends. 'Should we be seen with a girlfriend after school, we were ridiculed the following morning in assembly,' says Gerald Necklen, another of her former pupils. 'For forty boys at a time, it was an excellent substitute for having a girlfriend. And she was highly attractive. I think you could probably call her an English rose. She'd got a lovely skin, and hair attractively done, so we boys thought it was a great treat to have this young lady teaching us.'

She had no discipline problems at all, although with the strict regime at Central, there was none to speak of. Still, Necklen likes to think that 'perhaps controlling forty boys was a good learning step for her to control a cabinet. Perhaps we boys had a part in setting her on the right track.' In any case, 'She taught the subject well, as though she knew everything about it. I'm grateful that Miss Roberts came because I did quite well in my school certificate in that particular subject.' To him she was not a local girl, simply a teacher. 'She just exuded an air of confidence.'

Grantham was still being pounded by air raids. For a town of its size, it was damaged very badly because of the railway and the armaments factories. As these were close to residential areas, there were many civilian casualties. Terry Shelbourne remembers standing at the end of his street and for the first time in his life seeing grown men cry. 'But the people of Grantham – they just carried on. I don't remember my parents being panicky or frightened.' There were signs, however, that the war's end was coming. While Margaret was at Central, Paris was liberated and the headmaster called a special assembly.

She put her teacher's earnings towards a bicycle for her second year at Oxford. It is a sign of her thriftiness that during her first year, in spite of the need quickly to cover the ground between lectures and labs, she managed without a bicycle, which she now recognised as 'that luxury in Grantham but a near-necessity in Oxford'.[10]

In 1943 – a great honour – Alfred Roberts was elevated to alderman by the votes of his fellow council members. In 1945 he became Mayor of Grantham. For his formal portrait with robes of office, Beatrice made both her daughters new dresses – 'a blue velvet for my sister and a dark green velvet for me – and herself a black *moiré* silk gown'.[11] The official photograph supports local memories: Muriel looked like her mother, 'rather dumpy', and Margaret, head erect and hair rolled back in the 1940s fashion, had blossomed into a beauty.

Chapter 3

On vacations from Oxford, Margaret used to accompany her father to Quarter Sessions (trials of minor offenders) where qualified lawyers sat as Recorders. One such was Norman Winning, a King's Counsel; she joined him and her father for lunch. In the presence of the eminent jurist, she blurted out (according to her memoirs) that she wished she could be a lawyer but could not change her chemistry course. Winning told her to stick with chemistry. He himself had done physics at Cambridge. If she got a job near London, she could study law in the evenings later.

Nineteen forty-five was more than the year when Alfred Roberts became mayor. It was the year in which Clement Attlee became prime minister of a Labour government with a landslide majority. An extravagantly phrased expression of the general glee was written by an old Somervillian, Iris Murdoch: 'Oh wonderful people of Britain! After all the ballyhoo and eyewash, they've had the guts to go against Winston!'[12]

That was not Margaret's view. She was horrified that the country had thrown out its wartime saviour. In the run-up to the general election in July, she had worked hard for the Conservatives. Using the training in public speaking she had acquired at OUCA from a Conservative Central Office tutor, she gave warm-up speeches at village meetings. At polling booths in Grantham she worked alongside Margery Bradley, a girl from her grammar school, and was shocked. Bradley was working for the Labour Party – a KGGS girl endorsing the socialists!

Yet the country did the same. It was Margaret's first experience of electoral defeat and she (and many Tories thereafter) blamed it on the servicemen's vote. Roy Jenkins, however, in his biography of Churchill, says that the result was widely forecast – Labour was ahead all year in the polls – and that it was not swayed by the servicemen's vote, which was three weeks in coming.[13] Indeed, Attlee, as deputy prime minister in the wartime coalition government, had gone with Churchill to the Yalta Conference in January 1945 to discuss international arrangements in the post-war world.

Mayor Roberts, for his part, lost little opportunity to attack the new Labour regime. He deplored its controls on food prices, on industry and on imports, describing them as a 'malignant disease'.

Another era began in August 1945 when the United States dropped atomic bombs on Hiroshima and Nagasaki. Neither then, nor in subsequent years, did Margaret entertain any doubt about the rightness of the decision to use the bomb. The following year at Oxford she read and strove to comprehend the Smythe Report, *Atomic Energy for Military Purposes*, which explained how the fissionable fuel was obtained.

There had been an advantage for women in the shortage of men at Oxford: they advanced to heights previously unscalable. In 1945 Rachel Willink was elected first woman president of the Oxford University Conservative Association. Women were still excluded from membership of the Oxford Union, the training ground for aspiring politicians. But none of them minded; it was a given of the times. Willink says she 'rather enjoyed watching men sort of dress up and prepare themselves for public life, which obviously so many of them were'.

In her post-war years Margaret shared digs with Pauline Cowan and two other young women in Walton Street, near the college. Their house was run by what Cowan remembers as two 'old dears' who served a hideous breakfast of pilchards and mashed potatoes. Eggs and bacon were rationed and were served perhaps once a week. There was no bath; the girls had to have their baths in college.

If the Oxford student diet did not improve with the war's end, much else did. Men had returned from the services and the political scene was lively, for the Conservatives not least. Like the Young Farmers' Unions, Young Conservative Associations generally had a reputation for being something of a marriage market. More importantly for Margaret Roberts, the well-attended meetings, held at 'the Taylorian' – the Taylor Institute – were where useful contacts could be made.

Oxford undergraduates at that time were, by and large, moderately left wing. They were impressed by the Attlee government; there was a feeling that the whole socialist endeavour was in some broad sense right. Young Conservatives were bound by the suspicion that it was pushing the country 'in the wrong direction'.

In March 1946 Margaret became general agent of the Oxford University Conservative Association. Willink says, 'I think she regarded the OUCA as her apprenticeship, her toe in the water, and she was going to do it to the best of her ability.' If so, Miss Roberts's assessment was exactly right. The OUCA was a stepping stone, a place where useful contacts might be made. She felt she had a future in politics and aspired fairly high. She was not going to waste the opportunities available while she was at university.

Willink, whose father had been health minister under Churchill, was accustomed to condescension for being on the unfashionable right. Hitching a lift (perfectly proper behaviour in those times, especially for students), she found herself with two prosperous men who expressed surprise 'that in my youth I should be to the right of politics. That was a thing for the old and decaying.'

With her impeccable Conservative credentials, Willink nonetheless had the impression that Margaret Roberts disapproved of her. 'I was aware of what I believed to be her impression of me. There was a slight sort of lifting of the nostril and a curling of the lip because I was so unserious in my political interest. I might be competent, I might have people who thought I was doing a good job, but I was a lightweight . . .'

Searching for a reason, Willink decided that perhaps it was 'my general style . . . [and the way] I spoke – and so many people did in those days if you were in public school and born and brought up in London: one had this earlier version of the Queen's English, which was rather sort of high pitched. You get it in old films. But I think she was probably aware of my accent and that probably therefore I was a bit privileged, a bit light of purpose . . .'

Margaret did have a social chip on her shoulder. She said one day to her friend Margaret Goodrich, 'Don't you wish that when people asked you where you came from, you could say "Cheltenham Ladies' College" instead of "Kesteven and Grantham Girls' School"?'

This remark, which Goodrich passed on to various interviewers over the years, has been interpreted as a sign that Margaret was beginning to find her provincial background something of an embarrassment. Yet those who lack assurance cannot help but envy those with lots of it. Nina Bawden felt much the same. Going up to Somerville from a working-class Essex family, she was conscious of the contrast between her own flat Essex vowels and the confident public-school accents around her. Margaret Roberts, she remembered, 'spoke as if she had just emerged from an elocution lesson'.

Goodrich herself admits the simple awkwardness: 'When people asked you where you were at school, and you told them, they'd never heard of it, of course.'

Other people fell in love, went swimming in the nude, tried the usual undergraduate excesses, but, unless evidence is deeply hidden, Margaret Roberts did not. To Rachel Willink, she was 'a steady, useful, obliging person [but] I don't think she ever had that period of youthful flight which might have been a good thing for her to have at some point in her life . . .' Margaret did like to dance, however, and perhaps because of her musical ability and in spite of her upbringing, she did it well. Reports of a romance with a 'son of an earl' who dumped her have not been substantiated.[14] Willink paired her off with her own future husband, Michael Kinchin-Smith, for a dance at Lady Margaret Hall – 'very grand affairs to our innocent eyes' – that she herself did not wish to attend. Instead, she watched from the gallery. Pairing her boyfriend with the aspiring treasurer was 'not a wicked whim. I chose Margaret Roberts because I knew they had politics in common. He was, after all, an ex-president of the Conservative Association, he had the most excellent manners and he had quite an agreeable evening with her.'

So he should have done. With Kinchin-Smith and Stanley Moss during the Michaelmas (autumn) term of 1945, Margaret wrote a policy paper containing phrases and ideas that, with hindsight, sound the leitmotifs of the forthcoming Thatcherism. 'Individual enterprise is the mainspring of all progress . . . There is no empirical evidence at all for the existence, either as a real entity or as a true conception, of the mystic community, state or nation that figures in all systems opposed to this principle, such as the Nazi.'[15]

John Campbell, in the first volume of his Thatcher biography, remarks on the glaring contradiction between this belief in the individual ('more important than the system') and her own mystical-patriotic faith in Britain's 'greatness'.[16]

Margaret first became secretary, then treasurer of OUCA. As such, in March 1946, she addressed the Federation of University Conservative Associations at the Waldorf Hotel in London. Her most memorable phrase was 'Let us not forget the need for the uncommon man'. Delivering it, she may have been well aware that she represented just what the Tories now realised they needed – a widening of the class base of the party.

Churchill, after the Conservatives' first major defeat in forty years, had placed Lord Woolton in charge of reorganising the party to take advantage of the new post-war demographics. With the middle class expanding and suburbs growing, people wanted broader representation in Parliament and a downgrading of the importance of personal wealth. Until then a candidate's promise to pay his own way helped selection chances and had thereby restricted the opportunity of standing for office to a tiny section of the population. Almost every Tory MP had been to public school. It had become a patrician, old man's party.

In the Michaelmas term of 1946, Margaret became president

of the Oxford Young Conservatives, thus becoming the second woman to hold the office. 'It would have looked mean spirited if she hadn't at that point been made president,' Willink says, looking back. 'She was an absolutely reliable, honest, faithful servant of the Association.' She won by eleven votes to seven.

One of the deciding votes was that of the seventeen-year-old William (now Lord) Rees-Mogg. He voted for her because she was 'straight-forward and hard-working. I thought she'd do an extremely good job, and she did.' He was impressed by her interest in local government and practical matters: 'Not in broad issues, not in political ideas and beliefs. She was intelligent, focused.' To the future editor of *The Times*, she looked 'severe and serious – agreeable. We were all serious. Sherry was three pounds a bottle – the equivalent of £100 today. We couldn't drink.'

He saw her as a mainstream Conservative; that is, she believed in consensus and accepted those parts of the Labour programme, such as full employment and welfare provision, which people felt the country needed. The Tories, according to Rees-Mogg's retrospective view, recognised that they were one of the political forces behind the creation of the welfare state. As members of the coalition government, they had endorsed the Beveridge Report, and the Butler education reforms, the basis of the education service. While they disagreed with the nationalisation of iron and steel, they accepted that a large part of a national budget had to be spent on welfare.

Nonetheless, he insists, at that time among women undergraduates with political intent the outstanding figure was Shirley Brittain – later Shirley Williams. He recalled, 'If you had to pick an Oxford young politician who, of their contemporaries, was likely to become the first woman prime minister, they'd have said "Shirley" and not "Margaret".'

In October 1946 her OUCA presidency took her to her first party conference, held in Blackpool. She was, she says, 'immediately entranced'.[17] She was delighted to find that the rank and file were still proud of the label 'Conservative'. They would not change the party's name and were eager to rebel against the socialism that the 1945 general election had imposed on them.

Her presidential year was spent organising a full programme of speakers: Lord Dunglass (later the Earl of Home, then Sir Alec Douglas-Home), Robert Boothby, David Maxwell-Fyfe, Lady (Mimi) Davidson, who was the only Conservative woman MP, Anthony Eden and, in debate with the Labour Club, Anthony Crosland and Anthony Wedgwood Benn. She met the great names, took them to dinner at the Randolph Hotel before they spoke, and undoubtedly hoped they remembered hers. At that period also she began serious reading on the arguments against the planned society. She found 'unanswerable criticisms of socialism' in *The Road to Serfdom* by Friedrich von Hayek, an Austrian refugee at the London School of Economics, who traced the roots of Nazism back to nineteenth-century German social planning.[18] Colm Brogan's *Our New Masters* also contained phrases which delighted her. The Labour Party, Brogan wrote in 1947, was 'unfit to govern because of the intemperance of its mind and the childish unreality of its view of life'.[19]

Margaret's political ambitions were now openly expressed. On a visit home to Grantham, she attended a twenty-first birth-day party for Margaret Goodrich at the vicarage in Corby Glen. The party is remembered for the question being publicly put, in Goodrich's recollection, by her mother: 'What', she asked Margaret, 'are you thinking of doing when you go down from Oxford?' The answer was, 'I'm going to be an MP. I want to be an MP.'

The exchange stuck in everybody's mind, even the vicar's. Nobody was surprised because by then Margaret was so involved with the university Conservatives. What also remained in some memories happened during a game of charades – a game that calls for group leaders (usually self-appointed) to tell the others what to do. As Goodrich recalls, 'During the charades, she was pretty bossy. One friend, Theo Parker, lost her temper over this and said, "If you don't stop bossing us about, I shall tread on your foot."'

Political ambition did not relieve her of the task at hand. In the autumn of 1946 Margaret went back to Oxford for a fourth year to take her BSc. After doing her final exams in the summer, she could have left with a BA (Oxon.). Instead, she began the research project that constituted Part II, the fourth and last year of the chemistry degree. With a refugee German scientist, Gerhard Schmidt, and under Dorothy Hodgkin's supervision, she worked on the protein structure of the antibiotic Gramicidin B. They shot X-rays through crystals – the same technique that Dorothy Hodgkin had used to solve the structure of penicillin in May 1945.

The distinguished chemist was, Margaret's memoirs say, 'ever-helpful', and was to remain so over the years despite vast political differences between them.[20] Hodgkin, if anyone bothered to notice in those pre-feminist times, was a role model for the intelligent woman with ambitions in a man's world. During Margaret's third year, she was pregnant with her third child, Toby, born in May 1946. When Hodgkin discovered the structure of penicillin the previous year, her mentor and former lover, the eminent J. D. Bernal, told her she would get a Nobel Prize for the work. Hodgkin replied she would rather be made a fellow of the Royal Society. That, said Bernal, was harder.[21] It was not. Hodgkin was accepted into the Royal Society in May 1947 – the fourth woman in nearly three hundred years to achieve the honour. 'If a woman FRS can have three children, anyone might do anything' was one of the compliments she received.[22]

For Margaret, admission to the Royal Society would take longer. However, her research work yielded the data for a thesis on X-ray crystallography and won her a 2:1 degree: a 'good second'. In later years Janet Vaughan dismissed her famous graduate as 'a perfectly good second-class chemist, a beta chemist'.[23] Yet in the eyes of Rees-Mogg, Vaughan was 'a bit of an intellectual snob. As a person of the centre-left, I think she would have regarded Margaret Roberts as not intellectual in her way and too far to the right.' Dorothy Hodgkin was slightly kinder: 'I came to rate her as good. One could always rely on her producing a sensible, well-read essay and yet there was something that some people had that she hadn't quite got.'[24]

Starting from the same base, Margaret's fellow student, Pauline Cowan, did make a career of science and went on to become a distinguished molecular biologist at King's College London and the University of Sheffield. In their years at Somerville, even in their two years of shared digs on Walton Street, she never discussed science with Margaret, but believes they both received a good, if narrow, education. In Cowan's assessment, 'If she got a second, she was well trained.'[25]

Margaret Goodrich remembers her last conversation with Margaret at Oxford. She herself stayed behind to do a year's diploma in education. As they were walking down Parks Road, 'I said, "Congratulations, you've got your degree." She replied, "Yes, but I don't know. Chemistry isn't the subject for politics. I shall have to read law."'

Had Margaret Roberts been on the wrong track at Oxford the whole time?

4
The Joy of Kent
(1947–1951)

She had trained to support herself and now she began. Upon leaving Oxford, Margaret Roberts took a job as a research chemist with a plastics company in Colchester in Essex, the county on the unfashionable side of the Thames estuary. The BX (for British Xylonite) Plastics factory was not exactly in Colchester, rather ten miles from the town, where she took a room in the house of a widow. Life eased somewhat after four months when the BX research department moved just four miles from town.

Plastics was a heady word in 1947 and xylonite was a primitive form made from coal tar. What seems a quick jump in the chronology of Margaret's life actually spanned eighteen months of hard work – commuting, living in digs and being paid, as a woman, £50 a year less than the £400 p.a. the men were getting for the same job. Her assigned task was looking for a way of coating steel with polyvinyl chloride. Among her co-workers she stood out from the rest with her well-pressed clothes, her gloves, and her voice. The careful vowels, the precise consonants earned her various titles behind her back – 'Duchess' and 'Snobby Roberts', to name but two.

She joined a trade union – the Association of Scientific Workers – and, less surprisingly, the Chelmsford Young Conservatives, where her political ambitions were clear and often expressed. In 1948 she made what was perhaps her first trip

43

outside the borders of England when, as a representative of the Oxford University Graduates Association, she went to the Conservative Party conference at Llandudno, the Welsh seaside convention spot. There she had the break she dreamed of. A friend of hers, John Grant, introduced her to John Miller, chairman of the party in Dartford, Kent, who was looking for a Conservative candidate to represent the constituency in the next general election. This had to come no later than 1950, five years after the Attlee landslide.

Miller, when first approached to consider a woman candidate, immediately said no. Dartford was an industrial seat; the blue-collar vote was male minded. (Such women MPs as there were were mainly Labour. Only two women had ever been members of a British cabinet – a Labour cabinet at that; both were what was then uneuphemistically described as 'spinsters'.) John Grant suggested that the Dartford Tories meet Margaret Roberts first.

Only to a young Tory hopeful could the constituency look enticing. There was absolutely no chance of winning it. Dartford was basically an industrial stronghold with satellite districts, Erith and Crayford. Its manufacturers included Vickers Armstrong, an enormous factory that made submarines and aircraft, and Burroughs Wellcome, an iron foundry. With Henley Cables, Baltic Sawmills and similar works, there was a very strong union element in the constituency.

The incumbent Labour MP, Norman Dodds, what is more, had an unassailable majority of 20,000, bolstered by natural charm. Even so, there were five on the shortlist for the vacancy at the Dartford Conservatives' selection meeting on 31 January 1949, four of them male, all proud to have been chosen from many more applicants.

Kent, the route to London for the Romans, the Normans and the Eurostar, opened the way to Margaret Roberts as well. She held the selection audience in the palm of her hand and won approval by a unanimous vote. 'She was so fluent,' says Ken Tisdell, who was there. 'Everybody was astounded. We thought she was actually terrific.' 'She didn't appear as young as most twenty-two- and twenty-three-year-olds. She seemed old for her age. But she was better educated – there weren't many people with a university degree in the constituency.' Another onlooker, Christine Upton, remembers her as 'very pretty. With all her wonderful answers and her memory, you couldn't resist her. Her looks just helped her along.' A solicitor who was at the meeting came back to his office exclaiming, 'We've got this young woman and she's absolutely superb. She'll make a marvellous MP for us.' June Wood, the secretary and stalwart Dartford Tory who heard this accolade, entirely agreed once she herself met the candidate. 'The thing that really impressed me was the fact that she led us to believe that we could all do what she was doing. It triggered me later on to have the courage to do lots of things I wouldn't have done otherwise.'

On the platform at the Dartford selection meeting was Margaret's father. Her sex and her youth perhaps justified the protective presence, and no one minded when Alfred Roberts, who had driven down from Grantham for the occasion, unashamedly referred to the prospective candidate as 'my baby'. He described himself as a Liberal who recognised that the Conservatives now stood for what he believed in.

What they stood for, however, was uncertain, as Labour's new welfare state was very popular. In her adoption speech at the Bull Hotel, as John Campbell notes, Margaret was careful not to criticise the welfare state and claimed for the Tories some of the credit for setting up the Beveridge Commission which had led to it.

In the audience, waiting like a groom to claim his bride from her father, was the man the candidate would marry. That night Margaret missed the last train from Dartford to London, which she needed in order to catch the connection to Colchester. Up came Denis Thatcher, a director of a manufacturing firm in Erith called Atlas Preservatives. He offered her a lift back to London and she accepted. As a local businessman, Thatcher often had his photograph in the local papers and was interested in politics, but not in becoming a politician. When the Dartford Conservatives had approached him to stand, he recalled, 'I said no without hesitating,'[1] and he dismissed them out of hand. A divorced man-about-town, he commuted in his Jaguar between his flat in Chelsea and his factory in the Erith district of Dartford.

A few months after her selection in Dartford, Margaret changed jobs. She accepted a place in Hammersmith, west London, in the research laboratories of the catering firm of J. Lyons. In so doing, she exchanged one punishing commuting journey for another. The object was to live in her constituency and to nurse it in the evenings. Accordingly, she took digs in Dartford with a Mr and Mrs Woolcott. Her new routine required her to get up before six in the morning, leave the house by half past, catch a bus to the station in order to board the 7.10 train to Charing Cross, and then a bus across London to Hammersmith. Reversing the exercise at night, she would get home by seven in order to spend the evening canvassing or speaking at a meeting. Somehow she found time to spend hours over the ironing board to get the marks out of her good black velvet dress. All for an unwinnable seat: she clearly took a long view of her future.

'Tony Hancock said you only joined the Young Conservatives if you want to go dancing,' says June Wood. 'True enough, you did it because it was a marvellous social club, but it was also another opening into a world you wouldn't otherwise see. You got the opportunity to meet all sorts of people who were young Conservatives – people like Chris Chataway . . . someone you wouldn't rub shoulders with in normal circumstances.'

But one did have to dance. Margaret would come to the dances at the Bull Hotel and take part, and stay all through the evening. She made her mark: quicksteps, foxtrots, the Gay Gordons, even the conga. At one jolly occasion she was presented with a gift, a handbag. Probably it was of the monogrammed variety she preferred. Campaign photographs show her with an array of different handbags, all bearing a large 'MR' on the clasp. On the dance floor Margaret was partnered on at least one occasion by her Labour opponent. Norman Dodds was a chivalrous charmer who liked women and did not despise his Tory challenger, especially as she was young and pretty and would lead a conga line at the Bull Hotel.

On the other hand, Dodds learned the hard way not to tangle with Miss Roberts on a public platform. At first he did not seem to take her seriously. At one point when they appeared together she dismissed one of his answers as 'not good enough'. He countered, 'Well, if you can do better, you answer it.' So she did. That seems to have been the occasion when she had fifty-two *Economist*s spread out on the platform. To prove Dodds wrong, she went straight to the issue where she knew the answer would be and turned it up. This feat of memory strongly impressed the audience and terrified Dodds.

All during 1949 she campaigned in anticipation of the day when Attlee would call the general election. Working woman though she was, in her campaigning she played the housewife card to great effect. The Labour government, she said, should do what any good housewife would do if money were tight: look to their accounts. For the first time in her life, she was having fun: going to meetings outside factories, canvassing, rebutting hecklers. She never stopped or looked tired. She learned how to get through a day with only four hours' sleep. Adrenalin and ambition sustained her. With the others flagged out, she would ask what the plans were for the next day. When she was refused entry to a working man's club where women were not admitted except as paid staff, she signed on as a barmaid. She thereby earned herself a photograph in the *Daily Mail* on 28 June 1949: pulling pints, wide-eyed, plump and round-cheeked as any Victorian bar girl.

Her stamina was the talk of the neighbourhood where she lived. June Wood, who lived with her parents across from the house where Margaret lodged, thought they themselves were diligent Conservatives. 'We'd go to the meetings, or we'd go canvassing or whatever. We'd come back home and I'd go off to bed, and later on so would my parents. But in that little window opposite, the light was going. My father used to say, "There's that good girl, burning the midnight oil."'

What was she busy at? The Wood family thought they knew. 'More than likely, she was preparing her speeches for subsequent meetings, because if we'd been canvassing, then she would have been working all the evening. And, of course, all day. She was still at that time working at her job. She hadn't given up work.' They were impressed too that not only did her father come down to help but her sister came as well.

Strange as it may seem, in those pre-Coronation days before television kept people at home, political meetings were considered entertainment. Also, they provided the only way other than doorstep canvassing through which the public could get a look at their prospective MPs. Margaret Roberts was a crowd-puller. She drew as many as four hundred people out to a political meeting, whereas her Labour opponent, Dodds, was lucky to draw seventy. Her audiences were impressed by her mastery of the facts and figures of local industries. When she answered questions, June Wood remembers, 'you could hear her all over the hall because you didn't have microphones in those days. And that was an advantage: a lovely clear voice and straightforward answers; no nonsense.' The press quickly noted her prettiness and star quality.

She was Churchillian, even Kiplingesque, in her rhetorical references to 'this proud island race'. From her reading of Hayek, she also pointed out the straight line that led from socialism to communism to tyranny and world domination. She used her own father's words to attack socialism as a pernicious system. As reported in the *Erith Observer*, she declared that socialism turned the human spirit into a caged bird: 'It has food and it has warmth and so on. But what is the good of all that if it has not the freedom to fly out and live its own life?'[2]

She door-stepped as well. She did not shy away from can-vassing stalwart socialist areas like the Temple Hill estate, built by the Labour government. It had an Attlee Street for whose opening Prime Minister Clement Attlee came and cut the ribbon himself. It was so pro-Labour that even those who intended to vote Conservative put socialist posters in the window to avoid trouble with the neighbours. Margaret Roberts was undaunted. In any area, preceded by teams of canvassers and leaflet-pushers, she would drive herself to an agreed street. The canvassers would knock on all the doors. 'If they said they'd like to see the candi-date,' says Alan Wells, 'we used to call Margaret over and she'd spend time with them, putting her arguments forward as to why they should vote for her.

'She'd have a lunch-time meeting to speak to the workers somewhere, then in the afternoon she'd be back on the stump until about five. She'd be back about half past six ready for the evening meeting – or meetings – sometimes two, sometimes three. And that's how it was. She never stopped and she never looked tired.'

Hecklers? 'She loved to wipe the floor with them and to swamp them with all the correct facts.' 'Margaret had this facility to take heckling and turn it to her advantage,' June Wood recalls. 'The heckling that came from socialists was all related to the unions. When they would cry "What about the workers?" she responded brilliantly. She used to come back and say that she had helped her father in his business and she had gone away to university and she knew what hard, hard work was, and hard work could get all the problems that we had solved.'

She also grew accustomed to the taunt 'You should be at home cooking and cleaning and leaving this to the men to do'. To that her retort was 'You can do both'. And when women said, 'I can't vote for you because my husband doesn't vote Conservative,' she would come back and say, 'Well, surely, you vote as you want to vote.'

One man made the mistake of harassing her with the shout:

'I wouldn't vote for you if you were an angel in Heaven!' And the answer came back, 'If that were the case, I doubt if you'd be in my constituency.'

She lost, of course. In the general election of 23 February 1950, when the widespread disillusion with Labour drove Attlee's majority down to five, she achieved the considerable personal feat of reducing the majority of the much-liked Norman Dodds, from 20,000 to 14,000. Other Kent Conservative first-time candidates were more successful. Both Edward Heath in Bexley and Patricia Hornby-Smith in Chislehurst scraped in. With the election out of the way, however, she packed up her things and moved to London. She took a flat in St George's Square Mews in Pimlico – a move that made commuting to Dartford easier. It also allowed her to begin studying for the Bar.

Now the press loved her. She was no longer the 'brown girl' of her Oxford days. The *Sunday People* dubbed her the election glamour girl – a part she played well at a 1950 Buckingham Palace garden party when she wore a stylish white hat with a black-piped twisted brim curving up on one side and down to her shoulder – asymmetry according to the fashion then preached by the French designer, Jacques Fath.

Following the election, Attlee's position was weakening. In April 1951 two Labour stalwarts, Aneurin Bevan and Harold Wilson, resigned from the government over the introduction of charges in the health service. Another general election fairly soon was on the cards. As Margaret says in her memoirs:

I felt morally bound to fight the Dartford constituency again . . . I also decided to move to London. With a little more money to spend from my job with J. Lyons, I had found a very small flat in St George's Square Mews, in Pimlico. Mr Soward (Senior) came down from Dartford to help me decorate it. I was able to see a good deal more of Denis and in more relaxing conditions . . . I also learned to drive and acquired my first car. My sister, Muriel, had a pre-war

Ford Prefect which my father had bought her for £129, and I now inherited it.[3]

Aside from allowing her to pursue her long-held intention to begin reading for the Bar, the move to London also made it possible for her to accompany Denis to the theatre and to gala events such as the Paint and Varnish Manufacturers' annual dance. When, at Christmas, recognising perhaps her liking for cosmetics, he gave her a powder bowl of crystal and silver, she realised he was serious.

He represented a world removed from her strict upbringing, which may explain why some of her erstwhile constituents saw her as 'a happy girl'. In retrospect, they realise that she was beginning to fall in love. So much was true. What Margaret probably did not know was that she looked remarkably similar to Denis's beautiful first wife, also named Margaret (although known as Margot), or that he had been deeply hurt because of the break-up of the marriage from the wartime combination of long separation and infidelity.

He was in want of another wife, and he thought Margaret was not only beautiful but diligent and steadfast. The decision to propose seems to have come on a motoring holiday in France with a friend from his public school, Mill Hill. Driving, in his words, 'a sort of tart-trap sports car that I had in those days', he suddenly thought to himself, That's the girl.[4]

A good part of their courtship was spent driving around Kent in his more respectable vehicle, his Jaguar. While her familiar patch of Kent, in Dartford, consisted basically of working-class estates, it bordered on the 'garden of England' Kent of well-heeled commuters, golf clubs and country homes which stretched east to the splendours of Sandwich and Canterbury. Denis's personal friends – memorably William Deedes, later editor of the *Daily Telegraph* – were more typical representatives of what Margaret announced in a speech to the Association of Men of Kent and Kentish Men in January 1950 was 'my adopted county'.[5]

The Kentish men adopted her as well. Particularly useful was Alfred (later Sir Alfred) Bossom, chairman of the Kent Conservative MPs. He took Margaret under his wing. Member for Maidstone, he invited her, even though she was not an elected MP, to his Eve of Session parties at what she saw as 'his magnificent house' at 5 Carlton Gardens, near the Foreign Secretary's official residence.[6] Bossom promised to help her find a better seat to contest. 'He was most helpful to Margaret,' says June Wood. 'But then, of course, Margaret got help from her male colleagues because she was charming. She wasn't the iron lady in those days. She was absolutely charming.'

Not at the start, in the eyes of William Deedes. He was Conservative candidate for Ashford, Kent. Seeing her at candidates' meetings, he recalls 'taking an intense dislike to her at first acquaintance because she asked very bright questions. It was rather like at school, where you always disliked the boy or girl who shone in class and you didn't. Simple as that. She shone.'

She kept on nursing her Dartford constituency. One of her fellow Conservatives, Alan Wells, asked her whether she'd like to go to the pictures one evening. To him, she was a pleasant-looking woman, not a dazzler – 'not the sort of women you'd wolf-whistle'. But he did want to take her out. 'She very nicely turned me down, saying that she had much too much to do and couldn't really spare the time. I understood, and understood even more when I found out about Denis.'

As the romance with Denis progressed, Margaret took him to Grantham to meet her parents. He made a gaffe straight away. Looking at the gaudy turreted Guildhall, he wisecracked, 'I bet they're awfully proud of that.' His bride-to-be accepted the compliment: 'Daddy thinks it's wonderful.' Denis told himself (and later his daughter), 'Watch it, Thatcher.'[7] His inner reserves were further called upon when Alderman Roberts, looking for something to offer to drink, found an old bottle of sherry. (Although he was teetotal, he kept cherry brandy and sherry for guests.) Denis watched while his future father-in-law blew the dust off the top. Sherry was not Denis's tipple of choice.

This disparity between his facetiousness and her literal-mindedness never, as far as anyone has seen, brought them into conflict. She never saw him as a comic character and never talked down to him. What is more, he introduced into her life an element she had long been deprived of: fun.

In allowing him to become her mainstay, Margaret accepted an older man with a past, a fast car and an officer's salty vocabulary. Denis's opinion of Field Marshal Montgomery was: 'a first-class ****, although a great soldier'.[8]

He had a worse epithet than '****' in his vocabulary: 'socialist'. As a businessman, he hated socialism. His view of the 1945 election was that in the services people from totally different backgrounds had mixed in an unprecedented way and that the result was 'an acute twinge of social conscience and a demand for the state to step in and ameliorate social conditions'.[9]

Their engagement was announced (or outed) in the press on the eve of the 1951 election, which came in October. The Conservatives narrowly won, with a majority of seventeen. Attlee resigned and Churchill became prime minister once more. Margaret had to be content with the satisfaction of shaving another thousand votes off Norman Dodds's majority.

Denis retained a healthy detachment from the winds of political fortune. His view of the result: 'She stood for Dartford twice and lost twice and the second time she cried on my shoulder I married her.'[10]

5
Having It All
(December 1951–October 1959)

I've always felt that, but for Denis, Margaret would have
found politics ... not out of reach, I think she'd have got
there – but infinitely more strenuous. It was quite expensive
going into politics. I mean, politics might be in her blood but
you wouldn't find it very easy to finance. At the time, her
personal income – what she earned – was around five hundred
a year. Not more. And on five hundred a year, paying your
own expenses for an election, you'd be stretched. I've often
felt that Denis was – for many other reasons as well – an
important factor in her life.

William Deedes

William Deedes, close friend of Denis and MP for Ashford,
Kent, from 1950 to 1974, was entirely correct. Denis Thatcher
enabled Margaret Roberts to go into politics without financial
anxiety. But that was hardly the extent of the couple's affinity.
The photograph taken at their wedding on 13 December 1951
shows that, like many couples, the new Mr and Mrs Thatcher
had physical features in common: sharp noses, wide, thin smiles
and triangular eyes narrowed down at the corners, alert to whatever might be trying to escape their notice. Both look exceedingly
pleased with each other and the sexual chemistry between them.

The bride was twenty-six, the groom thirty-six. The wedding
took place at Wesley's Chapel, 64 City Road, London, EC1, not
in Grantham, where few of their friends would have travelled.
The Reverend Skinner, who had first shown London to the
twelve-year-old Margaret, assisted at the ceremony, which
was performed by a Reverend Spivey. The hymns included

'Immortal, Invisible' and 'Lead Us, Heavenly Father'. Dartford Conservatives were well represented, pleased to think that their candidate was marrying a local man. Christine Upton of the Dartford Conservative Association office remembers the occasion happily: Margaret 'wore a beautiful blue velvet gown with a large hat, and looked most attractive. Her father shone with his proud smile.' As Mrs Upton's husband was unable to attend, the bride sent him a piece of cake and a little card.

That she wore blue, not white, was perhaps an acknowledgement that the marriage was not Denis's first. As if in recompense, the gown had aristocratic associations; it was copied from a Gainsborough portrait of Georgiana, Duchess of Devonshire. As Carol Thatcher later wrote (with a daughterly edge) of her mother's choice: 'The dress was no gamble: while at Oxford she'd had an identical one made out of a length of black velvet she'd been given. As a bride she teamed it with a matching squashy-style beret, trimmed with a fluffy mass of ostrich feathers on the right-hand side.'[1] The fluffy mass smacks of Hollywood glamour, the feathers tumbling from brim to shoulder are giddy and flamboyant – the mark of a woman so confident in her looks that she is willing to risk silliness on her head.

The wedding reception was held at Alfred Bossom's mansion in Carlton Gardens – a sign to all that the new Margaret Thatcher, although not yet a Member of Parliament, now belonged on the national stage. Alderman Roberts in top hat and tails played father-of-the-bride with great dignity, yet he was not comfortable. The High Wesleyan ceremony had set off 'halfway to Rome' vibrations in his Methodist bones.

After the wedding the couple went to Madeira or, as Margaret recalls breathlessly in *The Path to Power*, 'Denis swept me off.'[2] The verb expresses the wind of change her husband was bringing to her life. The honeymoon was Margaret's first trip outside Britain. That she had never travelled abroad before was not owing to any intrinsic insularity, rather to the war. Had she been a man, she would have served in the armed forces and probably been sent overseas. Had she been five years older or younger, as a student she would probably have wandered across the Continent during her holidays, staying in youth hostels and *pensions*, and sampling cafés. In the late 1940s, however, by the time Europe had become open once again to English tourists, Margaret was too busy cultivating Dartford to set out for Paris and Rome.

She had never travelled by aeroplane before either. Naturally, the trip was a business trip as well. The Thatchers' first stop was Estoril in Portugal, where they met the local agent for Atlas Preservatives. Then they flew to Madeira, and in Funchal surveyed the economic scene and toured the Madeira Wine Company. Returning to Portugal by boat because of bad weather, the bride became violently seasick. There were business dinners in Lisbon before they moved on to France, and for the first time she saw Paris.

Upon their return they moved into Denis's flat at Swan Court in Flood Street in Chelsea. The new wife, beginning as she meant to go on, began to organise her kitchen. But the oven had no bottom. 'I'm not surprised,' Denis said. 'I keep the gin in there.'[3] (This retort, related later to his daughter, shows a man willing to send himself up, playing the role he defined to perfection: that of the man superficially outrageous but with his feet on the ground.)

There was nothing superficial about Denis's commuting. In their willingness to undertake a marathon daily journey, he and his wife were as one. Every morning at 8.15 a.m. he would leave Chelsea for the long drive east to Erith. Every evening he would return home between 7.30 and 9 p.m. and eat the dinner that was waiting for him. There is no record that either spouse ever reproached the other for late return. From the start, their quid pro quo was, in her words, 'Work is the most important thing and it comes first.'[4]

Work brought wealth. As a new wife with money to spend for the first time in her life, Margaret became very hospitable.

She and Denis gave parties (at which she insisted on doing all the catering herself; one of her specialities was lobster flan). In her memoirs, she effuses: 'To be a young married woman in comfortable circumstances in the 1950s must always be a delight if the marriage is a happy one, as mine was. But to be a young married woman in those circumstances in the 1950s was very heaven.'[5]

'Those circumstances' allowed her to enjoy the affluence that was replacing austerity. In British homes that could afford it, the cold storage cupboard was giving way to the refrigerator, the scrubbing board to the washing machine. Bananas and grapes reappeared in the shops; Italian restaurants and coffee bars sprang up on the King's Road. Well placed, she was able to say to her Grantham friend, Margaret Goodrich, 'Never come up to London and spend money staying in an hotel. Always use my flat.'

Naturally she said goodbye to her job in the J. Lyons research laboratories and was now free to concentrate on studying law. She gave up her Conservative candidacy too. Having tilled the stony field of Dartford for over four years, fighting two general elections in the Tory cause, she had paid her dues. Keeping in mind that she would look for a winnable seat before long, she gave first priority to her marriage: 'that was the most important thing in one's life sorted out'.

The second most important thing in Denis's life was rugby football. (Even at the start, the Thatchers gave each other what is now called 'space'.) Until 1963 every Saturday afternoon in the rugby season Denis acted as referee in one match or another, confidently making the instant decisions that can call down the wrath of the stands. Early in their marriage Margaret, no sports lover, did accompany him to a rugby match, but once was enough. He saw why: 'She didn't like the way sections of the crowd criticized the referee – namely me'.[6]

The newly-weds agreed on other domestic rituals. Breakfast was the most important meal of the day, because it was when they could count on being together and when Denis, a creature of habit, expected a cooked breakfast after starting with half a grapefruit, each segment incised to come out neatly without a bit of peel. The essential ingredient was bacon – 'cooked to ashes', according to William Deedes.

However, when Margaret proposed taking up the study of accountancy Denis put his foot down. One of the measures of their compatibility is that she obeyed. He knew how to save her from herself, from her habit of taking on too much. 'Her nature is really to pile a lot on to herself,' says Deedes. 'That was why Denis was so valuable. He was very much a kind of "don't overdo it, love" [man].'

After they married, when they went to Grantham, they did not stay with her parents (who had moved to a larger house on North Parade) but at the George – a hotel that never forgot (and still has not) that it was mentioned by Dickens as one of the best inns in England. These were trips made out of duty. She asked her old friend Margaret Goodrich, now Wickstead, married to a vicar and living in Lincoln, 'Do you find it a big bore to go back home these days?' When she received the answer no, she countered, 'Denis and I do really. We go back and we stay a night in the George and then see my parents, but really we're not interested in Grantham any more.'

On one home visit, Margaret took Denis out to the vicarage at Corby Glen for tea, to introduce him to her surrogate parents, the Reverend Goodrich and his wife. 'Please may I show Denis your library?' she asked. The Goodriches were amused; the 'library' was actually a large drawing room with shelves of books and they never called it a library. Margaret, obviously wanting to impress Denis, did.

Grantham had not lost the power it exerted over her life. In mid-1952 the new Labour majority on Grantham Borough Council stripped Alfred Roberts of his aldermanship. As an independent lacking party support, he was left stranded. Margaret's old pupil Terry Bradley, an unsympathetic observer, believes that Roberts should have seen it coming. 'It was all pre-arranged. He must have been prepared for it because everybody else was. Why should we worry? We'd had enough of him.' When the votes were counted, the result was announced by the town clerk, and all recognised the end of a political career. Roberts, as if leaving the pulpit, declared a valediction: 'I took up these robes in honour, and now I trust in honour they are laid down.'[7] His daughter was deeply moved by these solemn words, and stored them for future use. Reciting them on national television many years later, she wiped her eyes.

Margaret was well into her law studies when, towards the end of 1952, she applied for the Conservative seat at Canterbury. Despite strong backing from Conservative Central Office, which now considered her a good prospect, she failed to make even the short list. The waiting must have been uneasy. At that very time she was confronting the signs that she might be pregnant. She was. The birth, planned or not, was duly calculated for September.

Undaunted, she passed intermediate Bar examinations in May. The next big event was the Coronation of Queen Elizabeth II on 2 June. Because of Margaret's condition, and because, unlike their friends, they had no television set, she and Denis, 'passionate devotees of the monarchy that we were, decided the occasion merited the investment of a seat in a covered stand erected in Parliament Square'.[8] Thus, during the downpour that accompanied the ceremony in June, they watched the pageant in more comfort than most.

In that obstetrical dark age, the Thatchers had no inkling that more than one child might be on the way. Only when Margaret had premature labour pains and went into hospital six weeks early was she told, after X-rays, that she was carrying twins. A Caesarean was scheduled for the following day, a Saturday, and duly performed. Denis was not present. He was at the Oval watching the Test Match between England and Australia. When he did get a look, he was less than overjoyed at the sight of his newborn boy and girl: 'They look like rabbits. Put them back.'[9]

The twins were named Mark and Carol: the result, apparently successful, of a determination to find names that were nickname-resistant. From her hospital bed, the new mother was immediately alert to the threat behind the blessing. She saw how easily she could be trapped by motherhood and deprived of a law career. In hospital, in between telephoning the shops to order two of everything, she applied to take the Bar examination finals in December, less than five months away. She sent off the examination fee (according to her memoirs), 'knowing that this little psychological trick I was playing on myself would ensure that I plunged into legal studies on my return to Swan Court . . . and that I would have to organize our lives so as to allow me to be both a mother and a professional woman.'[10]

How often in later years, one must wonder, did she use this motivating device to push herself into overreaching? In any event, she was certain that good organisation was the key to what is now called 'having it all'. By having twins, she had already accomplished one feat of efficiency: her family was complete with one trip to the delivery room.

With her sharpened perspective, she recognised that an imperative for getting out of the house was the growing isolation of women. The home of her Grantham girlhood was 'a more social place, visited throughout the day by a wide range of tradesmen, from the milkman to the window cleaner, each perhaps stopping off for a chat or a cup of tea'.

Thus sidelined, Margaret could only watch women's slow advancement into national politics. In 1953 the first Tory woman, Florence Horsbrugh, entered a British cabinet. Horsbrugh, like her two Labour predecessors, Margaret Bondfield in 1929 and Ellen Wilkinson in 1945, was unmarried and, in her sixties, likely to remain so. Politics was still a male preserve. While Margaret's mind restlessly wandered over the range of winnable seats, she knew that to stand for Parliament with children was almost unacceptable. Yet what about the Queen? Elizabeth II was giving an example – as Margaret had pointed out in the *Sunday Graphic* in 1952 upon the young Queen's accession to the throne. Under the hortatory headline 'Wake Up, Women!' she preached that the idea that women could not work and have children was obsolete. They could do both. The family need not suffer. Women should aim high, in politics not least. 'Why not', she asked, stretching her imagination to its limit, 'a woman Chancellor – or a woman Foreign Secretary?'[11]

Taking her final examinations on the day that Margaret Goodrich married in Lincoln, she could not travel to her friend's wedding. At the end of December 1953, she was admitted to the Bar and joined the chambers of a criminal lawyer, Frederick Lawton, for an apprenticeship (or 'pupillage') of six months in common law. She then moved through a succession of pupillages and chambers – Chancery, company law – before she got to her goal, tax law. She was already so immersed in its intricacies that about a year after her marriage, when Janet Vaughan invited her back to Somerville, she dismayed her old Somervillians by delivering a lecture to them on tax. Not only the dry subject but the new accent irritated (and embarrassed) her audience. She spoke, wrote Ann Dally, in an accent that sounded like the then-Princess Elizabeth, who used to talk of 'May Husband and Ay'.[12]

Margaret was lucky in her home help. In Barbara, their first, she had a nanny of the finest sort. Trained at Dr Barnardo's, Barbara settled immediately and stayed with them for five years, running the household as well. To make space, the Thatchers rented the adjacent flat and Margaret enlisted Denis's help to indulge in one of her favourite recreations, wallpapering. The twins and the nanny slept on the far side of the adjoining door but Margaret was never loath to dash through and pick up a twin crying in the night. 'Basically,' Barbara told Carol, looking back, 'my one aim was to let her sleep because she was always studying so late that she rarely had a full night's rest.'[13]

As the twins turned into toddlers, the Thatchers adapted their quarters further. Bars went up on all the windows of their sixth-floor flat at Swan Court. Twice a day, on weekdays, weather permitting, Barbara took the children to play in Ranelagh Gardens. Margaret saw herself as spending a lot of time with Mark and Carol, especially at weekends, and reassured herself that, working not too far away, she could be home if needed within twenty minutes. (Traffic permitting, one must assume. The London Underground does not serve that part of Chelsea.)

Orpington in Kent was more than twenty minutes from home. Nonetheless, in December 1954, with the twins only sixteen months old, Margaret learned of a Conservative vacancy there, telephoned Conservative Central Office and asked that her name be put forward.

She made the short list of candidates and, with Denis at her side, presented herself at the Orpington selection meeting. His comforting presence was a sign, as Deedes saw it, that 'The marriage was ideal. He was exactly right for somebody as dynamic as her, somebody who didn't sleep, who did overwork. It was forward-looking of him to accept that his wife was going to go into this strenuous career with two small children.'

In the Orpington vote, she lost out to the local candidate, unable to match his jokey boast that he was the only candidate who knew 'the state of the roads in Locksbottom'.[14] But the brakes were off. Margaret began actively to search for a seat anywhere within a thirty-mile radius of her home, with a special preference for Kent. Constituency-less, all she could do during the run-up to the May 1955 general election, however, was to speak on behalf of other contestants. Second fiddle did not suit her. 'Once you have been a candidate,' her memoirs declare, 'everything else palls.' In the event, the Conservatives held on to power, under Anthony Eden, replacing Churchill, who had resigned in April.

*

Was Margaret a devoted mother or merely obsessional? Accounts vary. Carol Thatcher describes both parents as workaholic, stopping reluctantly, if at all, for family holidays. Barbara, the nanny, Margaret saw as attentive but also competitive. When Margaret knitted royal blue jackets for both children, Barbara interpreted it as a challenge to her own skill at knitting. 'She couldn't bear the thought', she told Carol, looking back, 'that anyone might say "I can do this, you can't".'[15] Of the two parents, Barbara gave Denis the edge. He at least would remember to look up at the nursery window when he left the Flood Street flat on his way to his car. 'Mrs Thatcher, whose mind was already on her job, would forget.'[16]

All the same, while Mrs Thatcher's concentration was always focused on the office, part of her mind was always at home, organising the children's activities, hoping that Barbara was keeping to schedule. For one birthday the maternal hand baked two elaborately shaped cakes – a train for Mark, a boat for Carol – and meticulously iced them.

As a mother she was as fastidious about their clothes as she was over her own – a fussiness that grated on her sister Muriel. In 1949 Muriel had married William Cullen, an Essex farmer. (In his biography, John Campbell relays a story that Muriel stole Cullen from Margaret, who introduced them at a dance in her Colchester days).[17] For whatever reason, the distance between the Roberts sisters was widening. Muriel, speaking to her fellow Granthamite, Margaret Wickstead, drew an unfavourable comparison between her sister and the Sovereign. 'Oh, Margaret will be likely to come around our pig farm in court shoes, you know. Shouldn't think she's ever worn wellingtons in her life. Unlike the Queen.' (That gibe was unfair. Landed gentry spend their childhoods wearing wellingtons in stables and on grouse moors. Tradesmen's children are expected to keep tidy, especially if they help in a shop.)

Yet Margaret Wickstead knew exactly what Muriel meant. Now married with children, she had the Thatchers, mother and twins, to tea. 'And they came to play. Mark was dressed in little velvet trousers and white satin blouse and Carol in a pretty dress. We had a sandpit in our garden and they all got in. My children were dressed in the sort of clothes you wear for a sandpit and the garden.

'When they came to go, after tea – I can see her now on the steps – she said, "Say goodbye to Timothy." And Mark said, "I can't do that, he's too scruffy." '

In the Thatcher household, 'May Husband and Ay' shared strong convictions. Both wholeheartedly supported the Anglo-French invasion of Suez in 1956 and cancelled the *Observer* because of its opposition to the attempt to seize back the Canal. They had no qualms about Britain's right to respond with force to Nasser's 'illegal seizure of an international waterway' and its failure came as a terrible blow.[18] Their view, says her autobiography, was that 'Britain was a great power which should not be pushed around by Nasser's Egypt'.

In January 1957, in the unhappy aftermath of Suez, there was a new prime minister. Anthony Eden resigned because of ill health, and was replaced by Harold Macmillan. In 1957 also, the Thatchers embarked on a new life. Margaret got her chance to don wellingtons at last. She and Denis bought a whitewashed five-bedroom house with a large garden in Farnborough, Kent – easier for the children to ride their tricycles, easier for Denis to get to Atlas Preservatives, but harder for her to slog into town every day to her chambers in Lincoln's Inn Fields. The Conservatives held some responsibility for the move, however; by withdrawing rent controls, they had allowed the rent on the double flat at Swan Court to be raised to what Denis felt was an exorbitant sum.

At their new home, called 'The Dormers', Margaret had a garden for the first time, and she threw herself into landscaping, weeding and planting a crescent-shaped dahlia bed. But the first task was a no-nonsense move to fill in the pool so that the children could not fall in and drown. She took advice from a local horticulturist, which was fine until he married Barbara. The new nanny, Abby, turned out to be just as competent at childminding and household management as her predecessor. When the time came, Margaret took her place with other local mothers in sharing the school run.

The children were taken to church too, but not as often as Margaret had been as a child. The move to Farnborough allowed an effortless slide from Methodism to Anglicanism. They all attended Denis's choice, Farnborough Parish Church. 'We both felt that it would be confusing for the children if we did not attend the same church,' Margaret explains in *The Path to Power*, adding the ecclesiastical gloss that John Wesley had always regarded himself as a member of the Church of England.

They also went on typically English seaside holidays – first to Bognor Regis, then, starting in 1959, across the Solent to the Isle of Wight, which they liked so much they went for several years running. One of the nicest pictures of the Thatchers relaxing shows them on the sand, Margaret in sweater, buttoned casual skirt and sandals, with her hair (for once) wind-blown, Denis in knickerbockers, while along the sea wall is perched a line of people who have the look of friends who meet in the same spot year after year. It is a convincing picture of normalcy and contrasts with Carol's description, in her biography of Denis, of workaholic parents who disliked family holidays and a father who managed to be in Africa for all of August, returning only in time for the rugby season in the autumn.

Moving from place to place was no chore for Margaret Thatcher. Once Margaret Wickstead went to visit her as she was packing up. She was labelling, 'in the most efficient fashion, various pieces of furniture to indicate what rooms they were to go in. She's very practical and very good at housework. If a curtain fell off a hook, she wouldn't wait for somebody else to put it up, she would do it herself.' As for decorating, 'she knows how to plaster a ceiling and paper a wall'. During the visit,

Wickstead recalls, 'she did manage to fry some bacon for us to have a quick lunch'.

In the early spring of 1958 another tempting Kent vacancy appeared. Alfred Bossom, Margaret's old patron, was retiring from the seat at Maidstone, one that would suit her very well. However, she was rejected fairly smartly, in part because she gave a poor answer to the inevitable question about how she would juggle her family and public responsibilities. Her reply – that as a Member of Parliament she would have mornings free for her family – ignored the fact that parliamentary committees met in the mornings.

The question, put only to women and never to men, seemed relevant at the time. It is hard to recapture the extent to which women were chained to the home by housework before labour-saving devices became commonplace appliances, not luxuries. Margaret was liberated by Denis's money but, as she was never shy of saying, she was unusually fortunate.

Finchley occupies a large swathe of north-west London, commanding four stops on the Northern Line. It is a suburb known for the sophistication of its residents, including a large Jewish community, and for its architecture. The neo-vernacular planned community of Hampstead Garden Suburb, built in 1906–7, and the modernist East Finchley Tube station, built in 1939, with curved walls and other strong Bauhaus touches, are places of pilgrimage for students of twentieth-century building. Although the constituency has changed its shape over the years, its political complexion has been consistent. With its high proportion of home-owners, professional people, children in higher education, and with few council estates, it is, in the words of the former editor of the *Finchley Press*, 'a True Blue area'. In 1955 the incumbent Conservative MP for Finchley and Friern Barnet was returned in the general election with a majority of nearly 13,000.

When in March 1958 Sir John Crowder announced his intention of standing down at the next general election, two hundred Conservative hopefuls reached for the gleaming plum. This time Margaret Thatcher survived the rigorous elimination contest. Out of eighty candidates recommended by Central Office, she attained the long list of twenty, then the final four.

In the light of subsequent history, it is not surprising that those who were present at the decisive selection meeting remember the night. John Tiplady, later president of the Finchley Tories, was looking for a successor to Crowder, who lived in the shires and who used to arrive in the constituency wearing top hat and tails, riding in a carriage: 'what one in 1958 imagined a Member of Parliament to be'. Colinne Martyn, a Young Conservative at the time, also went in with 'this preconceived view: "It can't be a woman, it can't possibly be." In those days women just didn't stand for Parliament. I [thought I] would feel safer with a man because he was wiser, was in business and would have the wisdom and the power and the strength. But when she came on, she was electric, electric. She had a terrific charisma and she spoke so well. She appeared to be speaking to you right at the back.'

And she spoke without a text. She impressed them with her fluency and thorough preparation. Rates were unfair, she said, for example, because only the householder paid them while other people enjoyed the education, the council services and everything else. She thought that other members of the family should contribute to the council tax.

On this occasion she easily sailed over the 'What about your children?' hurdle that had defeated her at Maidstone. She explained that she had the good fortune to have a husband who could afford to pay for an excellent nanny-housekeeper. She could, with careful organisation, combine being a good mother with being an effective Member of Parliament.[19]

She spoke before Dr John Bowlby, the famed child psychiatrist, who lived in the constituency, which was not far from the heart of London's psychoanalytic community, drove guilt into the heart of working women with his elucidation of 'maternal deprivation'. 'Mother' and 'mother substitute', to Bowlby, were not the same thing.

Colinne Martyn was utterly won over by the Thatcher performance. 'There were still people who believed it should be a man, that a woman couldn't do such a job – but she told us that she had someone to care for the children and that she'd always be there if needed.

'One got the feeling that it was a good thing because she would know of the problems of bringing up a family, and she would know of the problems of women in Parliament and how they had to cope.'

Her three opponents were all public-school men. The contrast was great: the audience saw her, John Tiplady says, as 'a very attractive lady'. Suddenly Crowder seemed old, inarticulate, fusty, a knight of the shires. He had been a good MP but, Finchley knew, he didn't speak in Parliament.

'When the time came for the final vote,' Tiplady recalls, 'every person on the selection committee had placed Margaret Thatcher one of the first three. The final vote was not unanimous; three people abstained – perhaps because it was a lady.' The second ballot gave her the candidacy by forty-six votes to forty-three.

Margaret wrote to Denis about her chances but he never received the letter. As at so many major moments of her life, he was abroad. South Africa was an important market for the products of Atlas Preservatives. He was now chairman of the company, which employed two hundred people. Presumably he had no objection to her taking on another marathon obligation to criss-cross London from the deep south-east to the extreme north-west as a regular routine. It was bad luck that they had just bought the house in Kent, but she was prepared to drive herself as often as needed to her new area of responsibility.

Denis learned of her selection (and therefore virtually assured entry into Parliament) from a copy of the London *Evening Stan-*

dard that surfaced incongruously on the empty seat next to him on an international flight from Johannesburg to Lagos.[20]

Her adoption meeting on 8 August 1958 was a kind of coronation, for she dressed with appropriate solemnity. She wore, as she proudly recounts, 'a plain black outfit with a small black hat'. For the *Finchley Press*, it was love at first sight:

Speaking without notes, stabbing home points with expressive hands, Mrs Thatcher launched fluently into a clear-cut appraisal of the Middle East situation, weighed up Russia's propagandist moves with the skill of a housewife measuring the ingredients in a familiar recipe, pinpointed Nasser as the fly in the mixing bowl, switched swiftly to Britain's domestic problems (showing a keen grasp of wage and trade union issues), then swept her breathless audience into a confident preview of Conservatism's dazzling future.

The task ahead was clear: to prepare for the general election whenever (before May 1960) Macmillan chose to call it. The Liberals were the immediate threat as their strength was growing. A few years earlier they had campaigned against the alleged exclusion of Jews from Finchley Golf Club – a club with which prominent Conservatives were associated. (Cleverly the Liberals had outwitted the custom of omitting party affiliation from the local ballot paper. Their candidates changed their name by deed poll to 'Somebody Liberal' and as such it appeared on the ballot. The ruse gave them a majority on the council.)

Margaret admired the Jewish community, recognising the same values of family loyalty, self-reliance, hard work and aspiration with which she had been brought up. To counter the Liberal rise, she made a strategic move. Knowing that the Liberals were striving for the Jewish vote, she enlisted an MP known to be Jewish, Keith Joseph, to come with her to Hampstead Garden Suburb. In his biography, John Campbell gives evidence that Crowder, still the incumbent member for Finchley, complained to Central Office that she was inviting speakers to the constituency without his knowledge.

In the long run-up to the unspecified election day, there were a number of public meetings in which all three candidates appeared on the same platform. The young Labour candidate, Eric Deakins, a Tottenham councillor, saw the coming contest as a fight for second place. Would he, or the Liberal, Ivan Spence, finish below Margaret Thatcher? But Conservative Central Office was worried about the Liberal rise. Nothing was to be taken for granted.

Deakins, just starting his political career, watched her with fascination. But not admiration. 'I got the impression then that she was a formidable person,' he says, 'someone with convictions – great convictions – and a brilliant debater. But someone completely lacking in any vestige of human warmth.'

Harold Macmillan named the date at last – 8 October 1959 – while the Thatchers were on the Isle of Wight.

Over the next six weeks, the Finchley Tories came to love her. They admired the campaign photographs of the happy family: Denis beaming proudly, the by now handsome twins with wide engaging smiles, as if all they wanted was to see their mother an MP. The campaign workers struggled to match her 'tremendous enthusiasm, tremendous energy'. How, Colinne Martyn asked herself, could the candidate do it? 'She had very little sleep and yet still appeared well groomed, on the ball, and she used to canvass – she led us out there, she'd knock on doors, she'd roll up her sleeves and join in.

'She charmed everyone and ladies as well. I think it was the way she spoke to people. She believed in telling the truth that if she thought something was wrong, well, she'd put it right or try to.'

From the opponent's point of view, Deakins was 'to a certain extent in awe of her. I had never fought an election before; she had tremendous electoral experience in Dartford in 1950 and 1951, where she had done very well in reducing the majority in a safe Labour seat. At the same time I had a gut feeling "she is not my type of politician at all".'

In the 1959 campaign she stuck very clearly to the 'You Never

Had It So Good' line enunciated by Harold Macmillan in his own campaign. She defended Suez, the nuclear deterrent, capital and corporal punishment, a stronger United Nations. As Deakins watched her he saw that her manner was stubborn adherence to the party line. He liked to think of himself as more flexible, 'often marginally deviating from what was then Labour Party policy' in his statements and answers to questions.

But her advantages were obvious. Deakins too noticed that she was 'always extremely well turned out'. (Saying this, Deakins apologised – 'one shouldn't be sexist on these occasions' – without allowing that, in 1959, one could.) He continues, 'But she always wore the right clothes for these big political occasions. And they *were* big political occasions: audiences of two or three hundred people. And here comes this lady dressed – well, brightly – and her husband was in business; a family person. She was very pleasant to listen to; she sparkled. She always gave the impression of wearing new clothes.'

If, with her constant emphasis on her husband's income, she appeared to be boasting, she made clear that she did not believe that working wives should be subsidised through tax allowances, or, as she says in *The Path to Power*, 'by the taxes paid by couples where the woman looked after the children at home and there was only one income'.[21]

Mrs Thatcher did not rely only on her wardrobe. Debating with her opponents, she played a card she would always use to great advantage: the barrage of facts and figures. Added to her good memory and natural literal-mindedness was her barrister's ability to master a brief quickly. There were no jokes and little camaraderie in her delivery, rather a torrent of fact.

Deakins learned the hard way. In Finchley a public meeting was held, chaired by the Bishop of London, following a Conservative government report on a massacre at the Hola camp in Kenya, where seven or eight people had been shot by British forces. A parliamentary inquiry headed by a judge had produced the report.

'So naturally,' Deakins recalls, 'the Liberal and I were very up in arms about this. Mrs Thatcher spoke third. She held up a copy of the report about half an inch thick, and said, "Mr Chairman, I must be one of the very few people in this hall who have read this report from cover to cover."' It was true.

Deakins realised he had been wrong-footed. 'She must have taken a gamble that neither my Liberal opponent, who was an ex-colonial magistrate in his sixties, nor I, as a young man, would have even seen the full report. She proceeded to quote from selective extracts favourable to the government, naturally missing out anything that was unfavourable. That taught me a great lesson: always to be properly prepared in a public debate.'

The strategy worked, although she was never in danger. When the results were announced, she had improved on Crowder's majority by more than 3,000 votes, racking up a majority of more than 16,000. The tally was Thatcher 29,697, Deakins 13,437 and Ivan Spence 12,260.

When the new Parliament convened, Margaret Thatcher, charming in a neat straw hat and belted-waist dress, apparently scrutinising a document, was caught by a photographer, standing against the backdrop of Big Ben. The picture was no accident: she had alerted the press to the time of her arrival for her first day in Parliament. Considering the novelty of her position and the mood of 1959, the caption in the London *Evening News* was appropriate: 'Mark's Mummy is an MP Now'.[22]

6

A *Woman*? The *Tories*?
(1959–1975)

Twenty-five of the 630 Members of the new Parliament in October 1959 were women. The reputation of the new MP for Finchley and Friern Barnet had preceded her: mother of twins, blonde, pushy. The secretary assigned to her met her at the entrance to the House of Commons and offered to show her around. It was not necessary. Margaret Thatcher knew just where she was going, and headed into the Members' Lobby to deal with the necessary paperwork.

Very soon she had a stroke of exceptional luck. In the ballot for Private Members' Bills, she came third. Her maiden speech, therefore, would introduce her very own piece of legislation, on the subject on which she had been weaned, local government. Her bill would reinforce the right of the press to cover council meetings. While the press did have statutory right of entry to public meetings, local councils had the habit of withdrawing into committee and excluding the press. The new bill would close off this escape route. Not that Margaret was an ardent champion of a free press; rather she wanted the newspapers to keep a closer eye on 'socialist connivance with union power' in local government.[1]

She did her best to ensure a good audience for her debut by sending 250 handwritten letters to Tory MPs, inviting them to turn up. When she rose to her feet on 5 February 1960 and the chamber heard the Thatcher voice for the first time (for a full half-hour), she navigated gracefully the convention that a maiden speech should praise the constituency. 'Finchley, which I have the honour to represent,' she said, 'would not wish me to do other than come straight to the point.'[2] She spoke without notes. Denis, for some reason, was not there to hear the speech.

By morning she was a star. Her performance won universal applause – not least from the veteran Labour MP Mrs Barbara Castle (late Baroness Castle of Blackburn) – for its clarity and brilliance. The Peterborough column of the *Daily Telegraph* commented that as a maiden speech it was unlikely to be excelled.[3] There was talk of her getting a front-bench posting very soon. How did she feel about that? the press wanted to know. One answer was adroit: 'I think I'll just try and be a very good backbencher first.' She gave another that she instantly regretted: 'I couldn't even consider a Cabinet post until my twins are older.'[4] (This was a gaffe, she concedes in *The Path to Power*, without saying why. Was she trying to conceal her ambition?)

It took only two years for the prime minister, Harold Macmillan, to give Margaret Thatcher the boost for which new MPs yearn by making her parliamentary secretary to the Minister for Pensions and National Insurance. To be sure, it was what everybody recognised as 'a woman's job'. As she once explained it, 'You'll notice that women are put to Ministers of Health, Housing, Pensions, Education. Anything to do with welfare or children.'

She still had her other woman's job; the twins were now eight. As the first mother of young children ever to hold government office, she knew she had to justify taking on extra responsibility. How would she do it? In answer to the persistent question (with its scarcely veiled implication that she was neglecting her children) she would reply that, thanks to her husband's income, she was privileged to have an excellent housekeeper-nanny to look after them when she was away – and moreover she telephoned home every day at six o'clock to see that they were all right.

Her new responsibilities were going to need 'even more organisation and method. I'm a great believer in those two things,' she announced. 'In any case I could never do it were it not for the fact that my home is within thirty-five minutes of Westminster.' A subtle reminder of her affluent circumstances appeared in her boast that she never used foreign au pairs – a boast that ignored the fact that these language students, who worked for mere pocket money and ample free time, were the main source of home help for the middle-class working mother. But Margaret insisted that she could never be sure that an au pair's English was adequate to call the hospital in an emergency.

Photographed arriving for her first day as a junior minister, she marched in unsmiling and regal, wearing a fur toque and a long-line New Look dress. A dress, and not a suit, was the appropriate business wear for the serious woman of the 1960s.

Ten months earlier, on 7 December 1960, Beatrice Roberts died at the age of seventy-two. The primary cause was coronary thrombosis; Margaret was motherless at thirty-five. Looking back, she wrote in her memoirs, 'Although in later years I would speak more readily of my father's political influence on me, it was from my mother that I inherited the ability to organize and combine so many different duties of an active life. She had been a great rock of family stability. She managed the household, stepped in to run the shop when necessary, entertained, supported my father in his public duties and as Mayoress, did a great deal of voluntary social work for the church, displayed a series of practical domestic talents such as dressmaking and was never heard to complain . . .'[5]

For all her own domestic talents, Margaret did not have to be at home to prepare her children's lunch. Even so, she did spend a lot of time with her children; weekends were sacred to family and she never travelled during school holidays. She cosseted them and never raised her hand in anger. Wishing them to have the luxuries she had been denied, she saw to it that they had dancing and riding lessons. As she explained to Miriam Stoppard in a television interview in 1985, 'I try to give my children a little bit more amusement, a little bit more to play sport. Everywhere they went they could play sports.'[6]

Although the twins squabbled, she appears to have been equally close to each of them. Over the years, especially as he came to draw press attention, Mark Thatcher acquired the reputation of mother's favourite. There is little evidence, however, that he was anything more than his mother's only son. The mother–daughter relationship is different from that of mother–son. Carol probably spent more time than Mark did with their mother. She lived at home longer, and Margaret paid constant and scrupulous attention to every detail of her daughter's life, from after-school companions to clothes, hair, diet and lessons.

Fairly early in Margaret's ministerial career, in 1961, at the age of eight, Mark became a boarder at Belmont, preparatory school for Mill Hill, Denis's public school, conveniently near Finchley (Mark went on to Harrow). Three years later Carol went as a boarder to Queenswood School in Hertfordshire.

One of Carol's school mates, Hilary Skaar, found her 'popular, full of fun. Always laughing, she was slightly rebellious at school. She didn't like what she thought were rules that were made to be broken, like going upstairs two at a time or running down the corridors. She was never really naughty, but she was fun to be with. Even then she was very good with words, she wrote well. Very articulate. She also worked very hard because her mother expected her to work hard.'

As boarders, the Thatcher children were so accustomed to their mother being away at work that they did not suffer from homesickness. But there were sacrifices. 'I always seemed to be the only child in the class with a working mother,' said Carol. At one Speech Day she had to sit with the Skaars because neither

1. Not a hair out of place: Margaret Roberts, left, aged four,
shown in 1929 with her sister Muriel, began as she would go on –
well coiffed and well dressed.

2. Alfred Roberts – shopkeeper, preacher, city councillor, political and moral model for his younger daughter.

3. Beatrice Stephenson Roberts – dressmaker, musician, Sunday School teacher. 'She was a very, very capable woman,' says Margaret Thatcher in her memoirs.

4. One North Parade, Grantham: the Robertses' world, where family life and business coexisted, to the constant noise of traffic.

5. 'I owe a great deal to the Church for everything in which I believe': four times every Sunday Margaret Roberts attended the Finkin Street Chapel.

6. Margaret Roberts, front row, right, is remembered as an assertive angel in a Grantham nativity play.

7. Are you the new schoolmarm?
An Oxford undergraduate, pretty
Margaret Roberts was a welcome
change from the usual science
teacher at Boys' Central School,
Grantham, in the summer of 1944.

8. Finest hour: Alfred Roberts, flanked
by wife and daughters, is inaugurated
Mayor of Grantham in 1945.
Margaret, home from Oxford, has
blossomed into a beauty.

9. After hours: Margaret Roberts,
chemist during the day,
Conservative candidate in the evening,
goes over political papers
at her digs in Dartford, Kent.

10. The firm of J. S. Lyons was a
pioneer in new technology and
Margaret Roberts enjoyed her work in
its Hammersmith laboratories.

11. At the Bull Inn, Dartford, Margaret Roberts found use for her pianistic skills.

12. In her fashionably asymmetrical hat and piped jacket, Margaret Roberts shines at a Conservative fête in Dartford.

13. Handbag at the ready, Margaret Roberts, canvassing for the October 1951 general election, shows she is the working man's friend.

14. On eve of the 1951 general election, the engagement is announced of the Conservative candidate for Dartford to a local businessman, Denis Thatcher.

15. 'The second time she lost [in Dartford] and cried on my shoulder, I asked her to marry me'.

16. Two for the price of one: Margaret Thatcher produced a son and a daughter in August 1953 and four months later passed her Bar examination finals.

17. Friends together: the Thatchers relaxed with other families who, like them, returned year after year for holidays at Seaview, Isle of Wight.

18. Carol Thatcher is less happy than her twin brother Mark is with the constant photo calls required of the Conservative candidate for Finchley in 1961.

19. New Look greets Old Look: Finchley's new MP arrives at Westminster on 20 October 1959.

20. Pleased to be in the shadow Cabinet, on 22 October 1969 the new Opposition minister for education does not sense the 'milk snatcher' row lying in wait.

21. Cover girl: ever willing to pose, wearing what looks like a remnant of her wedding hat.

22. Caught in the act: one of Thatcher's proudest boasts is cooking Denis's breakfast every day.

her own mother nor her father could come. Also, on the Sports Day when she won top prize in the junior school, neither Margaret nor Denis was there to see her receive it.

In 1966 the Thatchers sold their house in Farnborough and moved into a rented flat in Marsham Street, very near the House of Commons. The following year Hilary Skaar came home with Carol to spend a week at the flat during a school break. The House was still sitting, but Hilary found that Carol's mother 'had us organised down to the last minute'. Margaret met them herself at Liverpool Street Station. Because the train was late, she said that they would have to take a taxi rather than the Tube because she had to be back at the House. Even so she saw the girls home to the flat first before she went back to work.

The plan for one day during the holiday called for Carol and Hilary to go to the top of the Post Office Tower, where Margaret would meet them for lunch. During the morning, however, the weather turned grey. From her office Margaret called to issue new instructions. 'You'd better go shopping,' she said, 'and I'll meet you for lunch at Harrods instead.' Which she did. Having returned home, in the evening, she asked to see the results of the shopping expedition and insisted that Carol try her new clothes on. She also inspected and approved of the hairdo Carol had given herself. After that, she invited the girls into her bedroom to help her choose outfits for a trip she was about to make.

The same holiday programme included a boat trip down the river, and entertainment every evening, with the Thatchers turning out *en famille*. At *The Black and White Minstrel Show*, Mark let himself be drawn up on to the stage. Hilary noticed that Carol and Denis laughed but that Margaret feared he might be embarrassed. (He was not.) During the same visit Margaret did not laugh when, at dinner, Mark, pulling out Hilary's chair for her, pulled it out so far that the girl sat down on the floor. 'His mother was absolutely furious with him,' Hilary recalls, 'even though I thought it was an accident.'

The holiday week ended with Margaret driving Carol and

Hilary down to Kent where there was more organised sight-seeing, so ambitious that the girls did not have time even to swim in the pool.

From 1960 the four Thatchers began to take an annual skiing holiday in Switzerland. Lenzerheide is a small mountain village at 5,000 feet, between (but slightly to the west of) St Moritz and Klosters. In 1960 it had just three hotels and a single street of shops displaying 'ENGLISH SPOKEN' signs. Indeed, the place was full of English people, having become fashionable in the 1920s for school parties from Eton and Harrow. There was a ski club where English families would race. Denis went curling with the curling club run by an Eton master. There were tea dances, bridge parties, and every evening black-tie dinners.

All four Thatchers took skiing lessons, the parents privately, the children at ski school. Patricia Nicholson, known as 'Poo' (now Mrs Madge), who was about four years older than Mark and Carol, was in the same ski class and also at the same dining table. She retains the vivid memories of one who has observed celebrities before they were famous:

The Thatcher family were good fun on holiday. Denis was quite quiet but Margaret was up for everything. She was good fun and the children used to play cards in the evening with my family – we played pontoon – furiously, with matchsticks, and took no prisoners. Mark tended to be naughty behind his mother's back but played the goody-goody when he was in front.

At ski school the instructors were tough. They made the children walk long distances in the cold. When Patricia protested, her parents agreed not to send her back, 'but Mark wasn't so lucky':

Mark set off bravely the first morning but quickly became tearful. He was cold, he was miserable, he was small and he wasn't a happy chap. When we got back to the hotel at lunch-time, he vowed he was never going skiing again. But out he came the next day and pressed on with it. By the end of the week he was doing really well and wouldn't have anybody believe anything different.

Margaret was a no-nonsense mother and wasn't going to have Mark dropping out of the children's ski school. She felt he would be perfectly fine there and he had to suffer. He did not like it.

Patricia recalls that Margaret Thatcher seemed to enjoy the après-ski more than the slopes.

She used to decide what everybody was going to do after dinner. Her favourite occupation was sitting in the bar after dinner with a liqueur and debating with anybody who would sit with her. The fellow guests in the hotel on the whole enjoyed it. One of the few people who didn't particularly enjoy it was my mother, who liked to be the centre of attention. She used to say, 'Oh, Margaret's on her soapbox again,' and disappear off to another bar and spend her evenings there.

Margaret was known to be a Member of Parliament and presented the cups after skiing contests. In subsequent years, Mark's skiing improved, as did Carol's, and Margaret was very proud when they achieved something in a skiing race. She was also conspicuous among the women for being always the best dressed:

We all dressed for dinner but she had something special. She carried herself well and she was more sophisticated than we were. She did her hair in the evenings for dinner. She had on lots of make-up and she really took a lot of trouble over her appearance.

But Patricia noticed that Margaret preferred the company of men. 'They were more ready to listen to her. There were a lot of university professors and quite educated people who would listen to her and let her have her say. I think there wasn't a place for a woman in her circle at that time.'

*

Chapter 6

The poet Philip Larkin chose 'the end of the Lady Chatterley ban and the Beatles' first LP' as the markers for the start of the sexual revolution. In the 1960s Britain was changing. The mood of the voters turned against the Conservatives. On 15 October 1964 the Labour Party under Harold Wilson won the general election by the narrow majority of fourteen and Margaret entered the shadow cabinet as spokeswoman on pensions under Sir Alec Douglas-Home, Leader of the Opposition.

Labour's victory swept a new formidable woman into Parliament. Shirley Williams, the new Labour member for Hitchin (which she served from 1964 to 1974) found the House of Commons 'very territorial'; women MPs were tolerated, but not everywhere, certainly not in the Smoking Room. When a male colleague invited her for a drink, she was sipping wine when an elderly male MP (Tory) came by, leaned over her shoulder and said, 'This is obscene.'

Where Shirley Williams (now Baroness Williams) would encounter Margaret Thatcher was the Lady Members' Room. 'You'd go in, and there would be very often Mrs Thatcher ironing her dress for the evening or touching up the collar of her shirt.' Baroness Williams, perhaps conscious of her own reputation for tousled hair and a Fabian indifference to wardrobe, recalls of Margaret, 'She was always impeccable.' However, there was a bond between them: 'Mrs Thatcher was a member of that obviously beleaguered group of women MPs. She was not, certainly, one of the most companionable; she wasn't somebody who joined in the fun.' But she was aware of the importance of women in Parliament sticking together. She said to Mrs Williams conspiratorially, 'We have to show them that we're better than they are.' That, in the Williams interpretation, was not a party political comment. 'One of the things that I got to know or learn about Mrs T. was that she had a very strong sense that men were agreeable, playful and in the end not very serious creatures.'

*

Harold Wilson did take Barbara Castle seriously, as he had done since 1945. In his new cabinet he made her Minister for Overseas Development, and then promoted her to Secretary of Transport. Mrs Castle was on the rise. Mrs Thatcher's career was stalled. And so was her marriage. In 1964 Denis left the country for three months, in a state that his daughter has described as 'on the verge of a complete nervous breakdown'.[7] He was forty-nine. The nest was empty, children away at school, wife keeping late nights at the House. His doctor told him overwork was endangering his health. 'I got myself on a boat,' he told Carol later, '– it shook Margaret – and took myself off to South Africa.'[8]

His explanation of his collapse was that it was caused by fear that his company was under-capitalised and that he and his dependants might suffer under the Labour government's new capital gains tax. What would be the financial outlook for his mother and his aunts if anything should happen to him?

Denis was always happy in South Africa. From there he went on safari, toured game reserves in Rhodesia, took hundreds of photographs and miles of moving-picture film, and upon his return – without telling Margaret – sold Atlas Preservatives. The deal, according to his daughter's biography, netted £250,000, of which £10,000 was his personal share; according to John Campbell's biography of Margaret Thatcher, the sale made Denis a millionaire.[9] In the event, the move turned out to be not so much a retirement as a promotion. The buyer, Castrol Oil Ltd, gave him a seat on its board and an office in the Marylebone Road. Soon Castrol was taken over by Burmah Oil, which also recognised Denis's business acumen. Burmah gave him a senior executive post and an Audi in which to travel to work – no small blessing a few years later when Burmah moved its headquarters eighty miles away to Swindon. Denis then made the trip twice a day. The Audi, according to Carol, had no radio.[10]

*

After nine months of the Wilson government, in July 1965, Sir Alec Douglas-Home resigned as Conservative leader, to be replaced by Edward Heath. Margaret voted for Heath, on Keith Joseph's advice, although her own preference was for Reginald Maudling. She knew Heath fairly well, having campaigned for him in her Dartford days when he fought and won the seat in the neighbouring Kent constituency of Bexley. Their backgrounds were not dissimilar. Heath was the son of a carpenter and the first Tory leader to have attended a grammar school. His odd strangulated vowels soon earned him the nickname 'the Grocer' from those who, like all previous Tory leaders, were pleased with their public-school voices.

As Heath assembled his team, Margaret, continuing her peregrination through the women's jobs, was moved from junior secretary of Pensions to shadow secretary of Housing and Land.

Although the Thatchers had sold 'The Dormers' and moved to a flat in Westminster, Denis had to have a country retreat and it had to be in Kent. The large mock-Tudor house they bought in Lamberhurst near Tunbridge Wells was called 'The Mount' and, of all their homes, remained Denis's favourite. The Thatcher children, however, far preferred town to country and, growing older, often protested against going away at the weekend.[11]

Heath gave Margaret a job because he recognised he needed a woman for his team. When Jim Prior, then shadowing Agriculture, Fisheries and Food, told him, 'Of course, it should be Margaret Thatcher,' Heath responded that he had already discussed the possibility with William Whitelaw. 'And Willie says that if we take her, we'll never be able to get rid of her.'

Her father needed a woman too. In 1965 he married a widow from a village near Grantham. Cicely Hubbard was a Methodist and mother of four. Margaret took the traditional stepdaughter's cool view of the second wife who moves into the family home.[12]

In March 1966 another general election confirmed Labour in power, with a majority of ninety-seven. Heath, reshuffling, gave

Margaret a further step-up in his team. She was now deputy (to Iain Macleod) shadowing the Treasury, but not within the shadow cabinet. In October 1967 she reached the top rank at last. She became shadow secretary to the Department of Fuel and Power. 'Not so dumb blonde', the *Sunday Times* had complimented her earlier in the year.[13]

Margaret Thatcher never hesitated to deploy her feminine charms when it suited her purpose; she courted admiration and was delighted when she succeeded in getting it. There had been a memorable exchange in May 1965 with Niall McDermott, the Financial Secretary to the Treasury. Even though on the Labour side, he was, says John Campbell, 'the type of tall, smooth-tongued barrister for whom she always had a weakness'.[14] When she attacked him for levying estate duty on widows' houses, she said she would take him apart 'molecule by molecule' if he did not give in. McDermott was unable to ignore the dominatrix element in this playful threat. He countered that the honourable lady had such grace and charm that 'the prospect of being taken apart molecule by molecule by her has its attractions'.[15]

On the government side, as a member of Wilson's cabinet, Barbara Castle was demonstrating that a woman could be as forceful as a man and could disregard jokes about her hair colour (red). Even on the Labour side, as Margaret's former challenger from Finchley, Eric Deakins, noticed when he got into Parliament at last, 'we sometimes used to deride female backbenchers on the Conservative side, for their shrill voices or what they were wearing'. None of that bothered Castle and she remained a forceful presence. She was, however, childless, and did not have to cope with half-terms and other school holidays.

After ten years in Parliament, on 21 October 1969 Margaret Thatcher was appointed shadow education secretary: another woman's job (Shirley Williams was the Secretary of State for Education and Science), but an important one, at cabinet level.

Chapter 6

The following May, Wilson called a general election for 18 June. She had little to worry about in Finchley and always enjoyed campaigns. She showed a new confidence with a less matronly look about her clothes. Her skirts grew shorter. That summer she was seen in a sleeveless straight frock that owed its influence to Jacqueline Kennedy Onassis.

Election nights were fun. She would go back to Conservative headquarters in North Finchley, where there was supper for the party workers as all watched the results come in on the screen. One of the faithful, Colinne Martyn, says, 'She could kick off her shoes . . . because she always worked in fairly high heels, laugh, relax and comment on the meaning of various results.' They all felt relaxed in her presence: 'She was natural. She was human.'

By the following June, she was the real thing: Secretary of State for Education and Science. In the general election of 10 June 1970, the Conservatives won an unexpected victory, with a healthy margin of forty-three seats. At last she had a government department all to herself, and two under-secretaries and a raft of civil servants to go with it. Sadly, her father did not live to see her take her seat in the cabinet. Alfred Roberts had died in February at the age of seventy-eight.

The buzz in the DES office (on Curzon Street, Mayfair, until Education and Science moved to a new block near Waterloo Station in October 1973) was that she had a career in front of her. All the same, she received a condescending welcome. Nobody expected she would be Leader of the Opposition within four years. It was known that her Oxford degree was in chemistry – not in the same class as the history, classics, philosophy and other humanistic degrees held by the intellectuals who went into the civil service. At the head of her private office, in charge of her personal staff, was John Banks, recalled from secondment to the Home Office without enthusiasm; career civil servants do not reject such appointments if they are serious about advancement. To be made private secretary to a minister (even a chemist) was seen as a promotion.

Banks appreciated that there were not many ministers of education who had a scientific training. Yet it seemed to him that her discipline may have left her 'really quite narrow. She was correspondingly weak in the humanities, arts, music, literature, history, languages, which, in an education minister, was something of a handicap.'

He felt that she was 'like a very well-spoken nanny' to them all. 'Very polite, almost over-considerate; easy to get on with but not very satisfying to relate to.' On the other hand, 'she was in many ways an ideal minister. She was undoubtedly very sharp. She would probe, interrogate, and she learned very fast. She could master a brief as quickly as anybody.' At the same time, Banks swiftly saw that she was 'a person who generated a lot of tensions around her'. And she appeared to condescend to the junior staff, adopting with them 'a curious manner of speaking particularly slowly and clearly – as if somehow it was necessary to make allowances for their lesser intelligence'.

Perhaps she did not relate well to Banks as he was known to be a Labour supporter. From her Whitehall experience, she had acquired a deep distrust of the civil service, which she suspected of being inherently left wing. Banks lasted only a year before, at his request, the permanent secretary of the DES, Sir William Pile, removed him. Thatcher had told Pile, 'I make up my mind about people in the first ten seconds and I very rarely change it,' and she had clearly made up her mind about Banks. Nonetheless, during their year together, Banks was an acute observer of his boss. He noted that Denis, always so reticent in public, seemed to have aired his views forcefully at the weekends.

On Monday mornings, Banks recalls, she would come into the office with what seemed 'a whole new agenda'. That was the worst time to encounter her.

I tended to keep people away from her on Monday morning until we had got through this between ourselves, and I had coped with the questions and the new ideas that she had brought in freshly after the weekend. [These] seemed to be the result of discussion, probably with her husband over the weekend, or perhaps with other friends. But certainly Monday morning was a high point of tension for the week.

Once she asked for the organisation plan, the organogram of the department. She wanted to know whether all the under-secretaries had the same level of financial responsibility. It was a somewhat unusual question to pose about a department's organisation. Under-secretaries are not normally given exactly equal financial responsibility. Some posts have quite different responsibilities, which are not financial. There was a certain amount of accountancy in her approach, which obviously could have been derived from her husband.

Did Banks know, one wonders, that Denis was the co-author of *Accounting and Costing in the Paint Industry?*[16]

As her private secretary, Banks had occasion to drive around London a good deal with Margaret in her official car. Once they passed the Pimlico Comprehensive School. Banks mentioned that he had visited the school to consider whether it would be a suitable place for his son.

She reacted quite strongly. 'Oh, John, you wouldn't think of sending your son to that glasshouse!' (It was a school which had a lot of plate glass in its construction.) That rather summed things up. I think for her, for anybody from the middle classes to send their child to a state school if they had the money and the opportunity to send them to a private school, was somewhat disloyal, to her values at least.

Carol Thatcher at that time, largely through her own initiative, had moved back to London to live at home, and was enrolled as a day-girl at the academically distinguished St Paul's Girls' School, where she remained for the seventh and eighth forms.

(These, at St Paul's were reserved for girls doing A levels.)

Margaret made another, more public revelation of her social attitudes when visiting a large comprehensive school in north London. As television cameras followed her, the head of Highbury Grove School, the controversial Rhodes Boyson (a Conservative MP, later Sir Rhodes), showed her and her civil service escort, John Hedger, around the school. They did the usual tour – the swimming pool, the gym, the classrooms – and ended up in a chemistry class.

Might she take over? she volunteered eagerly. She started to lecture the class on the principles of elementary chemistry and to explain how chemicals reacted with metal. Searching for a homely example, she reminded the pupils, 'We don't now use silver spoons for boiled eggs. We use stainless steel because of what the egg yolk might do to the silver spoons.'

The teenagers stared back at her in silent bemusement. To Hedger, it seemed unlikely that any of them had eggs for breakfast, let alone silver cutlery. 'But the television crews' reaction was rather different,' as he recalls. 'The words "silver" and "spoon", delivered in those cut-glass tones, were like a candle to a moth, and they started moving to the front of the room. I don't think she realised what she had said.' To him it showed her insensitivity to the reality of ordinary lives.

She was insensitive too to Heath's discomfort at having her in his cabinet. Around the cabinet table she had a habit of expressing opinions on subjects other than education. Besides, Heath did not like her. Geoffrey Howe, then Minister for Consumer Affairs, remembers a discussion on who might be the next chairman of the BBC. When he put forth the name of the economist Andrew Shonfield as prospective chairman, Heath dismissed Shonfield harshly: 'But he's got much too high an opinion of himself.' And Margaret chipped in: 'Well, most men do, Prime Minister.' There was a sharp, uneasy exchange of glances between them.

Jim Prior, Agriculture, Fisheries and Food Secretary, was sorry for her. The seating arrangement at the cabinet table had the prime minister flanked by the civil service secretary to the cabinet on his right, and next to him sat Margaret. 'But the secretary was always leaning forward and writing,' Prior says, 'and thus Margaret's eye was not caught very often if she wanted to enter the discussion. I suppose one could say that, yes, she was cold-shouldered. She wasn't one of the top team within the cabinet.'

How to break in if no one will catch your eye? With your voice. In Margaret's case, that did her no favours. To Robin Butler, Heath's private secretary (later Sir Robin, and secretary of the cabinet), her interventions 'always seemed rather shrill and extreme'.

The Thatcher inexperience combined with sharpness and stridency made her colleagues uneasy. Yet they recognised that she had a difficult brief. As Education Secretary, she was required to preside over the forced comprehensivisation of the grammar schools. It was not a policy with which she agreed, yet Heath and the Tories were committed to it. In her time in charge, she approved most of the comprehensive schemes that came before her, 2,286 in all. She also inherited the budget cuts and spending plans the Department of Education and Science had already agreed with the Treasury.

Her first priority was to moderate Anthony Crosland's Labour policy of turning grammar schools into comprehensives. She did so by issuing a circular outlining her own plans for comprehensivisation. The document was too brief and too hasty, by civil service lights, and managed to offend both sides in the educational debate. Haste, however, was part of throwing herself into the job. Four months later she was nearly thrown out of it.

Carrying out a series of cuts agreed with the Treasury – in order to release funds for the expansion of nursery education and raising the school-leaving age to sixteen – she announced that free milk for schoolchildren over the age of seven would be stopped. It would still be available for those who wanted it, at a few pennies a half-pint. The decision was part of a general cabinet determination that there must be painful reductions in public expenditure. She herself believed that public spending had to be reined back; the post-war social consensus had gone too far.

Yet she made herself prey to a gibe coined, she believes, by someone at a Labour Party conference and picked up by the tabloid headline writers: 'Thatcher, Milk Snatcher'. The tabloid *Sun* followed with her picture under the headline: 'Is This the Most Hated Woman in Britain?' The milk-snatcher sound-bite was a low joke, combining a cruel rhyme for her surname with a Freudian thrust at the unwomanly woman: the giver of milk abruptly withholding it from little waiting mouths. Overnight she went from media darling to media demon. She was so pilloried in the press that, according to Kenneth Clarke, education whip at that time, Heath seriously thought of sacking her. Clarke says that he himself persuaded the chief whip, Francis Pym, that the move would be catastrophic – and unfair: 'She was doing perfectly all right.' Clarke believes that she had a narrow escape. But nothing stopped the party from letting the whole weight of the press's rage fall upon her.

To Pamela Mason, who had known Margaret at Oxford, the 'snatcher' taunt was particularly unfair because 'even during the war everyone knew perfectly well about the waste of milk'. Schoolchildren, certainly those of secondary school age, hated 'that warm milk'. At Mason's own school, she recollected, the headmistress used to collect the unused bottles of milk to make cheese.

Margaret's unadmiring civil servant, John Banks, also thought the criticism unjust. There was little room for flexibility in the education budget. Most of it was committed to teachers' salaries. She was forced to make a cut; there was serious difficulty in finding anything else that could be removed from the budget. 'And school milk was one such possible saving. Items like that may have to be sacrificed. It happened all the time.'

In the end, Margaret proved quite a good Education Secretary. When it came to getting more money for the department, she succeeded. By persuading the Treasury not to take back savings she'd made elsewhere in her budget, she extended nursery education, launched a programme to modernise primary schools and raised the school-leaving age to sixteen. She saved the Open University from its Tory critics.

The attack had a profound effect on her. She had done her best, there was no alternative to the cuts the Treasury had imposed, yet she had been made to suffer national notoriety. It was, says her friend and fellow Tory MP William Deedes, 'the most strenuous time in her political career – very, very wearing. She was much more easily wounded than you might think.'

This first experience of a hostile press hardened her. Was the Iron Lady born out of the Milk Snatcher? Very likely. She now knew that, once she was sure she was right, she would not budge, no matter how unpopular her policies.

She was not sacked. She held on to the post of Education Secretary for more than three years, from June 1970 until February 1974. Her time there yielded another Thatcher legend, once again with food at its heart.

One day she was seen leaving the building by the permanent secretary, who said (as the story goes), 'Leaving early tonight, Minister?' She explained that she was going off to buy bacon for Denis's breakfast. 'But Secretary of State,' came the rejoinder, 'we can find any number of people to buy the bacon for you.' She spurned the offer. No one else could do it. Her husband was very particular. 'Only I know the kind that Denis likes.'[17]

Breakfast was also high on the agenda when Carol's friend from boarding school, Hilary Skaar, came to stay. Then eighteen, Hilary found that not only did Margaret remember her and her school progress, but she wanted her opinions on the Rhodesia situation. Before Margaret left for the day, she asked if Hilary would like to have breakfast in bed. The reply came: 'Oh no, no, I can't have the Secretary of State for Education bringing me breakfast in bed.'

'That's perfectly all right,' the Secretary of State replied. 'I'm doing it for Mark anyway.'

In 1972 the Thatchers moved out of their Westminster flat, sold 'The Mount' in Lamberhust for £85,000 and bought a three-storey, neo-Georgian town house in their old territory, Flood Street, Chelsea, for £28,000.[18] For weekends, and Denis's golf, they rented a flat at Scotney Castle, a fourteenth-century ruin owned by the National Trust, in Kent.

At the end of 1973, after three years of Conservative government, the country was in crisis. Heath had given in to one miners' strike, with a generous pay settlement. Faced with the threat of a second strike, he put the country on a three-day week to save energy. In February 1974 he went to the country to ask 'Who governs Britain?'

In that general election Margaret had to work harder than usual in Finchley. Boundary changes and Jewish discontent with Heath's policies on Israel gave her much campaigning to do, and she rarely left the constituency. Finchley by now was 'family'; she knew the rabbis by their first names. She promised to continue Heath's economic policies, although privately she had doubts. She was much in demand as a speaker. In the *Times Higher Education Supplement*, Peter Hennessy described her performance: 'not a hair out of place', 'that whiter-than-white smile', and 'shimmering slightly and demonstrating, yet again, that Righteousness can be beautiful'.[19]

(Denis was popular in Finchley too and would stand in for her if she could not make an engagement. However, he was known for never entering into any political discussions. 'He just wouldn't. We used to try and get him to say something and he wouldn't. "Leave that to the boss," he would say. "The boss will tell you that."'

Heath was in trouble too – across the water. The province of Northern Ireland had been in turmoil since the civil rights marches by Catholic demonstrators in 1969, when James Callaghan, the Labour Home Secretary, deployed British troops. On 30 January 1972 the city of Derry suffered Bloody Sunday, in which thirteen unarmed civilians were shot dead by British soldiers. Soon after, Heath had introduced direct rule from Westminster after suspending Stormont, Northern Ireland's legislature. In an effort to find a solution, in December 1973 he called a conference in Sunningdale, Berkshire, in which all parties, including representatives of southern Ireland, called for a power-sharing executive for Northern Ireland. The executive was to include representatives of the (mainly) Protestant Unionists, the (mainly) Catholic, pro-nationalist Social Democratic and Labour Party, and the middle-ground Alliance Party. The agreement accepted that the SDLP aspired to a United Ireland and also that there would be no change in the status of the North without the consent of the majority – in other words, of the Unionists. But a new link with the Irish Republic would be established: a Council of Ireland, representing both parts of the island of Ireland and providing for the first time cross-border cooperation in policing and criminal courts.

The general election of February 1974 not only gave the British public a chance to express what they felt about Heath's tough stand against the miners' union's wage demands. It also gave the voters in Northern Ireland a chance to say what they thought of his power-sharing executive, in office for scarcely two months.

Who governs Britain? Not Edward Heath, said the voters. Not only did Labour get five seats more than the Conservatives; in Northern Ireland, eleven of the twelve Westminster seats went to Unionists. It was a vote of no confidence in the new power-sharing executive and the end of the traditional alliance behind the name: the Conservative and Unionist Party.

After the election, Heath tried to stay in power by forming a coalition with the Liberals, who had fourteen seats. But the Liberal leader, Jeremy Thorpe, said no. Heath resigned on 4 March.

On Northern Ireland Harold Wilson's new government fared no better. In May 1974 the Ulster Workers' Council organised a loyalist strike which brought the province to a halt. Electric power was shut off, factories closed – and the power-sharing administration collapsed. The success of the strike, according to the authoritative Belfast journalist, David McKittrick, allowed the thought 'to lurk in the Unionist psyche that the force of Protestant numbers can, if properly mobilised, thwart the wishes of British governments'.[20]

In the bitter aftermath of the election, to many (but not to Heath) Sir Keith Joseph was seen as a leader-in-waiting. Heath gave him permission to set up his own think-tank, called the Centre for Policy Studies, to analyse what was wrong with the British economy. The vain hope was that the new centre would not upstage the existing Conservative Research Department.

Joseph, a right-wing intellectual, had already come up with his own diagnosis of what was wrong with Britain. In his speeches, he identified inflation as the cause of Britain's ills, and inflation was caused by the government's failure to control the money supply. The Conservatives under Heath, by making U-turns in the party's traditional stance of non-intervention, had been making things worse. Striving for full employment; bailing out failing industries; giving in to wage claims: all of these, to Joseph's way of thinking, made Britain weaker.

In Joseph, Margaret Thatcher found another of the father-figures from whom she drew inspiration. To Jim Prior, it became apparent that she and Keith were taking a totally different line from the rest of the cabinet. 'I began to realise,' he says, 'at that stage that they were setting off on a rather different course.' Heath then, not incidentally, shifted her position from his shadow cabinet, where she had been briefly shadow Minister of the Environment, to be Treasury spokeswoman.

Wilson's narrow February victory necessitated a second general election. In October 1974, he won again. Labour's overall majority was now three, healthy enough to govern for some time.

The second defeat within eight months galvanised the Tories. A small but influential group on the extreme right took the view that democracy in Britain was fatally stalled. In *Pinochet in Piccadilly*, Andy Beckett describes the group thinking that a private militia might have to take over and run the country.[21]

When Parliament reassembled in October and the battered Tories surveyed the wreckage, says Edward du Cann, 'the mood among Tory MPs was absolutely incandescent. It was my job as chairman of the 1922 Committee to dampen that down. The overwhelming majority were for an immediate change of leadership – determined that [Heath] should go and go at once. I was almost alone in saying that would be a profound mistake.' Tory candidates canvassing on the doorstep had been hearing the sentiment: 'We have nothing against the Tory Party, but we can't stand that Mr Heath. He was cordially disliked; the dislike was almost universal.'

Various replacements were suggested. There was Willie Whitelaw, chairman of the party and an amiable mandarin who, under Heath, had been successively Leader of the House, Northern Ireland Secretary and Employment Secretary. Yet Whitelaw was on the centre-left of the party and not at all what the monetarists like Keith Joseph had in mind. Du Cann himself was another possibility. Also, Christopher Soames (married to Winston Churchill's daughter); Hugh Fraser (married to the not-yet-well-known Lady Antonia); and Julian Amery. And Joseph, certainly.

But was the party ready for the first Jewish leader since Disraeli? Keith Joseph killed the possibility with a ruinous speech in Birmingham in October 1974. In it he suggested that women in the lowest income groups were weakening the 'human stock' by reproducing faster than those in the better-educated classes.

This kind of eugenics theory had been fashionable among Edwardian and 1920s intellectuals, but it was intolerable after the fact of Hitler's extermination camps. The press seized on the compulsory-sterilisation implications of Joseph's woolly argument. After a few weeks Joseph recognised that the damage done was irreparable. On 21 November 1974, he withdrew his name from the leadership contest. The way was now clear for Margaret. She told him that as he would not run – and only because of that – she would stand herself because 'somebody who represents our viewpoint *has* to stand'.[22]

Until then the summit of her ambition had been Chancellorship of the Exchequer. No one had mentioned her as a candidate for leader. Denis told her she hadn't a hope.[23]

As Treasury spokesperson, number two to Robert Carr, the shadow Chancellor, she blossomed. She had always liked tax matters. Cecil Parkinson, a young Tory MP who had long admired her equally for her appearance and her mastery of taxation, was dazzled by her performance in the first Finance Bill in 1974, which, says Parkinson, 'made her, really'. She gave a speech, a witty, lacerating attack on the Labour Chancellor, Denis Healey, which set the party talking. 'She was constantly interrupted and she handled it absolutely brilliantly. At the end the whole House, even the other side, was impressed.' To Parkinson, 'it was a sign that a really big player had arrived on the scene'.

As the New Year of 1975 arrived with the leadership contest heating up, suddenly Edward du Cann withdrew. The media were drawing attention to the fact that he was a director of Lonrho, 'Tiny' Rowlands' Anglo-African trading company which Heath himself had characterised as 'the unacceptable face of capitalism'.[24]

Du Cann moved from candidate to king-maker. As previous party chairman and chairman of the backbenchers' 1922 Committee, he received leading figures in the Conservative Party who wanted to discuss possible contenders. One day he entertained a pair of surprising visitors: Denis and Margaret Thatcher. Together they asked him how a leadership election, were there to be one, would be organised. 'The pair were very nervous and she even emotional.'

He recollects that he was glad to see them: 'They were always good together and Denis's support of his wife was heart-warming.' Indeed, the visit reminded du Cann of his daughter and her fiancé coming to tell him of their intentions and to ask his blessing. In an earlier interview with Brook Associates for a television programme, *The Thatcher Factor*, du Cann, describing this memorable visit, compared their demeanour to that of 'a housekeeper and handyman applying for a job'.[25]

When the Thatchers departed, du Cann was as clear about Margaret's intentions as if she had said openly, 'I'm going to be a candidate.' Personally, he felt she was short of ministerial experience: 'being captain of the ship was very different from being first lieutenant'. She was way down in the pecking order. What was more, he was not a fan. He had noticed her at candidates' meetings – very attractive, very able, but always the first on her feet to ask questions. He noticed a lack of warmth between her and the audience, 'simply because, I think, she offended against the English canon: you should never be too keen'.

Indeed, by openly revealing her new ambition, Margaret was taking an enormous risk with her entire career. If she challenged Heath and lost, she would be thrown off his team. Where she was, she stood within striking distance of her dream: the Chancellorship.

*

From the backbenches emerged Airey Neave. He was known to be a wonderful organiser; his escape-from-Colditz credentials testified to that. (In 1942 he was the first British officer to escape from the Colditz prisoner-of-war camp and, as a barrister, helped prosecute the German war criminals at Nuremberg.) He did not get along with Heath at all and, according to Prior, was determined to find a replacement for him. Keith Joseph was his first choice. After Joseph's withdrawal, Neave set his sights on Thatcher.

Initially and cagily, Neave did not say who his candidate was. The Conservative former Opposition whip, Dudley Smith (now Sir Dudley), recalls being approached 'by the man from Colditz', who asked, 'Would you like to join a small committee that wants to sort out the problems with the leadership and choose the next, er, leader of the party?' Smith consented, feeling 'a little like the cabal that got together to assassinate Hitler. In a way.'

When, after Joseph's withdrawal, various likely names were considered and rejected, Neave produced his master-stroke. 'Well, then, why don't we have a woman?' he asked Smith. 'Why don't we have Margaret Thatcher?'

There was, Smith recalls,

an explosion of seismic proportions when it came to actually putting her name forward and having her on the ballot. There'd never been a woman prime minister before – hardly any in the world, and certainly not a Leader of the Opposition to begin with. Three or four people actually resigned from the committee because they thought it wasn't going to work.

He himself was a friend of hers, having come into Parliament at the same time and made his maiden speech supporting her bill.

The eventual outcome was, in du Cann's view, 90 per cent Neave's work. There were huddled meetings all over the House side of the pseudo-Gothic Palace of Westminster – tea room, smoking room, dining room, private rooms. Various factions would deliberately mislead the others. 'Dirty tricks, yes,' du Cann concedes. 'That was happening all the time and it was rather good fun, I thought.'

With his persuasiveness, Neave won over the Tory right-winger Norman Tebbit. 'At that time,' Tebbit admits, 'had there been a male candidate as good or almost as good, I think I would've gone for that male.' But there was not. Neave continued his campaign – wily, sophisticated and secretive. At one point Neave put it about that Heath was going to win by a mile, according to Bernard Weatherill: 'So to give him a shock some of the old boys transferred their vote to Margaret Thatcher.'

His task was considerably helped by the *Daily Telegraph*, which encouraged Margaret's candidacy very strongly. To William Deedes, who had just become editor, the mood at the *Telegraph* reflected the feeling that Margaret Thatcher was right because the old methods were simply not working.

Deedes, of course, knew Margaret very well as the wife of his golfing companion, and he knew her background. He felt that Thatcher's rise from grocer's daughter to the parliamentary heights illustrated

something almost more important to the Tory Party than the fact that she was a woman: that in the Tory Party you could rise from any family rank and succeed. In my early days in the Tory Party, it was almost embarrassing the extent to which the Tory Party – I have to say this – made working-class candidates a bit of a trophy. In the 1930s the Tory Party was seen to be a party of grandees. The Thatcher phenomenon was a sign that the Tories had become more egalitarian.

That was the avant-garde view, if the phrase can be applied to anything concerning the *Daily Telegraph*. Others had grave doubts. The head of the Conservative Research Department, Chris Patten, found himself in a slow, creaking lift with R.A. (Rab, later Lord) Butler. Butler for a time was referred to as 'the best prime minister we never had', for he was passed over twice in favour of weaker candidates; the choice of Sir Alec Douglas-Home when Macmillan resigned in 1963 is considered among the Tory Party's many self-inflicted injuries. To Patten, Butler said, 'We don't have to take this Thatcher thing seriously, do we?'[26]

But they did. During the run-up to the leadership ballot, the press did another hatchet job on her image. In an interview in a pensioners' magazine, *Pre-retirement Choice*, she was quoted as suggesting that old people could fight Labour's inflation by stocking up on tinned food, particularly the hearty proteins such as salmon, ham and sardines. Was she advocating hoarding? The press had as much fun with the tinned foodstuffs as it had had with the school milk. Margaret was ridiculed for her assumption that elderly pensioners could afford to buy tins by the case. Food and women: the ancient combination, a witches' brew, turned into a story that would never have run with a man as its protagonist. In wan self-defence, she invited the press to Flood Street to inspect modestly stocked shelves in her larder.

On 4 February 1975, the morning of the first ballot of the leadership election, she allowed the press to photograph her at home, cooking – what else? – breakfast. During the day Conservative MPs filed into Committee Room 14, where the 1922 Committee met every Thursday evening. With party executives watching, they filled out their papers and inserted them into the ballot box on the podium. When balloting closed, the box was taken into a private room and the contents counted. Du Cann went back to Committee Room 14 and announced the result. Neither Heath nor Margaret was there.

Airey Neave, Dudley Smith and a few others ran along the corridor to the secluded committee room where Margaret and a helper were waiting. Neave broke the news to her: she had beaten Heath by thirty-one votes. She burst into tears and kissed them all. In reality, she did not have the necessary majority; a second ballot would be needed in a week's time. But her position looked unassailable.

Denis arrived at the celebration drinks party and the media pounced. So he fully expected his wife to be leading the Conservative Party? 'I do.' How did he feel about it? 'Delighted. Terribly proud, naturally. Wouldn't you?'[27]

The confirming second ballot came a week later. Edward du Cann announced the result in Committee Room 14. On 11 February 1975 Bernard Weatherill took her into Room 14, where the Conservative Party was assembled. She mounted the podium. She asked for their prayers, their understanding and their support, their loyalty. He saw a number of members getting out their handkerchiefs and dabbing their eyes. 'It was a very, very emotional moment.'

As was her custom, she later wrote Weatherill a charming, personal note.

> Dear Bernard
>
> Thank you for your kind letter. Even now I'm not quite sure how it all happened . . . Perhaps there is a destiny which shapes our ends. I can only hope that from the same source will come the strength and inspiration to live up to all that is expected and required.
>
> Yours ever,
> Margaret.

For his part, Edward du Cann remembers being delighted:

She had the courage to grasp the opportunity, which not everybody else had. Here was somebody who was willing to stand up. Here was somebody who was willing to go for it. Here was somebody who had the self-confidence to do all of that. Those are leadership characteristics and they made a very broad appeal.

The break with tradition, to him, was entirely appropriate: 'The Tory Party's always been adventurous. It's thought of as the conservative party with a small "c" but we elected the first

Jewish leader at a time when that was a really surprising thing to do and we elected the first woman leader of a political party in this country. They were remarkable steps to take.'

But many others suffered morning-after symptoms. What *had* they done? Norman Tebbit recalls colleagues moaning, 'How are we going to handle this?' Dudley Smith heard the fears 'that we'd made a ghastly mistake, that people would say, "We don't want a woman, women are in too many things already."' Peter Carrington saw the choice as completely out of the party's character: 'Of all parties unlikely to have a woman as its leader at that time, the Conservative Party was obviously the one.' And when Cecil Parkinson looked at the size of the vote for Heath it was evident to him that 'none of the heavyweights in the party voted for her. All the party establishment, almost to a man or woman, went Ted's way.'

There were no mixed feelings on the Labour side. James Callaghan, the Foreign Secretary, surveyed the Tories' misstep and jubilantly predicted the consequences: 'We've just won the next election.'[28]

7
Stepping to the Right
(March 1975–May 1979)

'Somewhere ahead lies greatness for our country again. This
I know in my heart.'[1]

Margaret Thatcher (1979)

Among the elders of the Conservative Party the view was that,
after her inevitable loss of the next general election, nature would
resume its course and a man would take over as leader. Her
capture of the leadership came to be known as 'the Peasants'
Revolt', reflecting the Establishment's view that the lower orders
had temporarily seized the mansion.

Like it or not, Margaret Thatcher was now Leader of the
Opposition. Shrewdly, she surrounded herself with much of
Heath's old guard. Those who had been in Heath's shadow
cabinet were in hers. Of her appointments, only two, Norman
St John Stevas and Keith Joseph, were likely to have voted for
her in the secret ballot for leader. Conscious that she could not
shift the party too sharply, she gave the Treasury portfolio to
Geoffrey Howe.

William Whitelaw, suddenly reincarnated as her devoted servant, trusted adviser and deputy, seems to have persuaded her
that Joseph was too volatile for a major office of state. To Airey
Neave, to whom she owed her success, she gave the only job he
wanted, shadow secretary for Northern Ireland.

Relations with Heath were never good. Immediately, and to
the dismay of her colleagues, she sacked Michael Wolff, who
had been a loyal and decent chief executive at Conservative
Central Office. For her, he was too much of a Heathite. As

for the discarded leader himself, there was no place in her shadow cabinet. It was rumoured that she offered him the ambassadorship to Washington.

Little of her actual opinions was known. She had made few memorable speeches. Most of her colleagues assumed that, despite Keith Joseph's influence, she would, like Heath, remain in the centre. She did not. Now that she had power, she planned to use it. Geoffrey Howe noticed

a progressive transformation from the Margaret who'd been a member of Ted's cabinet, and was really a very loyal and almost an obedient carrier of the banner, to the Margaret who was emerging. What surprised us was the extent to which she was able to fashion other people's thinking and use it as her own . . . She gathered around her, and continued to do so, a series of very bright people, who could furnish ideas and who could shape them into language.

The bright people gathered around her were from the right, from a new base. In December 1975, Norris McWhirter, with other right-wingers who feared that Britain was becoming ungovernable, formed a pressure group, the National Association for Freedom, with the infelicitous acronym NAFF. Six Conservative MPs and the deputy editor of the *Sunday Telegraph*, the influential Peregrine Worsthorne (later Sir Peregrine), were among its members. Margaret spoke at its first fund-raising dinner.

Keith Joseph was still her main intellectual influence. He took himself around the country on a personal 'Campaign for Capitalism', haranguing students, preaching self-reliance and the enterprise culture, arguing his thesis that the government should neither borrow nor spend too much. He built up his personal fiefdom, the Centre for Policy Studies, and watched it grow to overshadow the Conservative Research Department as the party's source of ideas. Some of the CPS's initial financial support came from the Confederation of British Industries. Joseph placed Alfred Sherman at its head and recruited two powerful hard-right thinkers, Norman Strauss, an ex-Unilever executive, and John Hoskyns, an ex-military man and computer millionaire eager to turn his talents to Conservative politics. Through them the CPS would flesh out Joseph's determination to design a new political strategy to end Britain's economic dysfunction. Monetarism – an economic theory based on controlling the money supply – was not enough; collectivism had to be fought in its own right.

Margaret did not take much persuading to adopt Joseph's idea that radical new measures were necessary to clear up the wreckage left by her predecessor. Heath's tactic had been all wrong. Government could not create jobs; government should not get involved in wage settlements; 'consensus' was a false goal that merely created crisis. Margaret admired the economist Sherman, an ex-communist turned free-marketeer. To her, he was brilliant. Not only was he a profound thinker but he was also witty and versatile – as evidenced by his column in the main Hebrew-language daily in Israel. What is more, she applauded (retrospectively) 'his complete disregard for other people's feelings or opinion of him'.[2]

As Leader of the Opposition, she began to travel; 'abroad' was not her strong suit. She knew scarcely a word of another language (except, of course, Latin). She was conspicuously deficient in American experience. She had visited the United States for the first time in 1967 on a State Department 'leadership' tour. (From visiting Los Angeles, which had suffered riots in the black ghetto of Watts, she offered the comforting (and incorrect) diagnosis that the disturbance was the work of 'outsiders'.)[3] In 1969 she had visited Russia and a parliamentary Commonwealth conference in the Bahamas, but not much more.

During 1975, her first year as leader, she went to France, Germany, Romania, Turkey and, once more, to the United States. Her constant message was much like her election address to Dartford in 1950: 'Every Conservative desires peace. The threat to peace comes from Communism, which has powerful forces ready to attack everywhere.'[4] Controversially, while in the United States, she criticised her own country where, she declared, democracy was on trial.

Now that she was head of the Conservatives, distinguished visitors called to see her, among them the governor of California, Ronald Reagan, in whom, on her visit in 1975, she had found a kindred soul. His press secretary sent her transcripts of his fortnightly gubernatorial broadcasts and, her memoirs acknowledge, 'I agreed with them all.'[5] She had almost daily visits from Joseph and Whitelaw. The likelihood of a general election at any time was on all their minds.

A critical test for her in 1975 lay in her first speech as party leader to the annual Conservative conference. The speech, given in Blackpool, was preceded by late-night marathon writing and rewriting sessions with Ronald Millar, a successful West End playwright of strong Conservative sympathies who had been speech-writer for Heath and had begun to do the same for her. Millar noticed, as all did, that nothing tired her. She was as lively and bright at midnight as she was the next morning.

The speech was a triumph. Ann (now Lady) Shelton, wife of William Shelton, Conservative MP for Streatham and a friend who had worked on Margaret's leadership campaign and had watched her progress, was moved to tears. 'It was wonderful. You felt this wave of people finding a leader. That's what we felt, we'd found a leader.'

As if from the pulpit, the leader told the party faithful that Britain and socialism were not the same thing, and as long as she had health and strength they never would be. Her vision was of people working as they chose, spending what they earned, owning property – 'to have the state as servant and not as master'.[6]

She even managed to get a visual gag out of the occasion when a woman emerged from the audience to come onstage and hand her a feather duster. Margaret stared at it for a second and then used it to dust the party chairman, Peter Thomas.

Back at the Thatchers' hotel suite, Ronald Millar dropped by to offer congratulations. But her restless mind had already moved on. The speech had gone so well, what would she do next year at the party conference in Brighton? That could be a dreadful anti-climax. Millar heard Denis thunder, 'My God, woman. You've just had a bloody great triumph, and here you are worrying yourself sick about next year.' Millar confided to his memoirs: 'So long as she has this man around she's going to be all right.'[7]

Ironically, her first year as Leader of the Opposition coincided with Denis's retirement in June from Burmah Oil. Growing busier, she worried about what he would do with his time. One thing was clear; he was not going to give interviews. As the worldly-wise husband of a very busy woman, however, he was not long in making his mark. As his friend William Deedes noticed, Denis became adept at calling a halt to meetings that went on too long, to people who made excessive demands on his wife's time and to her own willingness to forgo sleep.

Margaret Thatcher may have pleased the party faithful, but not the insiders and the backbenchers of the 1922 Committee. To them, according to Bernard Weatherill, later deputy Tory chief whip, 'It was totally an invasion of the Tory Party to have a leader who was female.'

One obvious flaw was that she was not a good parliamentary performer. Her big challenge came on Tuesdays and Thursdays, when there were Prime Minister's Questions. Norman Tebbit, then a backbencher, describes how hard her team worked to prepare her for the questions on the order paper: 'a group of us were the picadors, supposed to plant the darts in the prime minister so that she as the toreador would come in and finish the job'.

The problem was that her weapon – her voice – was too

weak. Shirley Williams, whose career was blessed with a husky contralto, says that for a woman in Parliament a high, light voice is a big drawback: 'it's hardly heard in the Commons and it's very easy to be heckled down'.

Another obstacle was sheer snobbery. Among the smart young men at the Conservative Research Department, Matthew Parris recalls, there were constant references to the fact that she was from Grantham and that she was a grocer's daughter. 'The nickname that we all used for her was "Hilda". "Hilda" was her middle name and thought slightly lower middle class. So it wasn't "Maggie", it wasn't "Mrs T". It was "Hilda" and it was not meant kindly.'

Parris, who had been recruited by Airey Neave to become correspondence secretary at the research department, cast a cold eye on the party's leader: 'purposeful, bustling, always clutching a sheaf of papers'. Her walk was 'like a partridge with lots of little steps close together'; her gaze 'totally directed – staring at you and standing slightly too close'. In a conversation, 'she'd fix you with a bayonet-like glance and ask for a quick opinion. You knew that you had about fifty seconds to deliver it and it had to be clear, decisive, focused, or she would look away and talk to somebody else. We were terrified of her in the tea room – everybody hoping she wouldn't sit with them.'

Right from the start, perhaps because she felt defensive about being a woman leader, she made great play of the virtues and understanding that a woman could bring to politics. She would always insist on talking about housework. 'She could hardly forbear to,' Parris comments acidly. 'She could hardly resist telling us that she'd cooked Denis's breakfast this morning or that she must get back and see that he had something for supper.'

He found her one day in the shadow cabinet room, standing on a chair in her stockinged feet, running her finger along the top of the picture frames. 'I'm checking it's been cleaned,' she explained. 'It's the way a woman knows that a room has been cleaned properly.'

Margaret received a mass of correspondence from the general public – sometimes eight hundred letters a day. Parris's job was bedevilled by her insistence on dipping into the pile, writing suggestions in the margins, sometimes even answering the whole thing herself in her own hand. Like Queen Victoria she was an inveterate underliner, underscoring the words she wanted to stress: 'very', 'hate', 'love', even 'I'. Seeing her in action, Parris summed up the views of many when he concluded that she was 'an appalling person to work *with* but she was a wonderful person to work *for*. If my father had been ill, she remembered to ask how he was. If we needed a new typewriter she'd support us.'

William Deedes, who had known Denis Thatcher's wife for a very long time, observed the same contrast between the hard woman and the soft woman. 'The closer you got to Margaret, the more attractive you found her character because you heard about the small kindnesses to individuals, the consideration she showed to people whom nobody had heard of.'

She was always concerned, for example, that she might be keeping the official driver she had acquired as Opposition leader, George Newell, away from his family (drivers were civil service employees). Whenever she needed his services at weekends, she would give him the nicest of the flowers she had received and ask him to give them to his wife May by way of apology for keeping him away so long.

Deedes noticed also that Margaret capitalised on her femininity. She tended to surround herself with a little band of admirers: 'they were very good looking and she did flirt with them. I think she loved men, and good looking – and they loved her and they admired her.' But he noticed that even her closest allies were not safe from her sharp tongue. 'I remember', says Deedes, 'Airey walking out of a meeting saying that he'd never been spoken at so rudely in his life before.' (That superlative was impressive, coming from a man who had been in Colditz.)

Ever the politician, Margaret could answer whatever her public threw at her. A woman whose husband had died wrote and asked whether she believed in the afterlife, 'because if you do, it would give me encouragement now that my husband is gone that I may one day see him again'. Back came a personal letter. It conveyed condolences, then: 'Christians believe in the afterlife and I am a Christian. Yours sincerely, Margaret Thatcher.'[8]

As leader she was ripe for biography. She authorised George Gardiner, MP for Reigate, Surrey, and a member of the 1922 Committee who had been involved in the infighting that had got her elected. He and she were in sympathy. He believed, as did she, that abolition of the death penalty was a mistake. He wanted Britain to stand up for the whites in Rhodesia and he condemned opening his country to 'the floodgates of immigration'.[9] She talked to Gardiner (later, thanks to her, Sir George) about her childhood and early political career with a candour that made *Margaret Thatcher: From Childhood to Leadership*, published in 1975, essential reading for future students of her personality. She was never again as unguarded or unstilted.

When her old friend from Grantham, Margaret Goodrich, now Wickstead, was visiting her at the House of Commons, they bumped into the MP for Lincoln, Geoffrey de Freitas, a great friend of Wickstead's husband. There was an enjoyable exchange of conversation, but when he moved off, Margaret Thatcher said, 'He's such a nice man. Such a pity he isn't one of us.'

Swiftly she set herself to reverse Heath's policy of offering a national assembly – devolution – to Scotland. Additionally, she wanted nothing to fragment the United Kingdom she believed in. She set herself to rebuild the links between the Conservative Party and Northern Ireland's Official Unionists, shattered by the Sunningdale agreement and Heath's suspension of Stormont. That Northern Ireland would hold a permanent place in the United Kingdom, she had no doubt. As Airey Neave told Ireland's foreign minister, Garret FitzGerald, 'she is really a unionist at heart'.[10]

*

Yet she had an image problem. In fact, she had two. For some, the toffs and gentlefolk of the Tory Establishment, she was too much the grocer's daughter. For others, she was too much the South of England Tory lady, in little black dress and pearls – a possible turn-off to the working-class male voter, where Tory hopes lay. Her clothes proclaimed her social status as the wife of a businessman in the gin-and-Jag set. To be sure, those who liked her looks loved them. To Lady Shelton, 'She had lovely fair skin and these blue eyes, and she was always immaculately dressed. She looked lovely – I think everyone thought this.' But everyone did not. Julian Critchley, the Tory MP and wit, spoke about the possible need to write to the prime minister, c/o Dickins and Jones. Margaret noted the criticism and was particularly stung by the attack on her pearls. 'They were a wedding present from my husband and if I want to wear them I'm going to!' Ronnie Millar heard her telling the Carlton Club.[11]

She went on a double-barrelled attack. Rather than disguising her provincial origins, she now began to emphasise them. With both parents gone, she realised what they had meant to her. She told Granada's *World in Action*:

I represent an attitude, an approach, and that approach is borne out by the development of my life: going to an ordinary state school, having no privileges at all except perhaps the ones which count most – a good home background, with parents who are very interested in their children and in them getting on.[12]

(It was just as she became leader, however, that Margaret began to downplay Beatrice Roberts's role in her life; upon becoming Tory leader she gave an interview to the *Daily Telegraph* in which she was quoted as saying, 'I loved my mother dearly but after I was fifteen, we had nothing more to say to each other.')[13]

For her friend Dudley Smith, a Conservative MP, her provinciality was a plus. To have had a female version of the aristocratic Harold Macmillan would not have worked. He could see that large numbers of people up and down the country would identify with her.

John Campbell's otherwise excellent *Margaret Thatcher: The Grocer's Daughter* may be too harsh in claiming that she ruthlessly distanced herself from her roots until the moment in 1975 when they suddenly became a political asset. It could equally be said that elevation to the party leadership was her first chance to refer to her Grantham past. Lincolnshire lore was not much use in Finchley.

As for the sedate Tory-lady image, it was jettisoned by Gordon Reece, a successful television producer and ardent Conservative. 'In his way, he was a genius,' says Norman Tebbit. 'Style, dress, voice – he was enormously influential.' Reece talked Margaret out of hats, putting an end to the silly radar dishes and puffballs that she had been accustomed to wearing on her head, undermining her seriousness.

Reece also taught her to seek clean, sharp lines in her suits and, when appearing on television, to watch out for background colours that clashed with her clothes. He alerted her to the importance of the popular press and radio stations, and of never refusing lunch with an editor of a national newspaper.

Perhaps it was Reece's influence which persuaded Margaret, early in her leadership, to make time for *Woman's Own*, the women's magazine that was selling nearly a million a week. As the editor, Jane Reed, found herself leaving the interview, Margaret took her to one side and asked how she got her hair to curl back off her face (in the style of the day). The answer was Carmen electrically heated rollers, which were new at the time. 'She wanted to know all about them,' says Reed. 'She always had hair problems, she said, and the first thing she did when she got into a hotel room was crawl about the floor and under the bed looking for the electric plugs for her hairdryer.'

Then she said (rather shyly, in Reed's recollection), 'You do those articles where people go in looking dreadful and come out looking wonderful, don't you?' Indeed *Woman's Own* did. Would she like a 'makeover'?

A few weeks later the *Woman's Own* team piled into Flood Street: editor, fashion editor, make-up artist, hair stylist and photographer:

She gave us a whole afternoon and she loved it all – making tea for everyone in her impeccably tidy kitchen. One shot called for her to be photographed in a long evening gown but the sample that was sent was far too long. So she happily stood on two telephone directories, looking positively statuesque.

Leaving, Reed judged that the Leader of the Opposition 'had a sense of her own destiny and she was going to look good fulfilling it'.[14]

Hilda or Home Counties, the leader saw to it that her hair remained blonde. Seeing that Margaret Wickstead had gone grey, she cried, 'Where's that beautiful red hair of yours?' Never shy of offering personal advice, she declared, 'You should dye it!' Her own worry was the lines appearing on her neck. Her friend recommended polo-necked jumpers. (This sartorial ruse, later adopted by President Mary Robinson of Ireland, was so conspicuous that a columnist dubbed her 'Her Polo-ness'.)[15]

Soon she had a stronger image, one that was known worldwide. In January 1976, at Kensington Town Hall, Margaret gave a speech drafted for her by Robert Moss, a young, right-wing Australian academic who worked for *The Economist* in the early 1970s. A few months earlier Moss had helped in the formation of the National Association for Freedom. As the author of *The Challenge to Democracy*, a book that made the case (very popular with the American Central Intelligence Agency) against the Chilean socialist government of Salvador Allende, Moss's cold warrior credentials were impeccable.

The Kensington speech attacked both worldwide communism

and the Soviet Union. Margaret called the USSR 'a strategic threat to Britain . . . graver than at any moment since the end of the last war'.[16] The Russians, she declared, were bent on world dominance and were a superpower in only one sense – the military. They were a failure in human and economic terms. 'The men in the Soviet Politburo do not have to worry about the ebb and flow of public opinion. They put guns before butter, while we put just about everything before guns.'[17]

These fighting words drew the attention of *Jrasbata Zvezda (Red Star)*, the Red Army newspaper, which promptly dubbed her 'the Iron Lady'. All her spin-doctors could not have achieved such a feat. After less than a year as leader of the out-of-office British Conservative Party, she had been transformed into a world figure.

She seized the gift. Before a public gathering, dressed with all the art at her command, she invited the audience to admire her: 'I stand before you tonight in my Red Star chiffon evening gown, my face softly made up and my fair hair gently waved: the Iron Lady of the Western World!'[18]

Denis was not always so wise in his choice of costume. In 1976, travelling with his wife to India, he made the mistake of putting on a pink turban. The picture made the cover of *Private Eye* – as he knew it would. That did not deter him, his daughter Carol says, from trying in Sri Lanka to feed a banana to an unwilling elephant.[19]

The Iron Lady label brought many more invitations to travel abroad. In April 1977 she went to China and grimly looked at all the attractions the Mao regime showed her. At the People's Evergreen Commune in Suchow, she asked boldly, 'What exactly *is* a barefoot doctor?'[20] Even so, she was not blind to the beauty of Chinese porcelain (she was a collector) and silk paintings. She also took great care with her appearance. With sisterly generosity, she cast a worried look at the hair of Sue MacGregor of the BBC's *Woman's Hour*, one of a select band of British journalists who had accompanied her on the arduous tour.

'Would you like to borrow my heated rollers, dear?' she offered MacGregor.[21]

Also with her on the Far Eastern trip, which took in Japan and Hong Kong, was her daughter Carol. Carol, having qualified as a solicitor and working in the City of London, was on her way to Sydney, to begin work as a journalist with the *Sydney Morning Herald*.

In March 1976, out of the blue, Harold Wilson, the Labour prime minister, resigned. There was no explanation. (His motive is now thought to have been a fear that he might be suffering from incipient Alzheimer's, the disease of which his father had died.) James Callaghan, Foreign Secretary, immediately stepped into his place, after a struggle in which he defeated Michael Foot and Roy Jenkins.

Callaghan proved a tough opponent for Margaret in the House of Commons. Nowhere is British government more of a man's game than at Prime Minister's Questions. Even though his Labour government was coming apart, Callaghan always bested her at these ritual jousts, oozing condescension. It says much for her toughness that she battled on at the dispatch box, knowing what was in store. In his book *Chance Witness*, Matthew Parris recreates the scene:

She would rise with a critical inquiry, perhaps a shade too shrill. Wily, avuncular old Sunny Jim would reply that the Right Honourable Lady really must calm down: the Right Honourable Lady has worked herself into a rage about something that she does not entirely understand. This would throw her into a rage. Her voice would rise and sharpen. He would reply that the Right Honourable Lady must please stop shrieking, and would do best to go away and learn a little more about the subject before raising it in this House.[22]

Callaghan clearly enjoyed his role as prime minister; he had a pinstriped suit in which the stripes consisted of tiny 'JCs'. He sent enough material for a similar suit to President Jimmy Carter, another world leader who shared the evocative initials.

In August 1976 Keith Joseph decided that the time had come for Margaret to meet John Hoskyns. Hoskyns was just Thatcher's type of man: the epitome of her predilection for what the journalist Hugo Young, in *One of Us*, sums up as 'handsome, articulate, upright men of military bearing and with a good business record'.[23] Moreover, Hoskyns was ready to give her a clear policy framework for reversing Britain's decline.

In forming his diagnosis and cure, Hoskyns had been much impressed by the opinions of Terence Price, head of the Uranium Institute. Price, as a nuclear physicist and former government employee, including a stint as chief scientist for the Department of Transport, had spotted the paradox. British technology during the war had been superb; high technology should now be one of the country's prime assets. What was going wrong?

Price, in a speech to the British Association in 1974, offered his own answer. As reported in the *Financial Times*, he contrasted 'the denuded state of British industry compared with the prodigious intellectual wealth' he had left behind in the civil service. In his experience, civil servants were like dons: 'impatient of outside views because they are cleverer than those with whom they deal'. Their lack of experience in business and industry had been one of the hidden factors in Britain's failure. 'The public sector had drained the private sector of intellectual talent. In technology we have misdirected our effort.'[24]

If part of the problem was to get the government to restrain its civil servants from interfering with the market, another was to use the power of law to curb the trade unions. Margaret was quite ready to move in this direction. William Rees-Mogg, editor of *The Times*, saw this when he invited her to lunch at the newspaper, to sit down with union leaders. He had expected that she would still resemble the girl he had known at Oxford, and that the union men would see what a lovely person she was.

'Not a bit of it. She gave a short speech after lunch giving them a thorough bashing: they were damaging the interests of their members by their resistance to new methods, higher productivity and so forth.'

The Conservative Party at that time had no position on the closed shop – the union policy that prevented people in certain industries from working unless they were union members. However, when a fireman sent her a letter telling her his tale of woe (he had lost his job because he wouldn't join the union), the draft answer came back to Matthew Parris, who had to deal with the letter, with a fierce declaration written in the margin: '*I hate the closed shop*'. The handwritten words, underlined three times, looked 'as though the pen had been held in her fist'.

In March 1977 Margaret was ready for a general election. She called a No Confidence vote to oppose Labour's devolution bill. And why not? The Conservatives were leading in the polls by fifteen points; she was prime-minister-in-waiting. But Callaghan evaded it by persuading the leader of the Liberal Party, David Steel, to join Labour in a Lib–Lab pact. In this, the Liberals, with their thirteen seats, would side with Labour and have an influence they had not previously enjoyed.

At the Centre for Policy Studies that summer, John Hoskyns and Norman Strauss began to write a report spelling out how the Tories would lead the British economy out of its morass. Keith Joseph gave it its title, 'Stepping Stones'. The first step would be to wake up the public to Britain's crisis: socialism, thought since the war to have done so much good, was actually doing harm. The next step would turn public opinion against the trade unions, by demonstrating how their power was blocking the economy. With luck, the unions might then be transformed from Labour's strongest weapon into the Tories' biggest asset. Tough measures could follow, such as the imposition of compulsory secret ballots in union elections and a ban on secondary picketing. Thus a sick society might be transformed into a healthy one.

But the shadow cabinet was not dominated by the hard right. For most of them, 'Stepping Stones' was a step too far. Its members deliberated long and decisively. Jim Prior, as shadow employment secretary, was foremost among those emphatically opposed to making an open case for union reform or for compulsory strike ballots. The proposals were seen as too confrontational to help the Tories in the election that had to come soon. For its part, the Conservative Research Department, not well disposed towards its upstart rival, could not accept that the trade unions were central to the country's economic problems. In the event, 'Stepping Stones' was never published, but its influence was profound.

Margaret, drawn as she was to the Hoskyns analysis, accepted the need not to antagonise the unions. At the 1977 Conservative Party conference at Blackpool, she asked and answered the question: would the trade unions allow a Conservative government to govern the country?[25] 'A responsible trade union movement is essential to this country.' She found her own veiled ways to get her message across, such as making an economic law of the parable of the Good Samaritan. The Good Samaritan would not have been able to help the beggar, she preached, if he did not have money to give away.[26] The moral – wealth precedes charity – was, to her, obvious.

All during 1978 Margaret Thatcher was ready to face the electorate, but James Callaghan was not. The widely expected autumn election never took place. She used the time for more self-polishing. She had acquired yet another powerful image-maker in Tim Bell, an executive from the advertising firm of Saatchi and Saatchi. Bell could hear straight away that the voice needed more work. 'Nobody liked her voice,' he says. 'Nobody particularly liked her. Her manner was a bit bossy, a little bit schoolmarmish.'

Bell got her to a National Theatre voice coach, who taught her to practise her breathing. She had to learn to speak from the front of her mouth rather than the back of her throat. In time, with much coaching, she managed to lower her voice to a vibrant contralto.

The same effort led to taking tea with Sir Laurence Olivier. Bell felt the meeting told them mainly about Sir Laurence, who talked about himself the whole time. Margaret, in retrospect at least, nonetheless felt that she got something out of it. The great actor pronounced her voice (she says) 'perfectly all right' and said further that she had a good 'gaze'. Moreover, he acknowledged the vast difference between speaking someone else's lines and delivering a speech reflecting the speaker's own views and personality.

Tim Bell recognised Margaret's potential attraction to a very large number of people who had never considered voting Conservative. Woodrow Wyatt was a good example. Wyatt was a disaffected former Labour MP who had had a great falling out with Harold Wilson. Meeting Margaret when she had just been made leader of the Tory Party, he found her strident. But after a second meeting, over lunch, he was converted, and thought that she had original ideas that could transform the country. Larry Lamb, editor of the *Sun*, was another. Bell says, 'He was of working-class stock and that helped. I think [he liked] the fact that she was at grammar school. She had no side to her whatsoever. None at all.'

Margaret was conservative on more subjects than the economy. She used an interview on Granada Television's *World in Action* to call for 'a clear end' to immigration as the way to improving race relations. People's fears had to be respected. She foresaw that 'the fundamental British characteristics which have done so much for the world' could be 'rather swamped by people of a different culture'.[27] (In private conversation, she would speak of the size of the intake of immigrants as 'two Granthams' worth' a year.[28] Her home town remained the measure of all things.)

The 'swamping' charge made on *World in Action* was seen as ghastly by the moderates on her shadow team, all too reminiscent of Enoch Powell's notorious 'rivers of blood' speech in 1968. Whitelaw, as shadow home secretary in charge of immigration policy, nearly resigned. Almost as appalling to her associates as her spontaneous, unworkable call for a halt to immigration – Whitelaw himself had promised not to break up families when admitting immigrants – was Margaret's habit of making policy on the hoof. She had learned that if she raised an extreme idea when talking with her colleagues in shadow cabinet, she would be out-argued or persuaded to retreat. But once she rose to her feet in public, she could allow her own instincts full rein and go a good deal farther than her team had expected.

Still living at her home in Chelsea, Margaret did a lot of entertaining, not least of her Finchley constituents and party workers. All admired the way she prepared and served everything herself. Even as party leader, Margaret did not neglect her constituents. She still saw them at her surgeries, but she now reduced these to one a month. The *Finchley Press* was a great supporter. The editor, Dennis Signy, liked her because she always came to the Finchley annual carnival and because she was so good with local charities. Yet he could not deny that she was bossy: 'She took control. If you said, "Can we just have a photograph?" she said, "Get Denis in. Stand here, stand there," and she would do the line-up and say who was in it and who stood where.'

Events continued to slide her way. Unemployment rose from 600,000 in February 1974 to 1.5 million in 1978, figures that enabled her to call Callaghan 'Prime Minister for Unemployment'.

She now had the powerful Saatchi and Saatchi agency on her side. In the summer of 1978 the Saatchis, who were in charge of the party's advertising, devised a brilliant poster showing a long queue of people snaking into the distance, with the slogan 'Labour isn't working'. When her triumvirate of image-makers, Gordon Reece, Tim Bell and Ronnie Millar, first showed her the poster, she objected. With her literal mind, she missed the pun on 'working', and saw the advertisement merely as a use of Tory money to splash the Labour Party's name. However, she was won over, and when, from the Labour side, Denis Healey criticised the poster, saying that the people pictured were not genuine unemployed but rather young Conservative volunteers, the resulting publicity multiplied the media coverage (Bell thought) tenfold.

Meanwhile, still more work was done on hair, clothes, voice – even teeth. Capping her front teeth eliminated an irregularity on the upper right side, where a slight gap was noticeable in photographs. Margaret was now on her way (although further cosmetic dentistry may have followed) to a perfect symmetrical smile.

Callaghan began to appreciate the consequences of not calling the election before Parliament resumed in the autumn of 1978. The Lib–Lab pact was not going to be renewed. Yet he surprised everybody by declaring that he would carry on. It was a mistake. By the end of the year his government's pay policy had collapsed. Defying the 5 per cent limit on wage rises, for example, the Ford Motor Company, which had had a prosperous year, granted its workers a settlement of around 15 per cent. As a penalty, the Callaghan government withdrew government contracts from Ford because it had given in to the workers. Yet the penalty carried its own penalty: Ford was a major exporter. How to proceed?

Workers in other industries knew what to do. A storm of strikes broke out – road haulage drivers, National Health Service non-medical workers, such as cleaners and porters, the oil-tanker drivers and manual municipal workers. There could be no fuel deliveries to power stations, hospitals, schools or factories. On 22 January 1979 Britain saw the biggest walk-out since the

General Strike of 1926. Callaghan, unfortunately for him, was abroad at a G7 conference. The *Sun* turned against him, by putting the headline 'Crisis? What Crisis?' over the remarks he made as he returned from sunny Guadeloupe.

The misery of national collapse warranted the Shakespearean allusion, 'Winter of Discontent'. Yet for Margaret the disaster was a gift – all the more because she herself would have had to face the same unrest if she had become, as had been expected, prime minister the preceding October.

Callaghan staggered on until spring, barely surviving votes of confidence, until Scotland, by a small majority, and Wales, by a landslide, rejected the Labour government's proposals for devolution. After losing a No Confidence vote on 28 March, he called a general election for 3 May.

Two days later, Margaret was hit by a stunning blow. Her good friend, campaign mastermind and head of her private office, Airey Neave, driving out of the House of Commons underground car park, was blown up by a bomb planted under his car. Where the Nazis had failed, the Irish National Liberation Army succeeded. (Irish republicans perceived Neave, apparently about to become Northern Ireland Secretary, to be distinctly more pro-Unionist than his Conservative predecessors.)

Margaret was arriving at the BBC when she was photographed receiving the news that Neave had been seriously injured in the blast. Cancelling her broadcast, she returned home to Flood Street, where she learned of his death. In public, she kept her composure. When she faced the press, she was dry-eyed. Neave was 'one of freedom's warriors. No one knew what a great man he was . . . except those who were nearest to him. He was staunch, brave, true, strong, but he was very gentle and kind and loyal.' She then carried on campaigning.

Yet personally she was still not popular. Callaghan led her by six points in the personal ratings. This called for Bell to pull out all the stops. He got her back on to the popular *Jimmy*

Young Show on BBC Radio 2, where she explained once more her fortune in having a husband who could pay for a good English nanny. Under Bell's direction, she used a battle bus for campaigning and lent herself to awkward, contrived photo opportunities. Brought to a mountainside and presented with a calf to hold in her arms, she held it for endless takes until Denis warned the photographers that they would have a dead animal on their hands if they didn't stop. Bell remembers the tableau: 'what we were supposed to communicate was mother love', but 'I think she actually found it quite revolting.'

Ronnie Millar organised a campaign song, 'Hello, Maggie', and played a tape of it to her in a Glasgow hotel. When she heard the final lines, 'Give 'em the old one-two, Maggie, Maggie, we're right behind you all the way', she demanded to know, 'What does "give 'em the old one-two" mean?' Carol, who was listening, groaned, 'Oh, *Mum!*'[29]

At every opportunity, Margaret played the housewife card, particularly to explain the complex economic theories behind her policies. In this time of labour strife, she made mollifying party political broadcasts, appealing to the majority of trade unionists who, she knew, were peace-loving.

Her theme was reversing Britain's deterioration. 'I'm in the business to try and make Britain great again.' Woodrow Wyatt, now a *Sunday Mirror* columnist, was utterly persuaded. One day Wyatt told his daughter Petronella, a schoolgirl of about twelve, quickly to change into a blue dress. 'You're going to meet "the Woman",' she remembers him saying. What woman? 'The woman who is going to shape the destiny of this country. In my eyes, she's the Queen of Heaven.' The girl obeyed and went into her father's study.

And there was this woman, with her face towards the window. You could only see this cap of bright yellow hair and she was wearing a yellow dress. She saw my smiley badge and said, 'Oh, that's right, dear. Keep smiling.'

And my father behaved dreadfully. He left me alone with the Queen of Heaven, who, having no small talk whatsoever, said, 'So what is your favourite subject at school, dear?' And I said, 'History,' which was true. This was followed by, 'Who are your favourite politicians?' I'd seen this sort of handsome picture of him in my history book, and liked what I'd heard about his integrity, so I just blurted out, 'Robert Peel.' The reaction was instantaneous: 'Robert Peel – too many U-turns.'

At the end of voting on 3 May, on the ITN ten o'clock news, the ITN exit poll came through with its forecasts. David Wolfson, one of Margaret's businessmen recruits, knew what the figures meant. Victory was certain. But where was Margaret? He suspected, rightly, that she was having her hair done at the time in preparation for going up to Finchley. He managed to track her down, and so was the first to announce: 'You're the next prime minister.' Of course, there could be no celebration until she herself had re-won her seat. She went to Finchley and had a long and irritating wait until her own result was officially announced at about two o'clock in the morning.

Then it was back to Central Office in Smith Square, Westminster. On the drive back, Cynthia Crawford, the assistant whom Margaret had hired from Wolfson's office and who would remain with her for years to come, noticed that her main concern was whether there would be enough food at Smith Square for the party workers. Her family were with her: Denis, Mark and Carol (back from Australia for the campaign). Crawford heard her speak for them all when she arrived, with the unsurprising words, 'We're not in the least bit tired.'

Next morning she went to Buckingham Palace and formally accepted the Queen's invitation to form a government. Then the motorcade sped her to her new home, Number 10 Downing Street, where, in her Tory-blue belted suit, she faced the world for the first time as prime minister.

Her words were taken from a philosopher more than halfway

to Rome: St Francis of Assisi. Jim Prior recollects, 'I was nearly sick on the spot. It was so untypical of Margaret's attitude, and the tone in which she said it.'

Many felt the same, as Margaret, with an unearthly gleam in her eyes, recited the lines she had memorised at Ronnie Millar's instruction: 'Where there is discord may we bring harmony, where there is error may we bring truth, where there is doubt may we bring faith, and where there is despair may we bring hope.'

At the back of the scene, on the steps of Number 10, observing the jostling scene of cameras, microphones, lights and policemen, looking down with the quiet detachment of a genuine saint, was Denis Thatcher.

8

No Gain without Pain
(May 1979–March 1982)

———

Within forty-eight hours of becoming Europe's first woman prime minister, Margaret Thatcher was a minority in her own cabinet. Feeling it her duty to incorporate all strains of thinking in the party, she included her critics Ian Gilmour, Christopher Soames, Francis Pym and Peter Thorneycroft, all the Tory old guard vigilant to her right-wing tendencies. She was never comfortable with them, according to Cecil Parkinson, then a young Tory MP on the outside looking in. He told Brook Lapping, 'She didn't really like them and she felt that they didn't really like her.' He recalls one grandee of the party going to the City and announcing, 'We're a cavalry regiment led by a corporal in the Women's Royal Army Corps.'

As she started out, she had the comfort of knowing that she was backed by many people who had voted Conservative for the first time. In the 13,698,000 votes garnered at the general election, the party's biggest surge of new support had come from the skilled working class.

Tireless, less able than ever to relax, Margaret found 'living over the shop' (her joke) a positive advantage.[1] At the end of the day, staff could run up from their first-floor offices at Number 10 Downing Street and leave papers outside the door to the prime minister's private flat on the second floor. She would then sit in the drawing room overlooking Horse Guards Parade and read them all – as she was happy to explain:

I always tackle them at nights [sic], because I want to make sure I know what's in them in case there's anything that has to get done extremely quickly. But it isn't any trouble to do them. They're always interesting and I know the day will come when I don't have to do them and I know I won't like it when it does come.[2]

Being prime minister of Great Britain was the one job in the world that she wanted. She loved it. As she told the BBC's Michael Aspel, work was a pleasure. It helped that she had trained herself to get by on only four hours' sleep at night.

So immune was Margaret Thatcher to ordinary fatigue that she would say pityingly, 'Oh, you do look tired' to lesser mortals who showed signs of flagging when meetings ran on after midnight. These were invariably men; she had appointed no women. One of them, Lord Carrington, her Foreign Secretary, was unapologetic. 'I would say, yes, I am, and go to bed.' Himself an early riser, Carrington would find, if he went into the offices at Number 10 at half past six in the morning, that there she would be, perfectly dressed, immaculately coiffed, doing her boxes. Yet he understood that there was urgent business: 'We really were as a country going down the plughole.'

With opponents around her, she set about recruiting a loyal entourage. As her press secretary, she chose Bernard Ingham from the Department of Energy. Ingham, a bluff, colourful Yorkshireman, was a former journalist who had turned civil servant and worked for a number of government departments. A one-time Labour supporter, he was now non-partisan except for his loyalty to his boss. He saw his role as buffer between her and the press. 'She regarded journalism as the haunt of the brittle, the cynical and the unreliable,' he explains in his memoirs.[3] She was no news junkie. She did not read newspapers at all, except for the front page of the *Evening Standard*, which was left for her on the table outside her study at the bottom of the stairs leading up to her flat. Ingham concedes that possibly each morning she scanned the news digest on the front page of the *Financial*

Times. As for television news and current affairs programmes, they watched them only in snatches, and never when her own face appeared on the screen. 'Turn it off,' she would command.[4]

Her first order of business in the early summer of 1979 was to tackle inflation and stimulate economic growth. Her father had always stuck to his principles; she would stick to hers – or rather, those that were handed down to her by Keith Joseph and his Centre for Policy Studies thinkers, principally John Hoskyns, on whom she increasingly relied. The prescription called for controlling the money supply and cutting government spending, in particular by stopping the subsidy of inefficient nationalised industries. While others in her cabinet showed considerable resistance to these tough measures, she and Geoffrey Howe, her Chancellor of the Exchequer, in charge of carrying them out, were as one.

Howe began as he was to go on. His first Budget reduced income tax to 30 per cent from 33 per cent at the standard rate and to 60 per cent, down from 83 per cent, at the top rate. Exchange controls on buying and exporting sterling were abolished. To replace the lost revenue and to reduce public borrowing, however, more income had to be found. Howe virtually doubled value added tax (VAT) to a unified rate of 15 per cent. Thus the price of many goods, excluding essentials such as food and children's clothing, went up. This general price rise came at a time when inflation was running at 10 per cent and international oil prices were being increased. Unsurprisingly, workers in the public sector began to demand pay increases.

The alternative, favoured by many in the Thatcher cabinet, was for government to spend and borrow more. Those of whom she was most critical acquired the label of 'wets'. The people who were on her side, the hardliners, the non-wobblers, became known as 'dry'. Those on the other side, the vacillators, the compromisers and doubters, were 'wet' – collectively, 'the wets'. Chief among them was Jim Prior, who remembered from public school that to be called 'wet' was not a term of flattery. As Employment Secretary, Prior could hardly be unworried by the prospect of the massive job losses that would follow in the wake of cuts in government spending. And he did not like being called 'wet'. He saw himself as the very opposite: 'one of the few who actually stood up to Margaret at the time'.

A new home, a new outlet for compulsive housekeeping. Margaret's housewifely eye found much that needed her attention. The flat at the top of Number 10 had been converted from offices by Neville Chamberlain. The Thatchers' immediate predecessors, the Callaghans, had never really lived in it and the place appeared not to have been properly cleaned after they left. There were dead flowers, old plants and general dreariness everywhere. The layout was long and narrow, like a railway carriage. Off the corridor was the master bedroom with two twin beds pushed together, and with an en suite bathroom where she had her hair done several mornings a week. There were small bedrooms for use by Mark (who lived mainly at the Flood Street house) and by Carol on her visits from Australia. A small sunless room became an office for Denis; another at the end of the corridor was turned into a work space for Margaret's constituency secretary from Finchley.

Denis was happy enough with the move and piled golf clubs in the front hall. His main sacrifice was giving up his silver-grey Rolls-Royce; it was too conspicuous for the comfort of the security service. To their consternation, he tended, when not on official engagements, to walk to his appointments. Going to lunch in the City, he took the Tube. 'No one's going to waste the price of a bullet on me,' he would say.[5]

As the flat had no resident staff, Margaret employed her own daily cleaner from Flood Street. For meals, often as not, with the assistance of a deep-freeze and microwave, she cooked for herself and Denis in the small galley kitchen. Stephen Sherbourne, her political secretary sharing a meal with them in the flat, heard them talking about 'the government' as if they were a couple in suburban England criticising the politicians far away.

But the prime minister lived in the whole house. Number 10 Downing Street had no silver service. Caterers usually supplied their own. To fill the gap, Margaret contacted the stately-home owner of her youth, Lord Brownlow of Belton House outside Grantham, and asked whether he might consider lending the Belton silver to Downing Street for official entertaining. In the same borrowing mode, she asked also whether he would lend the little enamel casket with the picture of St Wulfram's Church he had been given when retiring as Mayor of Grantham in 1935. Brownlow duly provided these loans to the nation, presumably having family silver to spare.

She borrowed from national art collections too – a Turner, a Henry Moore, various portraits and busts of British artists, heroes and scientists. In the hall, she placed the large portrait of Sir Winston Churchill that had hung in her office in the House of Commons.

Before a dinner party in one of the state dining rooms, she would go round the table, like Anthony Hopkins in *The Remains of the Day*, checking the forks and spoons, the flowers and the lighting. Once she sent for a gold salver – 'my splendid gold salver' – from her study to brighten one of the tables. Her devoted assistant, Cynthia Crawford, who witnessed these rituals, explained to Brook Lapping, 'She didn't want us to be seen to be poor. She went to all these wonderful places – the White House, the Kremlin – and she just didn't want us to look like the poor relations.'

Margaret and Denis Thatcher became much admired as hosts at Number 10, good at making sure that people did not stand around with no one to talk to. Denis was particularly adept at taking the lone guest by the elbow and saying, 'I don't believe you've met the Home Secretary.' As they both liked to drink, they saw to it that empty glasses were quickly filled, if possible by themselves. Margaret's new Finchley agent, Andrew Thomson, said that one of the small things about the prime minister which he liked was the way 'she mixed all the drinks herself for guests, lining up beforehand the tonic with the gin, the ginger ale with the whisky'.

The Iron Lady was not just an export model. At the end of November 1979 Margaret declared to the House of Commons, 'I hope that one quality in which I am not lacking is courage.'[6] She then went to Dublin and battled with her fellow heads of government in the European Council, demanding a refund on what she saw as Britain's excessive contributions to the European Economic Community. Her obduracy and shrillness alienated some of Britain's European friends, as well as some of her cabinet. She wanted a billion pounds back; she used the phrase 'my money', at which Lord Carrington, then Foreign Secretary, remembers, Helmut Schmidt stretched himself out in his seat and closed his eyes.

However, she struck up – temporarily – a good rapport with the Irish Taoiseach, Charles Haughey, a studied charmer. She liked him, when he came to see her in May 1980, finding him less garrulous and more realistic than his opposite number, Garret FitzGerald. Also, he gave her a Georgian silver teapot. For his part, Haughey took to her because, as he told a group of British journalists visiting Dublin, 'she's not the type who likes to leave things lying around on the table'. With brisk determination like that, he began to hope, some progress might be made on ending the eight-hundred-year conflict in Ireland, based perhaps on a new concept of the 'totality of the relationship between these islands'.

Conviction and pragmatism are not incompatible. In early 1980 a strike started in the nationalised steel industry, when the management of the British Steel Corporation objected to the general wage increases demanded by workers. It was eventually settled by a court of inquiry and the award of larger increases in funding than the government had wished. The government's rationalisation was that the only alternative was liquidation and that BSC's bad management had been responsible for the crisis. An equally crippled state-owned industry was British Leyland. Faced with BL's possible bankruptcy and closure, with a massive loss of jobs, Margaret allowed Keith Joseph, the Industry Secretary, to dip into the public coffers and throw £450 million to the troubled motor-car manufacturer.

There was no giving in, however, to the demands of terrorists. At the end of April 1980 a group of Iranian dissidents had forced their way into the Iranian embassy in London and held twenty hostages. It was Margaret's first test in which human life was at stake, her chance to demonstrate that even though, like Queen Elizabeth I, she had the body of a woman, she could be as tough as any man when it came to giving the order to fire. The crack troops of the Special Air Service (SAS) understood that Mrs Thatcher did not want any of the terrorists to leave the building, with or without the hostages. While hoping to preserve the captives' lives, she determined above all that terrorism would be seen to be defeated. When after four days Willie Whitelaw, her Home Secretary, told her that the situation inside the embassy was deteriorating and that the hostages' lives were endangered, she gave the go-ahead for the SAS to storm the building. In full view of the television cameras massed in Hyde Park, the SAS men clambered down from the roof with ropes, smashed through the windows and shot four of the five gunmen dead. The fifth was taken prisoner. Margaret then went personally to the SAS barracks in Regent's Park to offer congratulations. 'The air was thick with testosterone,' recalled Richard Hastie-Smith of the cabinet office briefing room, who was there. With the men in khaki and blackened faces at her side, the prime minister watched the dramatic instant replayed on television. When one of them said to her, 'We never thought you'd let us do it,' she warmed to the compliment.[7]

As she received the telegrams of congratulation that poured

into Number 10 from abroad, she sensed, she says in *The Downing Street Years*, 'a great wave of pride in the outcome'.[8] How much prouder was Britain's experience than the protracted ordeal the Americans had suffered in Iran when hundreds were held for months in the US embassy in Tehran and President Jimmy Carter was humiliated by a failed attempt to rescue them. However, it was an advantage to be acting on home ground.

Stun guns were no help in the cabinet. As inflation rose and industries collapsed, some of her colleagues thought her economic strategy was entirely wrong. Too much, too fast, the ruthless moves were fuelling a slump and destroying social order. From the backbenches, Edward Heath himself mounted an open attack on her harsh policies. Would she change course?

The Conservative Party conference of October 1980 was the time to show her hand. It was preceded by an even later than usual speech-writing session; the team did not break up until five o'clock in the morning. Watching the endless drafts and fresh starts, Denis muttered, 'You're not trying to write the Old Testament, you know.' Thanks to the skill of the speech-writer and playwright Ronald Millar, they came up with something almost as durable. It involved a joke – always a risk with Margaret – and this one was built on not one pun but two. 'U' and 'you' sound alike; 'turning' and 'burning' rhyme. Whether or not she was aware of Christopher Fry's 1949 play *The Lady's Not for Burning* did not matter. Coached by Millar, she delivered what is probably her most famous sound-bite: 'To those waiting with bated breath for that favourite media catchphrase, the U-turn, I have only one thing to say: "You turn if you want to. The *Lady's* [pause] *not* [pause] for turning."'

Did her words cross the water? Later that month, on 27 October, certain IRA prisoners at the Maze Prison near Belfast began to refuse food. They had already begun the so-called 'dirty protest' – smearing their cells with excrement – to advertise their demand to be treated as a special category. Filth is one thing, suicide another. The hunger strike has an emotive history in the Irish struggle against the British – martyrdom as the weapon of last resort. But Margaret was not interested in historical symbolism, still less in negotiating the verbal niceties of the strikers' demands for changes in their prison regime. Her position was simple and clear. The strikers had chosen not to eat; that was their decision. They were offered food three times a day and could resume eating at any time.

Adopting the rhythms of Pope John Paul II's strong words to the IRA when he visited Ireland in 1979 – 'murder is murder is murder' – she intoned, 'Crime is crime is crime. It is not political, it is crime. And there can be no question of political status for someone who is serving a sentence for crime.'[9] Her intransigence was rewarded when the hunger strike was called off on 18 December 1980 when one of the men lost consciousness.

Very soon, however, she showed that she could abandon a fixed position when there was no alternative. By the end of 1980 a national coal strike loomed. The National Coal Board had proposed the shutting down of several dozen uneconomic pits; exactly how many was the subject of much controversy. Closure would mean thousands of miners deprived of the only livelihood they knew, whole communities endangered. Kim Howells, the MP for Pontypridd and later a Labour minister, recalled that, in South Wales, where bitter memories of the 1930s were still fresh, it seemed 'the wickedest of all things' that a prime minister should be indifferent to keeping men at work. 'She was the grim reaper taking away that part of the economy [manufacturing] which had underpinned our sources of employment.'

It took only a few months for her to back away from a coal strike. As Nigel Lawson, then a young intellectual economist, junior minister in the Treasury and MP, recalls, 'She caved in very, very quickly'. In February 1981 the country was ill prepared. There were no coal stockpiles at the power stations. Britain, unlike France, had not developed substantial nuclear alternatives for energy. Without coal the country would have come to a halt, just as it had in the Winter of Discontent of recent memory. Reading headlines such as 'Unions queue to test Thatcher resolve' and 'Government retreat may avert national coal strike', her press secretary, Bernard Ingham, winced. For two years he had watched the political correspondents 'spotting hunt the U-turn and they never found one. Then here there was going to be one.'

The U-turn came, manifested in an announcement by the National Coal Board that the closure proposals would be withdrawn and that coal imports from abroad would be reduced. The press interpreted it as a surrender and climb-down by the Thatcher government. The prime minister's view, as she later expressed it, was: 'there is no point in embarking on a battle unless you are reasonably confident you can win'. Defeat in a coal strike would have been the end of her economic revolution.

She was just beginning her revolution. The hardest battle was yet to come: the 1981 Budget. Geoffrey Howe prepared a draconian Budget. To fight inflation, he was going to carry on cutting public expenditure; the public sector borrowing requirement, PSBR, would be trimmed from £11 billion to £8 billion. Margaret agreed to brace herself for the protests to come. As Howe told Brook Lapping, 'We were convincing each other just how tough it was going to get. And there was no doubt in our minds that we had to do it.'

The rest of the cabinet was supposed to listen, not try to tinker. Howe told them what he had in mind only on the morning of the day when he would present it to Parliament. Jim Prior knew there was no point objecting to what he heard. It was too late for anything to be done. He found it 'a pretty objectionable Budget'. There was now a gaping divide within the cabinet.

Reaction was swift. *The Times* published a letter from 364 economists saying that the government was wrong. They wanted the introduction of Keynesian measures – essentially, increased public spending to create jobs – to pull the country out of its slump.

Of course, she would not budge. She was on a moral, almost religious, crusade. In a speech that was tantamount to a sermon, given in a church – St Lawrence Jewry in the City of London – she spelled out her philosophy to a Conservative Women's Conference in March. In it she equated Toryism with Christianity, the family with the state and, almost as explicitly, socialism with atheism. 'Creating wealth must be seen as a Christian obligation if we are to fulfil our role as stewards of the resources and talents the Creator has provided for us.'[10]

She spelled out her belief that 'the nation is but an enlarged family', declared that socialism was a threat to the nation's character, quoted in full her favourite Kipling poem, 'Norman and Saxon', and further, the words of the eighteenth-century evangelical minister John Newton, who said in a sermon: 'Though the island of Great Britain exhibits but a small spot upon a map of the globe, it makes a splendid appearance in the history of mankind, and for a long space has been signally under the protection of God and a seat of peace, liberty and truth.'[11]

John Bull's other island, however, was not so peaceful. Northern Ireland's troubles intruded once more. And once more there was no question of a U-turn. 'Never surrender' was her policy when a new hunger strike began at the Maze Prison on 1 March 1981. It was led by the young, long-haired leader of the IRA prisoners inside the Maze, Bobby Sands. That spring, as he lay weakened on his bed, his supporters outside managed to get him elected as Member of Parliament for Fermanagh and South Tyrone. (There was a by-election caused by the death of an Independent Republican MP.)

From the Thatcher point of view, there was nothing to negotiate. The Secretary for Northern Ireland, Humphrey Atkins (often considered one of her appointments based on debonair looks rather than command of the subject), had nothing to offer the strikers. If Sands's own mother refused to ask her son to save his life by giving up his protest, Mrs Thatcher was not going to do so – especially as, while the strike was in progress, there was a new IRA terror attack in London. A nail bomb detonated outside Chelsea Barracks, killing a bystander and injuring many soldiers in a coach.

After sixty-six days of fast, Bobby Sands died on 5 May. Margaret rose in the Commons that day to declare, 'Mr Sands was a convicted criminal. He chose to take his own life.' She made the point that it was a choice he had not allowed his victims.

The 'totality of the relationship between these islands' faded in the wake of these deaths and Thatcher's inherent sympathy with the Ulster Protestants came to the fore. 'I knew that these people shared many of my own attitudes,' she admits in *The Downing Street Years*, 'derived from my staunchly Methodist background.'[12]

Being Britain's prime minister, John Hoskyns noted in his diary, is an impossible job. In the summer of 1981 everything seemed to go wrong at once. Just as nine other hunger strikers at the Maze prepared to follow Sands to the grave, unemployment in Britain rose to 2 million, well above the level at which Margaret had taunted James Callaghan with being 'Prime Minister of Unemployment'. A new centrist political party, the Social Democrats, formed by Labour moderates who disliked the party's cloth-cap doctrinaire socialism, drew level with the Tories in opinion polls. Its four leaders were all ex-Labour ministers: Shirley Williams, Roy Jenkins, David Owen and William Rodgers. Not long after a German journalist asked the prime minister about the possibility of her policies provoking unrest, several of Britain's inner cities were hit by severe riots. The first was in Brixton, a south London district with a large black population. As the summer progressed, the riots spread to Toxteth, a poor area of Liverpool, and to Moss Side in Manchester. Television news showed ugly scenes; against a backdrop of flames, burnt-out cars and broken glass, looters cheerfully carried away television sets and other consumer durables. For Hugo Young of the *Guardian*, the Thatcher reaction was summed up by her reported remark, 'Oh those poor shopkeepers!'[13] For the Bishop of Liverpool, David Sheppard, her telling remark was that which was reported to him by Michael Henshall, the Bishop of Warrington. Henshall spoke to Denis and Margaret Thatcher, on a visit to the stricken city, of the need for compassion. Denis turned to his wife and said, 'That's not one of your words, is it?'

'I find it so condescending,' she replied. 'Compassion? That's not a word I use.'[14]

She had to respond. In early July a group got together to write a party political broadcast in which she would recognise the national crisis but convey that there was no link between the unemployment figures and the riots. The right words were not easy to find. In a heated moment in the drafting, John Hoskyns became so angry with Ronald Millar and Ian Gow, her parliamentary private secretary, that he forgot himself and used the word 'fucking' in the prime minister's presence. 'Why can't you just stop these fucking stupid arguments?' he shouted at Gow.[15] Catching himself, Hoskyns apologised, to which Margaret replied, 'I am quite accustomed to it.'[16] 'Denis', thought Hoskyns. 'Bless him!'

The resulting broadcast was considered a disaster. She appeared too poised, too well dressed and too pretty against a backdrop of flowers – she looked out of touch with the ugliness and raw emotion of events.

Hoskyns, an independent consultant with no political ambitions, was no admirer of Thatcher's ability. He agreed with Alan Walters, a World Bank economist and now chief economic adviser to Number 10, that 'She just does not know how to think.'[17] Her attitude when presented with studied analysis on the miners and the coal industry was 'too many questions, not enough answers'.[18]

She had surrounded herself with clever men and even they now began to tell her off. David (now Lord) Wolfson remembers warning her that unless she learned how to work with her colleagues her own position could be in jeopardy. Lord Thorneycroft, whom she had appointed chairman of the party, was not sure that either she or Geoffrey Howe would survive.

The public began to feel the pain without any sign of the promised gain: unemployment was rising as government spending was cut and subsidies to beleaguered industries were withdrawn. Much manufacturing went to the wall. Interest rates were high. Prices rose. Jobless figures now neared 3 million.

At the end of the terrible riot-torn summer of 1981, the cabinet's last task was to think ahead to the Budget for the coming year. In essence, 'Carry on cutting' was the prime minister's instruction to her Chancellor. Margaret backed Howe's demand for further spending cuts the following year. At this, the cabinet erupted. 'Even the right-wingers in the cabinet objected to it,' said Jim Prior. The scale of dissent astonished even Howe. The choice was between raising taxes and cutting government spending. John Biffen, Trade Secretary, suggested raising taxes to balance the Budget. Margaret said in effect that she would rather quit than entertain such an idea.

The Iron Lady then swung her lance. At the start of the year she had sacked Norman St John Stevas as Leader of the House of Commons, possibly because he, dipping into his rich Catholic lode, called her 'the Blessed Margaret' and 'the Leaderene'. Now she dismissed three prominent 'wets' – Ian Gilmour, Mark Carlisle and Christopher (Lord) Soames. But not Jim Prior, although the press expected it. 'I'll fight like hell!' the *Daily Mail* headlined an interview with Prior. Instead, she gave him the poisoned chalice of Northern Ireland.

In the place of the rejects she put a new trio of young Conservatives likely to support her, not least as the agent of their advancement: Cecil Parkinson, Nigel Lawson and Norman Tebbit. She also appointed a woman to her cabinet – Janet, Lady Young –

who became Leader of the House of Lords. She told Parkinson, 'I'm determined to get like-minded people around me, I just need that. There's such a job to do.' She saw that she wasn't going to get it done with her old cabinet.

But the sacked members were now free to speak out. Gilmour, in September, did not go gracefully. Believing that he had been too acquiescent in Thatcherism when he could see the damage being done to the country, he immediately announced that the government was leading the country 'full speed ahead for the rocks'.[19] Also from outside the cabinet, Chris Patten at the Conservative Research Department called for halting the decline in the economy. Meanwhile, the SDP gained ground. In November Shirley Williams overturned a 19,000 Conservative majority to win the parliamentary seat in Crosby, Lancashire; Roy Jenkins won in Hillhead, Glasgow.

But Margaret felt better. Kicking off her shoes at a private party in Downing Street, she stood on a chair and announced, 'I am the rebel head of an Establishment government.'[20]

Kicking her shoes off was a characteristic gesture. Being short, she needed high heels for height and authority. But after a time they hurt. When she went off duty, the shoes came off. Her advertising guru, Tim Bell, a man with an eye for personality indicators, called this habit 'one of her great things'. 'She would take her shoes off,' he wrote in his autobiography, 'and sit on her legs; that was a sign being sent to you that you are in, you are a member of the close community – "I drop my guard with you", which was very flattering.'

The men around her were easily flattered, as was she. It was obvious to all that Margaret enjoyed being the only female among men. In official photographs, she always held centre stage, the jewel in the crown, sparkling in the monochrome sea of males. Shirley Williams was one of many who noticed how resistant Margaret was to promoting able women. In the

Thatcher cabinet Lady Young was the only one, and as a member of the Lords she was outside, in Williams's words, 'the cockpit of the Commons'. In refusing to promote other women even to significant positions at the minister-of-state level, Margaret seemed to be protecting her own unique position as the outstanding woman politician in the Conservative Party.

Woodrow Wyatt, columnist for the right-wing *News of the World*, remained besotted. His daughter Petronella asked him why. 'Don't you understand?' he replied. 'She is what Napoleon said of Josephine – "She's woman, all woman."'

Wyatt and the prime minister seemed to talk every day on the telephone. Petronella herself considered that Margaret Thatcher hated women. When she came to dinner at the Wyatts' home, she would not address a word to the other women. When Mrs Wyatt tried to get a word in, the prime minister 'just looked at her and said, "Be quiet, dear. Your turn will come."'

When the ladies withdrew for coffee, Denis went with them, while his wife remained with the men, talking politics. As Petronella told Brook Lapping, 'She was regarded by my father as an honorary man. Denis must have been bored out of his mind. He was always fond of drink. And so was she, actually. It was spirits all the way – no nonsense about wine – stuff like Scotch and gin.'

Honorary man or not, Margaret was not averse to giving motherly advice. She warned Petronella: 'Be careful about marrying a man with no money at all. You'll soon find that you'll become very bored. All the conversation will centre on money and lead to terrible domestic rows.'

And Denis had the money. He used the money to help her, and it was a great marriage. She never talked down to him a bit, not in my presence. She always treated him terribly well. They're an extremely loving couple. It was one of the most successful political marriages I've ever encountered.

*

In the winter of 1981 her personal approval rating dropped to 23 per cent, the lowest ever recorded for a prime minister since polling began. Margaret Thatcher thus held two unique distinctions: those of being the most unpopular prime minister and the first woman prime minister. Were these by any chance related?

Undoubtedly. The persona of 'Maggie' inspired a special kind of hatred. As with the milk-snatcher row, her experience in 1981 showed that women are easily demonised for showing unwomanly qualities. Also, personal rigidity masked her own uncertainty. Hectoring was her way of proceeding in arguments whose complexity she could not follow. Fearful of seeming soft and unsure of herself, she showed a hard face to the world. Inflexibility was her best defence. The Iron Lady concealed the Little Woman.

That same year she made a brave attempt to show herself a good sport – and someone with a sense of humour – by accepting the advice of Tim Bell, her image guru, that the Thatchers *en famille* should attend John Wells's play, *Anyone for Denis?*, at the Whitehall Theatre, famous for its farce. The play had been constructed around the 'Dear Bill' letters in *Private Eye*, which continued to delight the nation. They were written with the help of a friend of the editor Richard Ingrams, a former schoolmaster and an expert on quips from the 1930s, such as being 'as much use as a one-legged man at an arse-kicking party'.

All the Thatchers sat together, while Bell, who had not taken the precaution of seeing the play in advance, squirmed in the row behind. The evening was excruciating for them all, not least John Wells, who played 'Denis' as a drunken, farting, foul-mouthed, trouser-dropping buffoon. The official contingent sat glassy-eyed. Later, to complete the public relations exercise that it was, they threw a party back at Number 10 for the cast. The prime minister, when questioned about it, had a good answer: yes, the play had been funny but it was not as funny as the original. Carol reviewed it for *News of the World*.[21]

In an attempt to appear to unbend, the prime minster even

allowed herself to dip into an East Midlands dialect in the House of Commons. Over-excitedly attacking Michael Foot, the Labour leader, just prior to the general election on 19 April 1983, she said, 'The Right Honourable gentleman is frit! He's frit!'[22] Dudley Smith recalled the reaction. 'Everyone erupted in a great eruption of sound and noise. Apparently this is a local term used by Lincolnshire people for "frightened". It sort of underlined her regard for the old ways of her time.'

Her image presented a tough problem for Bernard Ingham, who was supposed to look after it. He was well aware that

part of the image, of course, was hard as nails, utterly without compassion, which wasn't true at all, especially with the people around her . . . but she was quite incapable of showing it, as when visiting a Courtaulds textiles factory where there were job losses. Her voice, when she tried to sound sympathetic, became all breathy and insincere. I had to say, 'Please don't sound compassionate. It just sounds insincere.' She couldn't do it.

It must have been clear to Ingham that more than the tone of voice registered insincerity. Lines such as 'We're very anxious to do everything we can to help these people. We realise what a tremendous blow it is, both to individuals [and] their families' came from a woman whose unshakeable policy was not to intervene.

By the beginning of 1982 Margaret Thatcher was an established figure on the world stage. She had enjoyed a glorious visit to the White House in February 1981. Her friend, the Republican Ronald Reagan, had succeeded the Democrat Jimmy Carter as President of the United States. She could now look forward to her political philosophy and principles holding sway in the White House. Indeed, she was the first allied leader he received. Reagan was the supreme example of the kind of square-jawed, handsome man she liked. He had film-star charm and an engaging smile; also – perhaps even better – he evinced a kind of admiring bafflement at the torrent of factual detail that poured from her mouth. They were politically in tune, intellectually a world apart, but he let her speak for them both.

From world leader to nervous mother was an easy and automatic shift of gears. There was no disguising her feelings when in January 1982 her son Mark went missing in the Sahara Desert. At twenty-eight, sought by advertisers, not shy of trading on his now famous name on tennis outfits and Scotch whisky, Mark was driving a white Peugeot 504 in the Paris–Dakar motor rally.[23] That he had a beautiful French co-driver did not go unnoticed in the press. A week into the 6,200-mile journey, he failed to report to a check-point at the southern tip of Algeria. Neither troops nor aircraft, let alone the rally organisers, could locate him.

Six days passed without any word. Margaret was distraught. She rang Wyatt repeatedly, saying, 'What will I do without Mark? What will I do without Mark?' In one of the Thatchers' few recorded differences of opinion, Denis was not upset. The boy was not lost; he would turn up. According to various accounts, Denis was taking a bath when her personal assistant, Cynthia Crawford, heard Margaret shout at him through the bathroom door that Sir (now Lord) Hector Laing of United Biscuits had offered the loan of his private aircraft. Would Denis go and find Mark? Denis replied that he couldn't; he had a dentist's appointment. His wife told him to cancel it.

Margaret was red-eyed but composed through a cabinet meeting the following day but broke down later when, arriving for a lunch engagement, a reporter asked whether there was any news. When she replied, 'We're just waiting,' he rejoined, 'It must be a very distressing time for you, Prime Minister,' and the tears flowed and she leaned her head on her detective's shoulder. 'No news. My husband will arrive this afternoon.'

With Carol, she waited back at the flat, easing the strain by working on her red boxes. She was just settling down to watch the news, making a drink for herself, when Crawford took a telephone call. The speaker announced himself as 'Ron'. 'Ron who?' 'Reagan.' The prime minister, given the information, handed her drink to her assistant, saying, 'You need the drink, dear; I'll answer the phone.'

Within twenty-four hours of Denis's arrival in Algeria, Mark and his companion were found by a Hercules aircraft, fifty kilometres off the rally route. Seeing his father, Mark reportedly said, 'Hello, Dad. What are you doing here?' When the pair returned to London on the President of Algeria's personal jet, Margaret went out to Heathrow and hugged her son on his arrival. There was a press conference, at which Mark explained the trouble with the back axle that was responsible for his veering off course. While he spoke into the microphone, Denis faced the other way, his face showing undisguised exasperation at the spoiled brat whose mother fussed too much.

The episode was heaven-sent for *Private Eye*, whose 'Dear Bill' column had begun to turn Denis into a caricature of himself.

Dear Bill, Thank you for your condolences on the safe return of the son and heir from his Sahara car rally. Honestly, what a prize twerp! I washed my hands of the little blighter years ago, and when the Boss told me he was intending to drive across the desert with some fancy French bint he'd picked up in the pits, my response was that he could go to hell in a handcart for all I care. Next thing I know, M is hammering on my door at some unearthly hour to say that she had just heard on the *Jimmy Young Show* that the little bugger has been missing for four days and what was I doing to do about it? Answer: turn over and go back to sleep. Cue for maternal hysteria, call myself a man, etc., why is Yours Truly always so pathetic in a crisis?

Eventually I found my glasses and endeavoured to pour a bit of oil on the troubled H_2O, arguing that a) a bad penny usually turns up in the end, and b) that being inexperienced in these matters he had probably driven off on one of the B roads in search of a quiet layby to try a bit of hanky panky with la belle frogette. Need I tell

you that this last analysis went down like a cup of cold sick, water-
works turned on, male sex maligned, wailing and gnashing of teeth,
all culminating in Yours Truly agreeing to jump on the first Laker
standby to Timbuctoo in search of the Prodigal Son.

Margaret never feared to caricature herself. Just as she wanted
'her money' back from the EEC, she counted the pennies in her
daily life. Her Finchley agent noticed the way she made gift tags
for her Christmas presents by cutting old Christmas cards into
squares.[24] She often used housewife analogies for public spending. She had cut taxes, she told a Conservative Women's Conference in London in May 1980, because 'You spend your own
money more wisely than the government does.' And economies
had to be made. The public sector borrowing requirement had
to be trimmed way back from the ruinous £11 billion. No department was to be spared, not even the Ministry of Defence. Something had to give. John Nott, the Defence Secretary, who had
replaced the cuts-resistant Francis Pym, decided to shrink the
Navy, particularly the surface fleet. An extravagance no longer
justifiable was HMS *Endurance*, the sum of the British presence
in the South Atlantic. Margaret personally ratified the decision.
The ship was withdrawn, at a saving of £3 million a year.

A penny saved is a penny earned. At least, that was what they
said in Grantham.

9
Finest Hours
(March 1982–March 1985)

When Argentina invaded the tiny British dependency of the Falkland Islands on 2 April 1982, Bernard Ingham thought (but refrained from saying to his boss), 'Well, you've brought it on yourself.' The Foreign Office and the Foreign Secretary Peter Carrington had been justifiably worried about the effect of the withdrawal of HMS *Endurance*.

The Foreign Office had long appreciated the vulnerability – indeed, the virtual indefensibility – of these dots on the map down near Cape Horn. Argentina had claimed 'las Malvinas' for its own although Britain, having ruled them since 1833, had formally annexed the island of South Georgia in 1908. In 1976, the explorer Lord Shackleton suggested improving the island's main landing strip but that was rejected as too costly. In 1979, during Margaret Thatcher's first year as prime minister, a simpler practical solution was sketched out. Nicholas Ridley, a junior minister in the Foreign Office, visited Argentina and came back with a compromise. Argentina was to be given sovereignty over the islands, which would then be leased back to Britain for a lengthy period.

Leased back? The prime minister exploded at the thought. So did certain members of the House of Commons. Two years later, in December 1981, when a three-man junta headed by General Leopoldo Galtieri took power from the previous military government in Argentina, any hope for diplomatic bargaining vanished. The prime minister herself began to be alarmed about this dangling imperial appendage. A contingency plan was needed.

But events moved too rapidly. On 31 March word reached Downing Street that an Argentinian invasion force was closing on the Falklands. That night there was a sombre meeting of ministers and officials in the prime minister's room at the House of Commons. A late and important arrival was Sir Henry Leach, First Sea Lord, chief of the naval staff, and one of those opposed to the naval cuts. Not being in uniform, he had been delayed by the Commons security staff because they were reluctant to allow him access.

The prime minister looked him straight in the eye and said, 'Can we do it?' Her knowledge of the geography of the South Atlantic was hazy. When Leach said it would take three weeks to get a task force to the islands, she corrected him: 'You mean three days.' No. Three weeks. Again the steely gaze: 'Can we do it?' Leach's answer (as he recalled it) was blunt: 'Yes, we can. And we must.'

A glacial look demanded to know the reason why. The answer again was swift: 'Unless we do, unless we pull the stops out, unless we are entirely successful, then, in a very few months, we shall be living in an entirely different country – whose word will count for nothing.' That was the sort of advice that she wanted to hear and that he wanted to give. He was rewarded with her smile of relief, and his own surge of recognition that he was in the presence of a great leader. She gave Leach authority to prepare a task force.

A few days later when the 'Argies', as Leach called them, actually invaded the islands, she and her cabinet ordered the task force to set sail. She was outraged that a British colony had been invaded by a foreign power. It mattered not that there were only 1,800 inhabitants; what counted was that they did not want to be part of Argentina. Starting with two aircraft carriers –

setting out from Portsmouth with banners waving, bands playing, and families weeping and cheering – the fleet soon swelled to an armada of 100 ships and 25,000 men, making the long, slow journey to the South Atlantic. At the same time, intensive diplomatic efforts to reach a peaceful solution were under way.

Simultaneously, Carrington resigned as Foreign Secretary, but not out of a sense of culpability. Everyone knew that the Foreign Office had warned the government about 'sending the wrong signals'. But he saw it as fitting, he says in his graceful and frank autobiography, that when 'the nation feels there has been a disgrace', the disgrace be purged by the resignation of the minister in charge: 'That was me.'[1] His departure would put an end to the search for scapegoats and would also remove an embarrassment at a time when the government was heading for a rough passage. In his place, needing a man of stature and experience, she reluctantly put an archetypal Old Etonian Tory, a former shadow foreign secretary and one of the old 'wets', Francis Pym. As Leader of the House, Pym had been publicly pessimistic about the economic recovery, of which signs had been spotted, and about monetarism in general. He was, says the *Guardian*'s Hugo Young, 'the most perfect epitome of the kind of Conservative politician Mrs Thatcher detested'.[2]

As prime minister, she was now doubly endangered. If she lost the Falklands war, just as if she were to lose the battle against inflation, she would be swiftly thrown out. In her mind the two wars were much alike. She was full of religious certitude that her life was dedicated to the struggle for the triumph of good over evil, and to facing – even welcoming – strife, in the cause of making Britain great again. In Parliament she faced no serious opposition to her Falklands move. The Labour leader, the admired but ineffectual Michael Foot, who had replaced James Callaghan in November 1980, was at a loss as to how to respond. British territory had been attacked: what could he say? He gave his quiet support to military action to retake the islands.

But was it progress when, three weeks later, British troops recaptured South Georgia? This small island, although legally part of the Falklands, lies eight hundred miles to the south-east. To Mrs Thatcher, the British landing was a first step and she chose to announce it as a great victory, giving an impromptu press conference from outside Number 10. When a reporter asked if Britain was going to declare war on Argentina, she was dismissive. How like a journalist to look for bad news. Instead, he ought to 'rejoice at that news [of the recovery of South Georgia] and congratulate our forces and the marines . . . Rejoice.'[3] Even if she did not utter a Handelian cry, 'Rejoice! Rejoice!' that is the way her words have gone down in history.

The woman who loved extended meetings in the company of handsome men of authority now had a war cabinet that met daily, and sometimes twice a day. This inner elite included Cecil Parkinson, her favourite among her young recruits; excluded was Geoffrey Howe, the Chancellor of the Exchequer. Harold Macmillan, as a former prime minister, warned her that when prosecuting a war the last thing one needed were reminders of financial constraints.

But her military advisers were not so certain about her. Parkinson, the new party chairman, remembers the concern in the military about the prime minister's gender. 'It was unknown territory. How would a woman react when one of our ships was sunk, or when people were killed?' There was, he felt, forgetting Queens Elizabeth I, Anne and Victoria, no experience in Britain of a woman as war leader.

The country did not have long to wait. The fact that the war cabinet met at weekends at Chequers fuelled her Churchillian fantasies. It was at the prime minister's official country residence, on Sunday, 2 May, that the information arrived that the Argentine cruiser *General Belgrano* was 'zigzagging', with 'orders to sink a carrier'. She looked around the room. Should they allow their nuclear submarine, *Conqueror*, to torpedo it? Each man in turn gave his assent. The unanimous decision having been taken, they all went in to lunch.

The *Belgrano* was duly fired upon and sunk even though it was outside, and heading away from, the 'exclusion zone', the area with a 200-mile radius that the British had declared around the Falklands. It did not escape the Thatcher critics that the sinking occurred on the same day that the President of Peru had offered what seemed a workable peace plan. The military view – that war means casualties – became her own. She was sorry that hundreds of lives had been lost. But, as she noted later, the ships escorting the *General Belgrano* were more concerned with anti-submarine activities than with rescuing the men floundering in the sea.

It was a different matter two days later, when she received the news that an Argentine Exocet missile had sunk the British ship, the HMS *Sheffield*. Twenty-one men were lost. She was visibly shaken and had to fight to retain composure. Later she sat in the dining room of the flat and wrote to every mother or widow of the men who had died. She drew on her own anguish when Mark had gone missing in the Sahara. 'And that's how', she said in a broadcast interview, 'I knew what the Falklands mothers were going through.' The same identification, however, did not extend to the mothers of the 368 Argentine men drowned in the *Belgrano* and she was furious when anyone suggested that it should.

On the floor of the House, she was combative. But Matthew Parris, her former correspondence secretary who had become a Conservative MP, was unconvinced:

At the Despatch Box she was loud. She shouted. There was never any talk of surrender. But she looked quite scared to me. I did sense deep insecurity as to what the result would be. Nor did I sense that she was actually in charge of the military situation. Perhaps Prime Ministers never are but a man is sometimes able to seem as though he is. She didn't really. She sounded to me as though she'd been given a very good briefing by the generals. It was somebody else's that she was giving us.

Humble with military leaders, she was confrontational with the Foreign and Commonwealth Office for which she retained a distrust. Sir Antony Acland, the FCO's Permanent Under-Secretary of State, had trouble getting her to listen. 'She'd sometimes say, "What does the Foreign Office think?"' He would get halfway through a sentence when she would interrupt with 'I don't agree with that.' The only way to deal with her, he said, was to say, 'Well, Prime Minister, if you'll just let me finish – and I'll be very quick – perhaps you will agree with it at the end.'

As she distrusted the Foreign Office, so did she distrust the BBC. She was enraged by its even-handed news coverage of the war. She saw British troops as 'our boys', the others as 'the enemy'. When the BBC ran analytic programmes on *Newsnight* and *Panorama*, discussing both sides of the conflict and the case for a diplomatic solution, there were protests in Fleet Street and in the House by some Conservative MPs. Asked at Prime Minister's Questions how she herself felt about the BBC's coverage, she replied that there were 'times when it would seem that we and the Argentines are almost being treated as equal and almost on a neutral basis'. For her part, she quite understood the strength of feeling 'that the case for our country is not being put with sufficient vigour on certain programmes – I shall not say all – of the BBC'. Her comments were a poor portent for the BBC director-generalship of Alasdair Milne, which began two months later.

The South Atlantic was never far from her mind. At night she and her assistant and friend, Cynthia Crawford (whom she always called Crawfie), would sit together on the floor of the master bedroom in the flat at Number 10, listening to the BBC World Service late into the night. Crawford recalls how they would have a drink to steady their nerves – always whisky and soda. 'She'd say, "You can't drink gin and tonic in the middle of the night, dear. You must have a whisky and soda because it will give you energy."'

Contributing to her uneasiness about the uses of diplomacy was the American ambivalence on the Falklands. Where was her friend Ronald Reagan when she needed him? At the very point when British troops, having landed at San Carlos on the edge of the main island, were poised for the final assault on the capital, Port Stanley, Reagan rang her to suggest that a diplomatic initiative might work if taken prior to the capture of Port Stanley. The American President was torn between the special relationship with Britain, and American strategic interests in South America. Galtieri had been received warmly in Washington on his visit in 1981 and had returned to Argentina believing that friend Reagan would turn a blind eye to an invasion. Reagan's Secretary of State, Al Haig, had the task of shuttling between Washington and Buenos Aires, trying to explain to Galtieri why the United States would not back him and was intent on finding a peaceful solution.

The prime minister was well aware of Haig's trips and was determined not to be dragged into a dishonourable compromise. To Reagan, she was blunt, according to a transcript obtained by Brook Lapping: 'Look. I didn't lose some of my finest ships and some of my finest lives, to leave quietly, without the Argentines withdrawing.'[4] The President persisted. If she could perhaps hold back her troops 'until a binational or multinational force arrived . . .'[5]

The lady was not for turning. 'Just supposing Alaska was invaded,' she put it to him in terms she thought he could understand. 'It's a long way away from you, it's next door to the Soviets. You've put all your people up there to retake it and you've lost a lot of men and ships. You wouldn't do it.'[6]

Reagan replied that Alaska was not comparable. She corrected him: 'More or less so.'[7]

She won – the argument and the war. On 14 June, the Argentinians ran up the white flag at Port Stanley. The Falklands remained British at a cost of several hundred British lives. It called for a victory dinner at Number 10 Downing Street, where she presided over a table set for seventy of her leading officers, with the Chief of the Defence Staff, Sir Terence Lewin, at her right hand. Their wives were invited to arrive for coffee.

At the end of the meal, she rose and said gaily, 'Gentlemen, shall we join the ladies?'

One of her rare jokes, the question was as triumphal as any of her Falklands rhetoric. By proclaiming herself an honorary man, she declared her victory over her own sex, as if she alone had thrown off the shackles that keep women in the anteroom of history.

The Thatcher sense that any other woman was a rival extended to Her Majesty the Queen. The monarch was conspicuous by her absence at the service of thanksgiving at St Paul's Cathedral on 26 July. (When, at the multi-faith service, Robert Runcie, the Archbishop of Canterbury, spoke of the grief of mourners on both sides of the conflict, the prime minister was not pleased.) The Queen did not appear either at the celebratory lunch at the Guildhall in October. At the preceding military parade, it was the prime minister who took the salute with the Lord Mayor and led the singing of 'Rule Britannia'.

The nation as woman: an old idea. Ireland had its Cathleen ni Houlihan, France its Marianne. Thanks to what became known as the Falklands factor, Margaret Thatcher now personified her country.

Did it cross her mind before she embarked on the Falklands war that it could rescue her political career? Probably not at the start. The greatness of Britain, the sceptred isle, 'never, never, never shall be slaves' and so forth: her patriotism ran on tramtracks. The truth nonetheless was that before the Falklands war, the Tories were seriously thinking of finding a new leader before the next general election, which had to come no later than 1984.

Her rhetoric to many seemed too harsh. The clergy were alarmed by the message that her doctrine of self-reliance was sending to the have-nots; it seemed as if society did not care whether these unfortunates had no hope. Within the Thatcher team itself, there was also a battle going on about how far and how quickly the nationalised industries might be privatised. Jim Prior, the only economic liberal among them, warned John Cole, the BBC's political editor, that Mrs Thatcher was deadly serious about her Friedrich von Hayek–free-market ideology. 'Don't make any mistake,' he told Cole. 'This is a very right-wing lady.'[8]

Dennis Signy, one of her admirers and editor of the *Finchley Press*, looked back on this time as 'a period when the hostility was growing and where we called her TINA – There Is No Alternative; when they started that thing, "Thatcher's gotta go." Right from the start – this may have been a woman in a man's world – she was tough; her rhetoric was strong and tough and uncaring.'

The Falklands victory countered all that. Was it her finest hour? Not to Lord Carrington:

It was a great hour, but I don't think it was her finest hour. There was no question that any prime minister would have had to do the same thing. Whether they would have done it with the same panache that she did is another matter. Her finest hour really was with the economy and to change people's perception of what we ought to be doing.

Indeed, she never surrendered to militants except when it was expedient. An undiguised concession to terrorism came in September 1980 when the leader of the Welsh nationalists, the ancient and venerable Gwynfor Evans, vowed in six months' time to go on a hunger strike if the Conservatives did not keep a manifesto promise to give Wales a Welsh-language television channel. In previous years Welsh nationalists had been burning cottages and blowing up television masts in protest against their English-dominated broadcasting. William Whitelaw, who as Home Secretary had the radio wavelengths in his gift, caved in to this blackmail. Evans withdrew his threat and did not miss a meal, unlike the hunger strikers at the Maze prison, who were starting the fasts that would eventually result in their deaths. Martyrdom on the mainland was obviously more serious than across the water.

The Thatchers, Margaret and Denis, relaxed in their fashion by occasionally visiting David Wolfson and his wife at their home in Cornwall. The two men would play golf while the wives would go off for two-hour walks along the cliff – that is, if the prime minister was awake. Wolfson has given one of the rare descriptions of Margaret Thatcher sleeping: 'She used to come down and wind down completely for about four or five days, literally fall asleep at ten o'clock at night and sleep in the afternoon in the garden with a pile of books, which remained largely unread.'

But there was an election date to pick. She could, in fact, have waited another year. There was much discussion within the cabinet before 9 June 1983 was finally set as the day.

She prepared for the election by going to the Falklands. The decision to do so was not taken until after she had fixed on the election date and it was not announced to the press. It was a long way to go for a photo-opportunity, and meant spending thirteen hours in the belly of a Hercules aircraft. As it neared their destination, Denis was heard to mutter, 'Only three hours, thirteen minutes and twenty-five seconds before I can have a cigarette.' Matthew Parris, who was also on the journey (about which the accompanying journalists were sworn to secrecy), said that the consequence 'was everybody arriving totally zonked and dishevelled except Margaret Thatcher. They had towed a caravan or a Portakabin into the belly of the plane. She spent the entire journey there, where she had a little make-up desk, and when the plane arrived in Port Stanley, she tiptoed down the stairs looking absolutely impeccable – hair perfect and perfectly made up.'

She was given the freedom of Port Stanley and made a speech. But the reaction from the islanders disappointed her. Enthusing about all the jobs that would be created by the reconstruction of the city – roofs to mend and roads to rebuild – she had forgotten that she was talking to a group of sheep farmers.

During the campaign she concentrated on a business-as-usual image, going to international conferences and campaigning on her manifesto promise of 'rolling back the frontiers of the state'.

Michael Foot did not dare to make the Falklands war an election issue, even though there were important questions to be answered about the wisdom of the massive force deployed, about the preventability of the attack and about the sinking of the *Belgrano*. It took a member of the public, Mrs Diana Gould, to rattle the prime minister during the campaign by telephoning the BBC programme, *Nationwide*, on 24 May, to ask why the *Belgrano* had been sunk as it was outside the exclusion zone and sailing farther away.

The prime minister retorted that the ship had *not* been sailing away from the Falklands. But, as her well-informed questioner persisted, she became aware, on camera, that she had the actual facts wrong – a sin she found unforgivable in others. To be so humiliated served to increase her distrust of the BBC. She suspected, with some encouragement from her husband, that the BBC, like the Foreign Office, was intrinsically left wing and opposed to what she was trying to do. Denis had never made any secret of his contempt for the 'nest of vipers' and 'the bloody reds' – the actual words he used to describe the BBC to its new chairman, Marmaduke Hussey.[9]

The Conservatives were ahead in the polls from the start and went on to win the election on 9 June 1983. The total Tory vote was down slightly – and represented only 43.5 per cent of the vote. But that mattered little in the face of the party's majority, which increased to 144. The Social Democrats (SDP), in alliance with the Liberals, had taken a good chunk of the Labour vote but, for lack of proportional representation, had only twenty-three seats in Parliament to show for it.

The result was a clear example of the effect of 'first-past-the-post' voting or what some may call 'elective dictatorship'. Margaret Thatcher may have been a minority prime minister – based on the low percentage of votes – yet she had 100 per cent of the power.

In response to this supremacy, friends and enemies alike saw a change in character. Gone was the unconfident woman. In Jim Prior's view, she began to be openly domineering. 'She really didn't want to listen to anyone else.' In the view of Neil Kinnock, the new Labour leader who replaced Foot after the 1983 election, she 'started to strut. You only have to look at the movie pictures to see the change in demeanour.'

If her political opponents were dispirited, those in the trade unions were not. Four weeks later Arthur Scargill, leader of the National Union of Mineworkers, threw down the gauntlet. Sizing up the political scene, he announced, 'A fight-back against this government's policies will inevitably take place outside, rather than inside, Parliament.' Scargill said that what he and his minders intended to undo was 'Thatcherism'. Four years of it.

The battle lines were drawn. The country had, in effect, two leaders: Scargill, who had become president of the mineworkers' union in 1981, and Thatcher, whose re-election in 1983 had wiped clean the slate of her wobbly start.

But first she had to reshuffle her cabinet and get rid of the opponents whom she had suffered for too long. Parkinson, tall and smooth-haired, wealthy by his own efforts, was her favourite among her young protégés. He had been a valuable member of the war cabinet and, as party chairman, a skilled director of the recent campaign.

What better reward than to make Parkinson Foreign Secretary, vaulting him to one of the highest offices of state? Her dream was interrupted by a letter from the father of Parkinson's mistress, Sarah Keays. He thought that the prime minister ought to know that his daughter was pregnant. In consequence, she offered him the less high-profile Trade and Industry Department instead.

Margaret Thatcher, for all her strict upbringing, was surprisingly neutral on sexual behaviour. She was neither a gossip nor a goody-two-shoes, and she did not invite gossip about private lives. She didn't discuss morality at all, Parris remembered – with one exception. 'She really didn't approve of women who cheated on their husbands. She didn't approve of adultery and tended to blame the woman rather than the man.' Parris had the feeling that her prejudice was born of a feeling that such women might steal other women's husbands.

It seems that what she did not like was divorce. Her own beliefs were probably reinforced by Denis's bitter experience. It seemed to Parkinson, on the other hand, that the decent thing to do was to divorce his wife and marry the mother of his child. This was not decent to Margaret Thatcher. 'What about Ann?' she asked when he told her of his impending fatherhood.[10] She was relieved at his decision to stay married and leave Miss Keays to become an unwed mother. Unhappily, she accepted his resignation from the Trade and Industry secretaryship he had held only briefly. She saw it as a loss – one of her finest men sent into the political wilderness.

The reshuffle was ruthless. Out went the last of the wets she had dutifully kept round her, with Pym refusing the token leadership of the House she offered him. Geoffrey Howe went to the Foreign Office, Nigel Lawson to the Treasury, and a rising star, Leon Brittan, to the Home Office. Out too went the first and last woman ever to join her cabinet, Lady Young, who had been allowed a brief two years as Leader of the House of Lords. 'Janet', Margaret Thatcher wrote patronisingly in her memoirs, 'had turned out not to have the presence to lead the Lords effectively and she was perhaps too consistent an advocate of caution on all occasions.'[11] Not up to a man's job, in other words? Whitelaw got the appointment instead, and a peerage to make him eligible.

Since Arthur Scargill's initial provocative statement, Margaret Thatcher had been braced for a miners' strike. But she at least had had a rehearsal for what was to come. Having avoided the miners' strike in 1981 by backing down, she was not going to surrender again. Next time she was going to win.

Scargill waited until March the following year (1984) to call his men out. His signal was the confirmation by the National Coal Board that it would close uneconomic pits. The government was ready – almost too ready. Its preparations were conspicuous: the non-stop trains, laden with coal, moving stocks from the pitheads to the power stations. What's more, a leaked report published in *The Economist* gave full details of the government's battle plan to outwit the miners.

Neil Kinnock, now Leader of the Opposition, was in an awkward position, just as his predecessor, Michael Foot, had been over the Falklands. The Labour Party was committed, financially and philosophically, to supporting organised labour. Kinnock himself was from a South Wales coal-mining family. Yet he was stunned to hear that Scargill had officially sanctioned the strike without calling for a national ballot – even though the National Union of Mineworkers' constitution appeared to require a democratic mandate for a national strike.

Had Scargill called for a ballot, he might well have won; the NUM rules required only a 50 per cent majority for a strike to claim democratic legitimacy. But he ignored the constitution – and Kinnock said nothing. Kinnock's later justification was that South Wales miners had been working to rule for five months and that telling them to hold back from a strike might have seemed a betrayal. In retrospect, he regrets his silence. 'I'll never forgive myself for that,' he told Brook Lapping in 2001. It continues to haunt him that he did not point out that there must be a ballot and that without one there would be no solidarity of the kind needed to bring an end to the dispute.

When Scargill went ahead, insisting on his own interpretation that NUM rules allowed for a strike without a national ballot, Kinnock knew 'at that second, that, barring miracles, whatever industrial action they took was not going to have a positive outcome. In fact, it was doomed.'

For the prime minister, the miners' strike was more than an industrial dispute. It was another of the struggles of good versus evil that she felt it was her destiny to fight on Britain's behalf. She had come to office determined to curb trade union power. This was the big contest she had been waiting for. If the miners won, clearly no government would have been able to govern without the agreement of Scargill and his union. Dipping once more into her 1939–40 vocabulary, she accused Kinnock of 'appeasement' and called her opponents 'enemies within'. On Channel 4's *A Week in Politics*, she spelled it out:

'Enemies within are those who do not believe in the democratic system but who will use violence or intimidation – some means other than democracy – to attain their ends.'

But the miners were by no means united in their determination to stop digging coal. The lack of a national ballot split their ranks. An independent union, the Union of Democratic Mineworkers, representing those at the Nottingham and Derbyshire coalfields, refused to join the strike; its members continued to go to the pitheads every morning even though it often took a police escort to get them there.

The ensuing violence made ugly scenes on the television news. Angry pickets surrounded the working mines and the power stations as police took workers through the picket lines, against a screaming chorus of 'Scab! Scab!' In the memory of Kim Howells MP, at that time research officer and editor of a miners' union newspaper, 'Anybody who tried to get through picket lines in those days was either the bravest person on earth or completely crazy or a combination of the two.' The miners were not only 'at war with Thatcher' but at war within their own communities: 'the most terrible and weakening thing'.[12]

Howells would not have believed that the prime minister would employ the whole apparatus of the state to defeat the Scargill union. But she did. Police were drafted in from other parts of the country to protect the working miners, and they presented a dehumanised picture on television. Thanks to the riots in Toxteth and other inner cities in the summer of 1981, they were now kitted out for urban war, with plastic helmets, shields, armoured vehicles and sophisticated communications. Howells saw 'a kind of medieval battle taking place'.

The worst and bloodiest battle came in the summer, at the Orgreave coke works in Staffordshire. Five thousand picketers, trying to stop coal reaching the Scunthorpe steelworks, showered the police with bricks and darts. Many were injured. The show of force demonstrated that, in the end, the massed power of the law was bound to prevail.

To be victorious is not the same as being admired. The people being knocked about by the police on the Thatcher government's orders were citizens ordinary in every sense other than their fierce support for the strike. Fearful of uniting other trade unions against it, the government did not even use its new laws against secondary picketing – picketing by those from outside the pit involved. An immediate threat was a national dock strike. However, after walkouts at certain ports, that strike collapsed after ten days.

Nevertheless, the coal strikers retained much public sympathy. Their picketers were visibly not antisocial looters and car-burners, but representatives of heart-of-Britain mining communities for whom the public felt a sentimental *How Green Was My Valley* affection. 'There was the impression', says Kinnock, 'that people who were down were being stamped on.' Miners' wives certainly felt so, some joining their men on the picket line. One woman shouted at a television camera: 'I'd like to tell Margaret Thatcher there's no way we'll give in, and she's not living like we're living. She's not feeding three children like I'm feeding them on about twenty pound [a week] for groceries.'

Those miners who remained at work received grateful letters from Margaret Thatcher, and some financial support from behind-the-scenes senior Conservative Party figures. But the prime minister knew she was right. She rose to Gloriana heights of rhetoric (albeit with some repetitiveness): 'I will never negotiate with people who use coercion and violence to achieve their objective. They are the enemies of democracy. They are not interested in the future of democracy. They are trying to kill democracy for their own purposes.'

'Trying to kill democracy for their own purposes.' She used almost the same words on Friday, 12 October 1984, when she spoke at the Conservative Party conference at Brighton. She appeared at precisely nine o'clock in the morning even though a few hours previously an IRA bomb had blasted the Grand Hotel where she was staying, killing five people. She had come to the conference an hour earlier – dressed and well groomed as usual – saying that the proceedings must start on time. Her principal private secretary Robin Butler was appalled. There was no need to be so punctual when the ambulances had scarcely left the scene. 'But she was right and I was wrong,' he told Brook Lapping.

Margaret knew very well that the bomb had been aimed at her, as well as members of her cabinet, all of whom were staying at the Grand. It was mere chance that, with the callous inefficiency of terrorism, the plot's main victims were not the primary targets but bystanders. One of the dead was Roberta Wakeham, wife of John Wakeham, Conservative chief whip. Terribly injured was Norman Tebbit's wife Margaret, who was left permanently paralysed. Both Thatchers escaped even though their bathroom was destroyed. Had either been in it they would have died. But Denis had gone to bed and Margaret was in another room, engaged in her usual night-before speech-writing exercise.

The conference had got off to a good start. The government was riding high and all were waiting for the annual set-piece, which she did so well, the prime minister's address. All the more reason, therefore, for the intensive writing and polishing routine the night before. This never varied, and it took a lot out of her aides, as well as Denis. In the recollection of John Whittingdale, then of the Conservative Research Department:

You started at the beginning. You went through to the end, and then you started again at the beginning, and you went through it time and time again. Then she would turn around and say, 'No, it's absolutely hopeless, the whole thing is useless.' She would chuck it away and we would then have to try and slowly reinsert all the passages that she'd rejected back into the speech. The goal was her declaration: 'Oh, it's much better now.'

During this ordeal Denis, who liked to go to bed at a normal hour, would sit up in a corner of the room, eyelids drooping, because he knew there was a role that only he could perform. '"I don't think we're going to make much further progress on this tonight," he would say. "Why don't we all go to bed now and see what it looks like in the morning." She would sometimes take this advice from him, never from anybody else.'

On the night of 11–12 October, Denis had retired long before the elusive goal of the leader's satisfaction with the speech was reached. At twenty minutes to three, just as the final draft had been handed to the typists, a loud thud shook the room, followed by flying glass, falling plaster and the ringing of alarm bells.

Butler moved Margaret away from the windows; she made for the bedroom to find Denis. Her immediate fear was that he wouldn't put his slippers on and would stumble across the broken glass. He was fine. Although the bathroom had disappeared, he emerged, pulling a pair of grey flannels over his pyjamas. She then checked to see if the three secretaries were all right, and said, referring to the bomb, 'That was for me.'

For the next forty-five minutes, David Wolfson, Margaret's economic adviser, also staying at the hotel, recalls, 'It was a recovery operation. Should the prime minister climb out of the window? Should the firemen put up a ladder or should she walk through the hotel? Was the hotel going to collapse? And then everybody went off to Lewes Police Station and it wasn't until the next morning that we knew about the casualties.'

In the prime minister's suite, too, the immediate concern was for the practicalities. 'Where shall we put the speech?' asked her diary secretary, Tessa Gaisman, before deciding to put it in the prime minister's handbag, 'because we knew she was never going to let go of her handbag'. The loyal Crawfie picked out two suits, one for Margaret to wear the next day. All then made their way down the main staircase, still unaware that anyone had been killed. Taken to the Lewes Police College, Margaret changed into a navy suit – she had been in evening dress – and in a room shared with Crawfie she slept for an hour and a half. At half past six in the morning on breakfast television she watched the shocking scene of Norman Tebbit, the Trade and Industry Secretary, being carried out on a stretcher, his pyjamas and bare feet covered in dust and plaster. On the way to the conference hall they saw the gaping V-shaped hole slicing through the front of the hotel. Only later did she learn that Roberta Wakeham and Anthony Berry MP were among the dead.

Determined to carry on, she did. If she was in shock, there was no sign of it. There was work to be done. Obviously the speech had to be rewritten. She and Ronnie Millar worked to take out the jokes and the Labour-bashing. On cue, she took her place on the platform. 'The fact that we are gathered here now, shocked but composed and determined,' she declared, 'is a sign not only that this attack has failed, but that all attempts to destroy democracy by terrorism will fail.'[13]

An Italian journalist who was in Brighton to cover the conference was overwhelmed by this display of the British capacity for composure. Had the bomb been in Italy, he conjectured (speaking to an Italian–British round-table conference in Rome two years later), the reaction would have been somewhat different. Indeed, he could not imagine any other country where the conference would not have been cancelled.

The trauma did not relieve her of the miners' strike. In refusing to give in to the miners, she was up against her old dilemma: woman's heart versus man's muscle. The cabinet secretary, Sir Robert Armstrong, believed that she identified closely with the miners' wives, trying to feed their families on scant strike pay. He could see, however, that 'it was very difficult to combine that sort of compassion with the strength that you needed to show in dealing with the miners' union'. Inasmuch as she took the women's point of view, to Armstrong she appeared to think that 'it was up to the miners' wives to tell their husbands to be sensible'.

The strike, although waning, dragged on longer than anyone had dreamed. At Christmas 1984, miners' families were sent gifts of food and toys and other charity from a public sympathetic to their hardship. The New Year saw a straggling return to work – several thousand a week; by March, the miners were exhausted and broke, and the strike collapsed. It made a sad scene, says Kim Howells: 'men crying, whole families crying, marching back to the pits and marching back to Mrs Thatcher and to the conviction that we were in for a very, very bad time because we weren't going to have work in the pits for much longer.'

Howells was right. Some 150,000 mining jobs were lost. Whole communities died. All the same, from the perspective of the next century, it is a mystery why anyone should weep for the right to work 300 feet underground in cold and darkness. Or, why no one foresaw the new industries of information technology and electronics, which would provide cleaner, better-paid jobs in many former mining areas.

Today, when fewer than two dozen coal mines remain open in Britain, the Big Pit Mining Museum in Blaenavon, Gwent, a World Heritage Site, stands as a memento of two hundred years of industrial past. With preserved shafts, pithead baths, blacksmith, lifts and all, the museum provides an opportunity for anyone over five years old and one metre tall to don a helmet, cap-lamp and battery pack and to descend 300 feet underground for 'a real sense of life at the coal face' and, when they surface, to buy 'quality souvenirs' at the gift shop.

Was the miners' strike of 1984 worth it? Norman Tebbit, not the softest-hearted Tory, told Brook Lapping of his sadness today at seeing the desolate mining communities of Yorkshire and Derbyshire. Looking back at the strike, he now thinks it was 'immensely sad and not necessary for it to have been so harsh'.

In the end, the mining industry was sacrificed to market realities – a fate not yet allowed to descend on British farming. Green fields and rosy-faced farmers have a greater hold on the national heartstrings than did the hymn-singing, brass-band-playing, grimy miners.

During the miners' strike Margaret Thatcher used the language of war as she had during the Falklands, but without the same rewards in the public opinion polls. She was proud of both victories. Never good at disguising her true feelings, she obviously meant what she said when she addressed a group of Conservative councillors. 'Of course people told me I shouldn't gloat. Well, I am gloating. I am gloating.'[14]

She had reason to feel pleased with herself in 1985. The economy was slowly turning round. Inflation was dropping. The sale of British Telecom in November 1984 had gone well; Britain was now leading the way to privatisation, which the other bureaucratic bastions of state monopoly – Europe's various post and telecommunications authorities – would slowly follow. With her Trade and Industry minister Kenneth Baker, she had mounted a crusade for information technology and ensured that there was a computer in every school. Her policy of selling publicly owned council houses at a discount to tenants was proving popular. And few wept (at least, not at the time) at the abolition of the Greater London Council and other metropolitan giants of local government. Socialism had indeed begun to look fusty, a post-war relic out of tune with the go-ahead 1980s.

All during her prime ministership Margaret Thatcher had been lucky. During the Falklands war at least thirteen Argentinian missiles hit British ships but failed to explode. At varying times the *Hermes*, the *Invincible* and the *Canberra* were either thought to have been hit or narrowly missed. If any of these ships had been sunk, Sir Antony Acland believes Britain could not have won. In the same way, if the Union of Democratic Mineworkers had not splintered from the NUM and had instead allied with Scargill, she couldn't have won the miners' strike, even with the coal stocks she had.

Above all, she was lucky in her opponents. From the unpopular Heath to the weak Michael Foot to the autocratic and wrongheaded Arthur Scargill, she was up against men she could defeat. As she entered 1986 and her sixth year as prime minister, she was lucky once more. Neil Kinnock was now the man she confronted across the chamber of the House.

10

Not a Hair out of Place
(1984–1987)

'Your hair will send significant messages to those around you.
It will tell people who you are and what you stand for.'
Senator Hillary Clinton, Senior Class Day Address,
Yale University, 20 May 2002

Seeing 'Carmen Rollers' in the prime minister's diary one morning, somebody wondered who Carmen was. It was no mystery to her diary secretary. The entry was shorthand for having a comb-out. Male aides were never allowed to see Margaret Thatcher during this procedure, when she would work on her papers and be down in the main office by 8.30 a.m.

To *The Times*, looking back from 2002, 'The semiotics of Baroness Thatcher's hair shrieked "Strength! Power!"'[1] That was the intention. She was what Roland Barthes called a face object: like many film stars, she had a diminutive stature offset by a big head with strong, symmetrical features topped by a full corona of hair. Backcombed and sprayed into immovable shape, her hair was never photographed wind-blown unless the occasion demanded, such as riding in a tank-turret. When travelling in service helicopters where passengers were given earmuffs to dull the noise, Bernard Ingham observed that Mrs Thatcher used to wear them upside down, with the headrest under her chin, to avoid spoiling her hair.[2]

It is scarcely possible to exaggerate the importance Margaret Thatcher placed on looking her best at all times. It was as if her hold on office, her power over her cabinet, the House of Commons and heads of foreign governments, depended on being impeccably attired in the right suit with the right brooch, neck-lace, earrings and bracelet. Before a trip to France, she would have calls made to the British embassy in Paris to find out in great detail what colours, what sleeve shapes and hemlines were in vogue that season. Her principal private secretary understood. 'She attached very great importance to being well turned out, and she had a remarkable eye,' says Robin Butler. 'She could sketch a dress she had admired so that her own dressmaker could make one like it.'

Hair was of supreme significance. When after the general election of 1983 she summoned Nigel Lawson to her office and appointed him Chancellor of the Exchequer, the only briefing she gave him was to get a haircut. Nobody ever had to give that advice to her.

Her personal assistant for many years, Cynthia Crawford, dismisses any suggestion that Margaret Thatcher was vain. 'She has a very small face but her hair makes up for everything. Particularly when TV cameras came into the House, we had to make sure that her hair looked terrific. We decided that although she had her hair washed every Monday she would have it combed out again on Tuesday and Thursday so that she always looked her best.'

She travelled abroad a great deal – in 1986 alone she visited Japan, Korea, Israel and the United States; remaining well-coiffed on foreign trips was a special challenge. On a trip to Turkey, a hairdresser arrived with an interpreter, shaking and perspiring at the awesome task ahead. The man was so agitated that Crawford, thanking him profusely, asked him to leave and did the job herself.

To be sure, attentiveness to wardrobe and appearance was not only required by the job but was a form of relaxation. She considered it a luxury to have time to look at beautiful clothes. When she got bored – and her staff dreaded a bored prime minister because she would go round hunting for things for them to do – they would ring up Margaret King, her fashion adviser at Aquascutum, and ask for some clothes to be brought round for inspection.

Not that Margaret Thatcher confused style with substance. Rather, she appreciated that style *was* substance. How you looked announced who you were and how you meant to do business. It also announced to a male world that your femininity was under control. She became prime minister at a time when women and their embarrassing bodies were still regarded as incongruities in Parliament. In the mid-1980s less than 4 per cent of MPs were female. When a woman would start to speak, certain Tory MPs would hold their hands out before them, palms up, as if weighing melons.

The Thatcher dress sense was also a weapon in the ongoing battle to stand out from other women. She didn't like being upstaged. When Charles Powell became the private secretary for foreign affairs at Number 10, Robin Butler feared trouble. Carla Powell, Powell's Italian wife, was always spectacularly elegant. Butler's fears were misplaced. A connoisseur recognised superior flair when she saw it. The prime minister took Mrs Powell up to her bedroom, displayed her own wardrobe and asked for advice.

The task of wardrobe mistress fell on two women: her personal assistant Cynthia Crawford and her dresser Amanda Ponsonby. The prime minister was, in Crawford's words, 'very high maintenance'. When she asked in the morning, 'What am I wearing today?' she expected a full briefing, just as she would get from a civil servant on policy matters. The dress plan for the day was outlined, from morning to evening wear, and the outfits assembled with the appropriate accessories. Like an opera singer, the prime minister was a specialist in quick changes between scenes. Butler was constantly amazed. 'You never had to make any concessions to the fact that she was a woman and needed to get herself ready. She could be ready within ten seconds between one costume and the next.'

This agility required organisation. Crawford kept a card for each ensemble. All the essential accessories – shoes, blouse, jewellery, bag – were packed with it in a garment bag. She and the prime minister had code names for certain favourite outfits. The dark burgundy full-length evening suit worn on Terry Wogan's *Children in Need* show was 'Wogan'. The green coat made for a visit to Poland (on the basis of information that to the Poles green was the colour of hope) was 'Poland'. Evening bags in gold, silver and black, as well as four or five other colours, were pre-packed with lipstick, handkerchief, comb, powder compact and a pound coin for the attendant in the cloakroom. In a flash the prime minister could grab the right coloured bag and know that it held all that she needed.

The highlight of the sartorial year was the annual Lord Mayor's Banquet and the grand arrival at the Guildhall with police escort. This occasion called for a dramatic gown that could hold its own against the robes and other fancy dress of the City of London luminaries. She always looked wonderful in black, her advisers agreed – but how to vary it? One year Margaret King of Aquascutum had a brocade evening suit made for her in gold and black; trimmed with fur, the hem sported godets that flashed black velvet as she walked. Each year, King would go to Number 10 to help the prime minister dress in this ceremonial garb, after which she would take Polaroid photographs and then call in Denis to pour on praise.

He never failed. His admiration for his wife was boundless. One year he was watching the Trooping the Colour ceremony from the stand outside the back entrance to the Number 10 garden, with Cynthia Crawford at his side. 'Doesn't the prime minister look lovely today, Mr Thatcher?' she asked.

'Crawf,' he answered, 'she's looked lovely for the last thirty-five years.'

In the Thatcher psyche, no shift of gears was required between being the leader of the country and the fashion-plate clothes horse. The male and female sides of her personality coexisted comfortably. Head of the Foreign Office, Sir Antony Acland, calling on her one day at Number 10 to discuss Libya, found her preparing for a European summit meeting on oil price rises and trying on clothes at the same time. She would break off their discussion, disappear upstairs, and come down to ask, 'What do you think of this outfit?'

Acland learned that she also expected other people to look their parts. When he came to discuss senior appointments with her on one occasion, she frowned at the name of a particular candidate. 'He doesn't look right,' she declared. 'He looks like a second-hand car salesman. Doesn't look like an ambassador.'

Delicately, Acland ventured, 'We can't help what we look like, can we, Prime Minister?'

That was the wrong argument to use with Beatrice Roberts's daughter. Self-presentation, like self-reliance, was the duty of every Briton. If Margaret Thatcher could do it, so could the rest. Disregarding Acland's shrewd comment, she kept repeating that the candidate 'didn't look right and she couldn't see him as an ambassador'. In the end, he managed to persuade her 'that the man in question – a very intelligent, able person' – should go to a good post, 'and he did very well in it'.

There is no doubt that Margaret Thatcher manipulated her feminine attractiveness for political ends. Douglas Hurd, who served her as front-bench spokesman on Europe, Home Secretary and Foreign Secretary, reflects that, although she lived in a masculine world and was accustomed to dealing with men on masculine terms, 'she was quite capable every now and then of – almost deliberately – turning on a feminine charm.'

Some leaders got a larger dose than others. While she respected the President of the European Commission, Jacques Delors, in the presence of the French socialist President François Mitterrand, she blossomed. 'Of course, he likes women, you know,' she commented after their first meeting. In Hurd's view, 'Mitterrand understood her, was fascinated by her, and although she disapproved of him – not for his morals but for the things he stood for – she also quite admired him and enjoyed his company.' Clearly Mitterrand's deathless remark – 'Mrs Thatcher has the eyes of Caligula but the mouth of Marilyn Monroe' – was based on close observation.

She loved flattery. Men who approached her in this way were rewarded with seeing her face light up. Hurd winced to hear the Spanish foreign minister interrupt his discussion with the prime minister with 'Madam, may I just say something? People have told me of your bright intelligence, but no one had warned me of your beauty!' Such an unctuous compliment, Hurd suspected, would be a disaster. Not at all. 'She swept it aside, of course, but clearly it had been a hit.'

Her susceptibility to compliments left her open to manipulation. According to Mark Hollingsworth, biographer of her public relations guru Tim Bell, Bell always included a minor criticism in his compliments to avoid seeming obsequious. 'Margaret, I do love that outfit you're wearing,' he would say. 'It really does suit your figure. But can I just say one thing? Your jacket is a little long.' Or, he would kneel lovingly at her feet, tell her how wonderful she was and then show her some advertising that the chairman of the party had thrown out several times and had instructed him never to show to the prime minister. He knew she liked visitors and a glass of whisky at 'Slipper Time' – about 10.30 in the evening. She would tease him about his weight. 'I'd lose weight, Prime Minister, if you had an election.' She replied, 'I can't call an election just for you to slim.'

By the middle of the 1980s, Margaret Thatcher had come a long way. Britain had weathered the recession. She had taken on the unions and the Argentinians, and had won. Months before he was made Soviet leader, she had met Mikhail Gorbachev, entertained him at Chequers and pronounced him a man she could do business with. She had (reluctantly) signed a deal with China on Hong Kong.

Yet success carries the seeds of its own destruction. Having liberated herself from the restraining influence of the Tory elders in her cabinet, she became intolerant of dissent and increasingly overconfident in her own judgement.

In the country at large, she was less popular than her party, being seen as schoolmarmish, 'old bossy-boots' and uncaring. Many felt that she was more interested in making a few people richer than the whole country harmonious and happier. All during her tenure, Chris Patten at the Conservative Research Department had kept a cool distance from the leader. Looking back, his view is even cooler. The prejudice against her, in Patten's assessment for Brook Lapping, was not based so much on her class or her gender, but rather on her simplistic political convictions:

I don't think Margaret Thatcher had a coherent philosophy. She had some quite simple views about the world, which might have been exemplified by Rudyard Kipling and the gods of the copybook headings: balancing the books, family values, national pride, patriotism, rule of law, all policemen are honest – a fairly predictable set of views. To these she stuck on a series of other people's philosophies and opinions which agreed with hers. You would find her handbag stuffed with little bits of paper on which were written down some wise comment by Milton Friedman or William Simon or somebody, which happened to fit into her world view.

Her critics included men from the Church of England who felt she was dividing society, basing it on greed and selfishness. A group of them said so in December 1985 in a document called *Faith in the City*, calling for urgent help for the urban poor. The document was in response to a commission set up by the Archbishop of Canterbury, Dr Robert Runcie, which, after two years' work, placed the responsibility for the turmoil of Britain's inner cities on the Conservative focus on the individual, thus sacrificing the sense of social responsibility for the community.

What was needed was increased funds for job creation, child benefit and welfare payments.

What did this sound like to the ardent Thatcherite? 'Pure Marxist theology' in the words of a senior government figure, quoted in the *Sunday Times* under a headline 'Church report is Marxist'. On Channel 4 Television the Conservative Party chairman, Norman Tebbit, claimed that no one with right-wing views was represented in the report. When the Right Revd David Sheppard, former Bishop of Liverpool, countered that it was hard to find thoughtful Christians on the right who knew about urban issues, Tebbit walked out of the interview.

At the apparent height of her career, Margaret Thatcher faced the greatest challenge to her political survival from within her own cabinet. There she was surrounded by ministers of her own making – younger men who owed their political rise to her. Now they were starting to assert themselves and to put forward ideas contrary to her own beliefs.

Michael Heseltine had been in her cabinet since the start. In 1979, he was Environment Secretary, then from 1983 Secretary of Defence. At fifty-two, seriously rich, socially secure, with an even fuller head of hair than Cecil Parkinson – his nickname was 'Tarzan' – Heseltine was one of the first examples of a colleague restive under Thatcherite ideas that he did not like. As Environment Secretary with responsibility for inner cities, he had been active in the restoration of Liverpool after the Toxteth riots. He believed in public–private partnership between government and business rather than rolling back the welfare state, and he also felt that Thatcher's reproving attitude towards the turbulent underclass was too harsh.

Heseltine knew, if the prime minister did not, that she could not remain leader for ever. He wanted to succeed her, but to win the party leadership he knew that at some point he would have to make a stand against her. He would prefer to do that from outside the cabinet. At some point, therefore, he would almost certainly have to resign.

Over the Christmas period of 1985 a fierce conflict – between himself and the prime minister, and between his own Defence Ministry and the Department of Trade and Industry – hit the newspapers. The future of the West Country helicopter manufacturer, Westland, was at stake. Westland, Britain's only maker of helicopters, said it would go out of business without government assistance. It wanted also to sell a large minority shareholding to Sikorsky, the American aerospace maker of Black Hawk helicopters.

Heseltine wanted a European solution. He backed a rescue bid, involving a large minority stake in Westland by a European consortium, European governments having agreed that they would try to make their own helicopters and buy from each other. Margaret preferred an American bidder for the shareholding – Sikorsky. On her side was Leon Brittan, made her Secretary for Trade and Industry in September 1985. To them, the European consortium that Heseltine favoured was an artificial construct of European governmental defence procurement agencies, which would inevitably depend heavily on member governments giving it contracts.

Nigel Lawson, Chancellor of the Exchequer, sided with Brittan and the PM. He would make no public money available to bail out a company that now did not even need it. Let the shareholders decide what to do and let the government stay out of it. This seemed a perfectly satisfactory solution, particularly as Westland was now in the hands of an able new chairman, Sir John Cuckney. Above all, a cornerstone of the Thatcher economic policy – with which Lawson was in total agreement – was that the government should not put any more money into industries that could not keep themselves alive by their own sales.

At a Christmas party Heseltine walked up to the Archbishop of Canterbury and said: 'Your bishops have got it all wrong. Things are much worse than they say.' Over the New Year break the press carried a letter he had received from Lloyds Bank, warning of the dire consequences of accepting the Sikorsky bid. Revenge, if that is what it was, was not long in coming. In a matter of days there was a leak to the press of a letter to Heseltine from Sir Patrick Mayhew, the Solicitor-General, pointing out factual inaccuracies in the letter from Lloyds.

The Westland crisis reached its climax at a tense cabinet meeting on 9 January 1986. The prime minister announced that, from that moment on, all statements on Westland must be cleared with the cabinet office – in other words, with herself. Heseltine would accept no such gagging order. She replied (in Nigel Lawson's recollection), 'No, that is what has got to be.'

That was the signal Heseltine had been waiting for. He stacked his papers together, like a television newsreader at the end of the bulletin. 'In that case, Prime Minister,' he said, 'I can no longer stay in this cabinet.' It was a dramatic moment: the first cabinet minister for a century to resign during a cabinet meeting. Inside the room, after a short recess, the prime minister coolly resumed the agenda and announced at the end of the meeting that the new Defence Secretary would be George Younger. But just beyond the doorstep of Number 10, Heseltine announced his resignation to waiting journalists and promised a full statement later in the day. That the statement then took the form of a detailed twenty-two-minute presentation suggests that his resignation had been premeditated.

The government was angry. But how had the Mayhew letter, a private communication between a senior law officer and a cabinet minister, reached the press? Someone must have authorised the leak. The Industry Secretary Leon Brittan, whose anti-Heseltine stance was supported by the leaked letter? The press secretary of the Trade and Industry Department, Colette Bowe? Had it been done with the subtle encouragement of the press chief at Number 10, Bernard Ingham? If so, who gave him permission? Perhaps, the rumours flew, the order came from the prime minister herself in order to discredit her rebellious minister. The scandal made such big news that Ronald Reagan called

his friend Margaret from Washington to say that he was furious
that anyone had the gall to question her integrity.[3]

Brittan had to defend himself and his Trade and Industry
Department in the House of Commons. In answer to a cruel
question thrown at him by Heseltine, he used an opaque legalis-
tic form of wording that only made matters worse. Brittan had
to come back and apologise for having appeared to mislead the
House. All the while, the prime minister maintained that she
knew nothing of the origin of the leaks. If so, then she was blind
to what was being done behind her back – hardly flattering to
the supreme controller of Britain's government.

On 24 January 1986, Brittan resigned. To have lost two ministers within a fortnight began to look like carelessness. The Opposition smelled blood and called an emergency Commons debate
for Monday, 27 January. All through the weekend, the Thatcher
speech-writers worked on the reply that she would give in her
defence once Kinnock, the Labour leader, had led off with the
case against her. On their way to the Commons, the prime
minister said to the cabinet secretary, Sir Robert Armstrong,
'You do realise, don't you, that by six o'clock I may no longer
be prime minister?'

As the debate began, Alan Clark, MP for Plymouth Sutton
and a brilliant diarist, was watching eagerly: 'Every seat in the
House had been booked with a prayer card, and they were all
up the gangways. For a few seconds Kinnock had her cornered,
and you could see fear in those blue eyes.'[4]

Within a few minutes, however, she was safe.

Neil Kinnock, who had defeated Roy Hattersley as the replacement for Michael Foot as Labour Party leader after the 1983
general election, was welcomed by the party as young, likeable
and prepared to move against the Scargill hard left. The son
of a Welsh miner, his Labour credentials were impeccable. He
personified his party's hope for the future.

Unfortunately, he was not a great House of Commons

man. A product of the University of Wales rather than Oxford or Cambridge, he had no flair for the cut-and-slash of Commons debate. As he faced Mrs Thatcher twice a week, he was particularly inhibited in his attack because she was a woman and considerably older than himself. Looking down from the press gallery, Matthew Parris, parliamentary sketch-writer for *The Times*, saw Thatcher versus Kinnock as a gift for the columnists:

They were both in their different ways equally unappealing. We called him Kinnochio and the Welsh Windbag; he went on and on and wouldn't come to the point. What is less well remembered is that she wasn't a great speaker. She didn't have a great line in putdowns. She just shouted. Relentless like an electric drill at the despatch box. They looked like a man and wife railing against each other. Each knowing the other pretty well. Each sick to the teeth of the other, and neither with anything new to say any longer.

There are many accounts of how Kinnock muffed the Westland debate. To Parris, 'he moved in for the kill and – it was his motion of censure – he waffled it away. It was like seeing someone advance to the net and then drift off sideways.' To Alan Clark, Kinnock began well: 'But then he had an attack of wind, gave her time to recover.'[5] In Kinnock's own analysis, he made 'a huge error'. Against his usual practice, he wrote out his speech beforehand; then, on the Monday morning, he added a page and a half of preamble. To Thatcher's speech-writer Ronnie Millar, the long build-up sounded as if Kinnock were reciting the same section twice.

When it became clear that Kinnock had swiftly blown away his chance to bring down the government that very day, the Conservative backbenchers released a fusillade of noise. The press accounts next day were savage; they said that the prime minister had performed pretty poorly too.

Kinnock did turn in a dreadful performance, yet his target was hazy. The British public cared little about the fate of a small helicopter firm in Bristol (whose shareholders eventually accepted the Sikorsky bid). As for the who-authorised-what scandal, it was so labyrinthine in detail as to make accusations of guilt hard to stick.

Why Westland mattered was because of what it revealed: a prime minister out of control of her cabinet, possibly plotting with some of her ministers against others. In his autobiography, John Cole, then political editor for the BBC, neatly sums up the Westland 'crisis': 'Michael Heseltine's resignation was only a symptom of the grumbling weakness of an otherwise impregnable Prime Minister: she was rubbing more and more people up the wrong way.'[6]

Sir Antony Acland says that he sometimes wondered whether she realised the impression she was making on people.

She certainly was confrontational in manner. She'd come into a meeting, almost before she had sat down she'd start banging her fists, saying, 'I don't agree with this recommendation. This is what we ought to do.'

She needed to be challenged clearly and quickly. You had to be quite tough, quite almost rude. She didn't mind that. She spoke toughly to you, interrupted you when you were halfway through your sentence and she didn't mind being answered back. She wanted to challenge her prejudices, her instincts against arguments.

Douglas Hurd saw through her techniques. 'If you were having an argument with Margaret Thatcher and she wasn't actually winning it, she would go off into some completely separate piece of detail. If she could catch you out on that, she would use that fact to turn the tables on the argument she was having.'

He saw how easily she was angered, and how she sought culprits. If something was wrong, somebody must be at fault. In 1975, as a relatively new Member of Parliament, Hurd was asked to accompany her on her trip to China because twenty years earlier he had lived there as a British diplomat. 'It was her way to hold me personally responsible for everything she disliked [saying] "Douglas, did you see that!" – as if it had been in my power to prevent all this happening.'

Her Chancellor, Nigel Lawson, found her more and more authoritarian. From March 1987 the two of them clashed on monetary policy. He wanted sterling to shadow the deutsch-mark, and Britain to join the exchange rate mechanism – the band of European currencies that rose and fell together. She did not, out of her loyalty to the pure Britishness of the pound and her instinctive fear of anything that threatened to dilute British sovereignty.

A serious casualty of the Westland affair was the career of Leon Brittan. Still hurt from being demoted from Home Secretary to Industry Secretary in the 1985 reshuffle, Brittan believed that he had been authorised by Number 10 to permit the leak of the Mayhew letter to the press. Had he chosen at the time, he could have defended himself much more strongly, even going on the attack as Heseltine did and placing the blame for the leak on Number 10 – perhaps on the prime minister herself. Honourably, he did not but remained silent.

There was an unpleasant whiff of anti-Semitism in the parlia-mentary reaction to Brittan's role in the Westland affair. In the 1980s (and beyond) the casual between-the-wars anti-Semitism in English life persisted. Alan Clark's diary, for example, describes the colour of someone's gold Rolls-Royce as 'Jewish Racing Yellow, as apparently the colour is termed in the Mess at Knightsbridge'.[7]

Brittan's performance in defending himself was considered over-clever, sly and devious; he was described as acting as if 'cornered like a rat'. After leaving Parliament in 1988, Brittan never again found high political office outside of Brussels, where he served successfully as senior European Commissioner for many years.

No one ever accused Margaret Thatcher of anti-Semitism –

quite the reverse. When Keith Joseph left the cabinet, Lord (David) Young and Malcolm Rifkind entered. The *Spectator*, ever watchful of Jews in English life, carried a cover story 'Thatcher Chooses the Jews'.[8] Her apparent predilection for Jewish associates was explained by a non-Jewish colleague to the *Observer* columnist Alan Watkins: 'No mystery at all. They work jolly hard. There's no nonsense about them. Most of them have made their own way. Broadly they share her approach to life. Above all, they run her constituency for her in Finchley.'[9] Quoting this in his 1989 'psycho-biography' of the prime minister, the Jewish Labour politician Leo Abse was scathing about the Finchley Jews who kowtowed to their eminent MP.

'She finds in them', Abse says, 'the same sickly pious celebration of the work ethic which was at the very centre of the smug non-conformity characterising yesterday's East Anglian Methodism.' To him, 'Thatcher and her Jews, in their odious stresses on individualism, are in fact casting aside the most valuable elements of their Judaeo-Christian heritage, the "group ethic"'. Jewish morality, Abse maintains, 'lays all its stress on the well-being of the group, to which individual self-aggrandisement and individual salvation must be subordinated'.

Margaret Thatcher did like Jews, but preferred them tall, handsome and entrepreneurial – like David Wolfson and David Young, a property millionaire whom she made a lord and Employment Secretary in 1985 and whose brother Stuart Young she made chairman of the BBC.

Brittan, square, pudgy and intellectual, was not of this type. She contented herself in her memoirs with calling him 'this civilized but not very streetwise politician'.[10] About the 1985 reshuffle, which had been so painful for Brittan, she says, 'I replaced Leon at the Home Office with Douglas Hurd, who looked more the part.'[11]

Scarcely noticed in the Westland furore was the publication on 28 January 1986 of a green paper outlining a new plan for financing local government. Drawn up by Kenneth Baker, Environment Secretary, the 'community charge' would replace the rates levied by local government (based on property values) with a resident's tax. This alteration would cure what Margaret Thatcher saw as a long-standing injustice. Under the rating system, people who owned no property had the benefit of schools, rubbish collection, social and other local services – without contributing to their cost, while the bill was paid by those living in their own homes (widows were a favourite example), even though their households tended to be smaller and they made little claim on the community. The revised form of finance would also achieve another Thatcher objective: curbing what she saw as the overspending of local councils.

The green paper caused little stir although, within the cabinet, Hurd believed it would be difficult to sell and Lawson was totally against it from the start. As local government finance was a matter for the Environment Secretary rather than the Chancellor of the Exchequer, however, Lawson's veto counted for nothing. There was no hint at that time that the poll tax, as the community charge came to be called, would be the prime minister's undoing.

Six months after Westland, things were going wrong. It was the low point of the second Thatcher government. Two attempts at denationalising state industry – British Leyland and the water supply – had failed. So had a proposal to switch university students from grants to loans. Unemployment stubbornly remained above 3 million. Labour took the lead in the opinion polls, Kinnock's performance was improving and he was purging the party of the hard left. A spectacular upset in Brecon and Radnor in July 1985 saw the Alliance candidate snatch what had been a safe Tory seat. Analysis showed that the 'TBW' ('That Bloody Woman') factor had played a part in the ousting of the Conservative incumbent.

Margaret Thatcher seemed arrogant in her power and

indifferent to public opinion. There was a huge outcry when, on 15 April 1986, she let her old friend Reagan use British airbases for American planes to bomb Libya. Anti-Americanism flared, already fuelled by the Westland deal and the prospect that Land-Rover, an icon of the British motor industry, might be sold to American owners. Two out of three people polled thought that the prime minister had been wrong. Senior Conservative journalists raised the possibility that the Libyan raid could cost her the next election. Not surprisingly, Norman Tebbit prepared a dossier of evidence against the BBC, accusing its news of unbalanced coverage of the bombing of Tripoli.

But the signals were misleading. The economy was growing slowly and steadily, average weekly earnings were up and inflation stood at or below 5 per cent. In the autumn of 1986 the 'Big Bang', created by relaxing regulations, had given a big boost to the City of London. Personal taxation was edging down towards the Conservatives' goal of a 25 per cent standard rate. Despite all previous preaching about reducing government spending, Lawson found 'new money' for expansion in health, housing and education. Little was heard of old monetarism, Chicago economics and the wise men, Milton Friedman and Friedrich von Hayek. The sale of council houses had been immensely popular and the national percentage of homeowners soared. As people felt more prosperous, unemployment lost its 1930s image as the measure of misery. Above all, those who believed that there was an anti-Thatcher majority in the country forgot the vital fact that the Conservatives faced a divided Opposition, with Labour and the Alliance inevitably weakened by fighting each other.

The more powerful and domineering she grew, the more did Margaret Thatcher's reputation grow – within a small circle – for little acts of kindness, as if to demonstrate that within the Iron Lady there still beat a warm heart. She knew that Sir Antony Acland's wife was dying of cancer. As Acland arrived for an official lunch at Chequers one Sunday, she came hurrying across the room to ask, 'What's the news of Ann?' When Acland said, 'Not very good,' she insisted that he leave early. Arriving at the hospital to see his wife, he found that a large bunch of roses from the prime minister had preceded him, with a card in her own handwriting: 'I hope that these roses will bring the scent of an English garden into your hospital room. We're thinking of you. Margaret Thatcher.' Acland suspected that she had picked the flowers herself.

Similarly, when her long-time chauffeur George Newell died suddenly from a heart attack, the prime minister dispatched the second driver from Number 10 to assist Newell's widow May. She herself made do with a temporary driver from the civil service pool, and made a point of attending the funeral in south London. After that, according to Penny Junor's biography, 'Six months later, quite out of the blue, she asked one of the girls in the office to ring May to see how she was; and again at Christmas time, she would make discreet enquiries to make sure May was not alone.'[12]

At Christmas the prime minister gave gifts to each member of her personal staff, as well as the staffs of Number 10 and Chequers. Her assistant Cynthia Crawford did the shopping and wrapping. Late one night, tired and facing a pile of parcels, Crawford decided to postpone the chore of putting ribbons on them until morning. When she arrived for work next day she found that every single gift had been tied with ribbon and a bow, and each carried a tag written in the prime minister's hand.

Thatcher acts of obsessive housekeeping became almost as legendary as her thoughtfulness. In March 1987, before she arrived to open a Sainsbury's supermarket in north London, her personal secretary warned all in the reception party that on no account must the prime minister be allowed to shop. The warning was in vain. Passing the meat counter with a flotilla of executives and party workers, the PM cried, 'I need meat for the weekend!' She proceeded to buy three pounds of mince from which, she declared, she would make a shepherd's pie for Denis. However, unlike a housewife and more like royalty, she did not carry money. Embarrassed, she insisted that Sainsbury's, despite all protestations, must send her a bill. There was no way that she would accept the packet as a gift.[13]

Even at Chequers, the prime minister's country retreat, staffed and run by the Royal Air Force, she insisted on organising every tiny detail. If she felt that the large, high-ceilinged drawing room was cold, she would kneel down and build up the fire herself, inviting guests, such as Colinne Martyn from Finchley, to watch and learn: 'This is the way to put logs on the fire.'

She was generous in sharing Chequers with people who had helped her. She invited her party workers from Finchley for a meal and gave them a tour of the house. Among them was Dennis Signy, editor of the *Finchley Times*, who recalls finding the prime minister's husband 'plonked in front of the fireplace, standing, legs apart, very erect, with a drink in his hand. So we went up and engaged in small talk. We asked after Mark, and he said, "Oh, he comes here once a week. Brings his bloody washing with him. She does it for him, you know."'

Denis Thatcher loved Chequers. 'Chequers is why you get the job,' he explained to his daughter, who was writing his biography. 'We depomposized it [*sic*]. I used to say to people coming to lunch on Sunday that if they were early they shouldn't sit in that lay-by in the lane but come in because my woman didn't like me to start drinking before the guests arrived.'[14]

'My woman': not words likely to come out of the mouth of Prince Philip, Duke of Edinburgh, who was, in many ways, Denis's model for the role of consort. Addressing his wife directly, Denis would call her 'Beloved' or 'dear'. (She called him 'DT' or 'dear'.)

Denis said in praise of Chequers that it was the only place where the *Radio Times* was open to the programmes for the day when you arrived. (The Thatchers always watched *Miss Marple*.) The Chequers staff loved the couple, as did the staff at Number 10. The caretaker, Vera Thomas, instructed the staff: 'If the Prime Minister or Mr Thatcher want moose on toast at midnight, then they get it.'[15]

So much for their private life. The public image was different. She had won through on the Westland crisis but it did not make her lovable. Or trustful. The effect of Westland was that she began to distrust her immediate colleagues and rely more on her loyal courtiers – Powell and Ingham.

Nigel Lawson said: 'Westland had a very bad effect on Margaret Thatcher because it made her feel that she couldn't trust her colleagues. Her attitude towards her colleagues changed perceptibly from that time. Any one of them could plunge the dagger.'

She began to be caricatured on the satirical television show, *Spitting Image*, as a tyrant in pinstripes, barking orders at all her menials. In a famous sketch, she is seated at a table surrounded by her ministers when a waiter asks, 'Would you like to order, sir?' She says, 'I'll have a steak, please – raw.'

'And what about the vegetables?'

'They'll have the same,' she says.[16]

Her party's chairman since 1985, Norman Tebbit, saw that her nannyish image was a liability. At one stage the Conservatives were in third position behind the Liberal Democrats. At that time there was tension between him and the prime minister – a ludicrous situation because they were politically more in sympathy with each other than with the rest of the cabinet. It had entered the prime minister's mind that Tebbit was using Central Office as a power base and there is little doubt that, like Heseltine, he had hopes of succeeding her.

In any event, Tebbit was the last person from whom she wanted to hear the unpalatable truth about her personal unpopularity. In April 1986 he was present at a tense session at Chequers when there was a presentation of Saatchi and Saatchi's findings that 'That Bloody Woman' and 'old bossy-boots' was perceived as part of the problem. Her unsurprising reaction: 'I am what I am and I am not going to change to suit your research.'

But she did. Over the next few months preceding the 1987 general election, she put herself through a surprisingly candid examination of her own public image. Since girlhood, she had been adept at reinventing herself again and again.

No one, Tim Bell admits, looking back, liked her voice. But she had done a lot of work on it and it had responded to treatment. Thanks to her humming exercises, it was lower – a throaty authoritative contralto. According to Hugo Young's biography, *One of Us*, a political scientist who had analysed recordings of Thatcher speeches calculated that by her second term she had lowered her pitch by 46 hertz: half the average difference in pitch between male and female.

And she accepted, with some nudging from her fashion advisers, that her clothes needed more attention. From her first years in office, she had worn neckline bows, mainly out of loyalty to a particular dressmaker who made her dresses and blouses when she was first in office. Her assistant Cynthia Crawford recalls: 'I never mentioned the bows. She looked pretty, but it seemed every time she did anything she had a bow. It was time for a change because power-dressing had just come in; she was power.'

Out went the fussy bows and pastels. In came stronger colours, squarer-cut suits, bolder checks and darker blues. Her jackets were edged in contrasting piping to ensure that they gave a crisp, sharp image to photographers.

Margaret King of Aquascutum, who had helped before, now took a more active role (and thoroughly enjoyed it):

She was a delight to dress. She loved trying on clothes and would twirl around like a little girl. She loved materials and buttons, and told me about her mother Beatrice who was a dressmaker. She was very proud of the fact that her mother knew how to make clothes.

23. The statutory woman with the statutory hat: Prime Minister Edward Heath in 1970 regards his Secretary of State for Education and Science.

24. Followed by her campaign manager Airey Neave, Margaret Thatcher in 1975 faces the first ballot for the Conservative Party leadership.

25. Denis Thatcher, 4 May 1979, waits patiently for the new Prime Minister to finish her 'St. Francis of Assisi' remarks so that they can take possession of their new home.

26. Gordon Reece, public relations guru, remade Margaret Thatcher for television, got her to give up the garden-fête hats and helped to lower her voice.

27. Anything for a photo-opportunity: Thatcher's public relations advisers thought that holding a calf would communicate mother love and a liking for animals.

28. The body language says it all. Father and son at press conference after Mark's disappearance in the Sahara, January 1982.

29. Being called a 'wet' was no joke for James Prior, Employment Secretary 1979–1981

30. Two of a kind: Margaret Thatcher's admiration was boundless for Sir Keith Joseph, her closest political friend and mentor.

31. 'Everyone needs a Willie': said Mrs Thatcher, losing hers on William Whitelaw's retirement in early 1989.

32. Charles Powell, Number 10's adviser on foreign affairs, was one of the most influential in the prime minister's inner circle.

33. 'The best press secretary in the world' Margaret Thatcher had complete trust in Bernard Ingham to speak for her.

34. Favourite recreation, home decoration: the Thatchers painting their flat at Scotney Castle, Kent in 1975.

35. 'Chequers is why you get the job', said Denis. The Thatchers loved the Prime Minister's weekend retreat in Buckinghamshire.

36. Both Thatchers like a drink, but sometimes . . .

37. 'The Englishwoman's Wardrobe': Margaret Thatcher, with her fashion adviser Margaret King of Aquascutum, shows off her clothes on BBC television, 20 November 1986.

38. Her shoes off, a sign of relaxation, the Prime Minister nonetheless keeps her pearls on while doing her boxes at home at Downing Street.

39. The European Summit in Hanover, West Germany, 1988, included Jacques Delors, Poul Schlueter, Margaret Thatcher, Helmut Kohl and François Mitterand. Her antipathy to West German Chancellor Kohl did not extend to the French President Mitterand of whom she observed, 'He likes women'.

40. Flanked by Geoffrey Howe, *left*, and Nigel Lawson, the two cabinet ministers who would eventually topple her, Margaret Thatcher poses with her Cabinet on 12 October 1989. Her unsuspected successor, John Major, stands directly behind Howe.

41. Very special relationship: the prime minister loved visiting her friend President Ronald Reagan but would not dress down – even for Camp David.

42. Shall we end the Cold War? Soviet President Mikhail Gorbachev seems delighted to welcome his good friend on her visit to Moscow in March 1987.

43. Public tears, for the first time since her son was lost in the desert, as Margaret Thatcher, with Denis, is driven away from Number 10 for the last time as prime minister.

44. Half a century on, Denis Thatcher still admires 'my woman'.

That's one thing people have never appreciated about Lady Thatcher as she now is. She never forgot where she came from. She was proud of her mother and of her father and she likened herself to working people.

But the clothes had to be British. This feat of patriotism was accomplished by sketching a design she liked if it were foreign and having a Mr Hong at Liberty's make a copy. (Asked what she thought of the flamboyantly sexy designs of the designer Vivienne Westwood, the prime minister replied enthusiastically, 'Isn't it nice that she's British?')

In the end, Thatcher got it right. She mastered power dressing before the phrase became common, finding the female equivalent of the male business suit without ever looking mannish. Suddenly photographs taken in her early career looked dated, fussy, those of a timid little Tory lady from the shires, in contrast to the assertive world leader.

Throwing caution to the winds, the prime minister lent herself to a BBC programme on 20 November 1986, *The English-woman's Wardrobe*, in which she showed off her clothes neatly arranged on coat racks. For the camera she held up various outfits like a gardener showing off his best plants. Of a neat suit, she said, 'This one came through the Falklands war,' as if it were a tattered battledress. She then confided in the nation that she bought her underwear at Marks and Spencer: 'Doesn't everyone?'

Perhaps she was even developing a sense of fun. At Chequers at Christmas in 1986 she wore the multicoloured sunshade with flashing lights that Carol had brought back from an assignment in Disneyland.

She started the election year of 1987 with the satisfaction of seeing the new chairman of the 'nest of vipers' (the BBC) fire his director-general. Marmaduke Hussey, a solid Tory and former *Times* executive, had replaced chairman Stuart Young who had died suddenly the previous August. On an historic morning, 29 January 1987, Hussey called the director-general, Alasdair Milne, into a private room just before a BBC governors' meeting and demanded his resignation on the spot. This brutal and unprecedented dismissal of a lifelong BBC man, responsible for such past successes as the *Tonight* programme, marked the end of the old Reithian BBC. The sacking expressed the Tories' despair, after a series of crises which Milne managed badly, that no one was really in charge at the BBC. Milne's successor, Michael Checkland, chosen by the board of governors, was eminently satisfying to the prime minister. Checkland, an accountant who had spent twenty years with the BBC, soon began talking of the organisation in the kind of language that Thatcher could understand: it was, he said, 'a billion-pound-a-year corporation'.

An election was in the air, four years having passed since she defeated the hapless Michael Foot in June 1983. Nigel Lawson's Budgets had been sounding the signal: he cut a penny off income tax in 1986 and another tuppence in 1987.

The ideal pre-election warm-up was in her diary: a five-day visit to the Soviet Union in late March. What to wear? Making a special effort to look well when meeting her friend Gorbachev on his home territory, she took to heart Crawford's information that Mrs Gorbachev 'wore a lot of Yves St Laurent'. She would not be outdone.

There was another spur to change: a new daughter-in-law. On St Valentine's Day, 1987, at the Savoy Chapel in London, after a three-month engagement, Mark Thatcher married Diane Burgdorf of Dallas, Texas, where he had moved in 1984, in order, says Mark Hollingsworth, co-author of *Thatcher's Gold*, to escape the British press after the scandal over a Cementation contract in Oman. Awkward questions were asked about how a young man with modest O levels and a failed accountancy career was able to use the Number 10 address, his mother's contacts and her signed photographs to pursue international oil deals in the Gulf states, thus turning himself into a multimillionaire. The new Mrs Thatcher was Texan, blonde, well-to-do, and a good shopper. In London she bought a coat at Aquascutum, which her mother-in-law loved so much that she immediately wanted one like it. Word was sent to the chairman of Aquascutum to say that the prime minister needed a coat for her visit to Russia.

Margaret King went round to Downing Street with an armful of clothes, including a coat brought back from Paris, with fine detailing in the shoulders. It was decided that a version in black would be ideal. King pulled out all the stops. She had the coat made, with slimline stitching, and to it she attached a bijou brooch from Italy and antique glittery buttons to give sparkle, topping it all with a huge black fox-fur hat. She told the prime minister: 'This is the coat you will arrive in'.

King told Brook Lapping: 'She put these things on – she couldn't believe the hat and the coat – and she stood in front of the mirror and you could see absolute joy.' Then King asked permission to make a further comment. From watching the prime minister on television, she had observed a tendency to walk fast, looking down. Instead, King suggested, the prime minister should pull her stomach into her ribcage and stand up straight. When emerging from an aeroplane, she should first stand on the platform and look around; then, holding the rail, descend the stairs while slowly glancing at the crowd. 'Don't look at your feet,' King instructed. 'This is how you've got to walk in this coat; otherwise, the hat will drown you.'

This coaching paid off. When Margaret Thatcher stepped off the plane in the Moscow darkness, with the lights flashing on the black fox corona on her blonde hair, she became a superstar. The primitive associations of fur with the Russian bear and Cossacks worked their magic. (To be fair, the art of wearing the right hat for a dramatic entrance on to the Moscow scene had been demonstrated by Harold Macmillan with a white astrakhan cap in February 1959.)

The clothes made news. To Ronnie Millar, 'The Russian people loved the clothes that weren't available to them and loved her for wearing them.' Crawford rejoiced: 'She came on like a modern tsarina: the first popular breakthrough to the East by a Western leader and it was the British prime minister who made it.'

Perhaps Aquascutum deserves some credit for bringing down the Iron Curtain. In any event, the black hat, plus a camel-hair version together with another fur hat, were a great success – as was the prime minister's combative performance on Soviet television, cowing into silence three well-known male presenters.

It was an element in her dressing-up that she and the Soviet leader had developed an unexpected rapport on his visit to England in 1984. Then a senior member of the Politburo, Gorbachev had spoken informally, without notes, not in the usual stilted Soviet-speak, and he was sharp, likeable and direct. By her visit in 1987, he had become her Russian Reagan: they sparked off each other and exchanged knowing smiles, even when she was lecturing him about the evils of communism.

While in the Soviet Union, she also played her scientist role by visiting the Soviet Academy of Sciences' Institute of Crystallography. The director Boris Vainshtein reported back to Dr Dorothy Hodgkin at Oxford: 'Everybody here was fascinated by this clever and charming lady, who, despite her numerous political duties, is still very keen on science.'[17]

Margaret Thatcher had always admired her old tutor, now a Nobel laureate, whose portrait hung above her study desk at Number 10, even though Hodgkin was an ardent campaigner for nuclear disarmament. Uncharacteristically, the prime minister accepted that they were at opposite political poles and that Hodgkin's leftism sprang from idealism: 'She couldn't dissuade me and I couldn't dissuade her,' she told Hodgkin's biographer, Georgina Ferry.[18]

Her old tutor was one of the few women she did look up to. Hodgkin, Chancellor of Bristol University since 1970, had protested in a letter to her old student, now the prime minister, about harsh cuts in education, which reduced Bristol's budget by 11 per cent. Thatcher replied: 'Please do get in touch if you want to have a talk about the issue you are raising with Keith Joseph [Secretary for Education] or indeed any other issue. I do so much value your advice and guidance.'[19] But she did not restore the funds. These savage cuts to higher education, with the sorry effect they had in hastening the emigration of trained scientists, was one of the reasons why Oxford University denied Margaret Thatcher an honorary degree in 1985 – the first prime minister to be so humiliated. Oxford's refusal deeply pained her, reflecting its disdain for her modest degree and her failure to finance universities adequately.

On a high after the Moscow visit, and after successes in the early local government elections, the prime minister bustled into the cabinet room, wearing a light grey suit and a blouse tied in a bow at the neck over a double strand of pearls, where she called her third general election.

Margaret Thatcher believed that third-term Tory governments, says John Cole, tended to run out of steam. It was a radical manifesto: the opting out of schools; an attempt to break down local councils' grip on rented housing; changes in the health service; and her long-promised vow to abolish the rates in favour of the community charge.

In the campaign of late May and early June, Labour focused on the personality of their leader. A Labour Party political broadcast, made by Hugh Hudson, director of the film *Chariots of Fire*, emphasised the youth of the leader and his love for his wife as they walked hand in hand through Welsh scenery. It ended with the plea, 'Vote Kinnock'. In contrast, the Conservative strategy organised by Tebbit treated the prime minister almost as an embarrassment. She was kept in the background.

A week before election day, Labour was only four percentage points behind in the polls. Carol, returning from a journalistic assignment in Jordan, was shocked to see the superiority of the Labour campaign. She warned her mother: 'You had better get your act together or start packing.' Panicked, the prime minister enlisted her own, rival team of Tim Bell and Young and Rubicam to handle campaigning during the final week.

Bell was all too willing. As he told Brook Lapping, 'She felt the team wasn't on her side. They were in favour of a Conservative victory but they weren't in favour of . . . They didn't see her as the important weapon. Those of us who were very close to her couldn't understand why they weren't using this most powerful weapon they had got and we forced her back into the campaign.'

In any case, she had the tabloid press on her side. She had knighted the editors of the *Sun*, the *Sunday Express* and the *Daily Mail*, papers long loyal to her. She also knighted the two principal political inquisitors of the BBC and ITN – Robin Day and Alistair Burnet – although some of their journalistic colleagues worried that these titles might compromise their independence.

She went on the attack, producing a barrage of radio and television interviews and speeches, broken only by a trip to Venice for the G7 summit, which did no harm in terms of press coverage. In her public utterances, she was defiant. Her policies did not encourage greed, but success. Only if wealth were created could everyone enjoy a better life. By election eve, her campaign was in full presidential mode. The climax was a final rally at Wembley stadium, with streamers, balloons, laser beams. Ronnie Millar was pleased with the preparations: 'The dress was fine, the hair was fine.'[20] He took a risk in having her 'half speak, half sing' a mocking reference to the Alliance's uneasy leadership by the 'two Davids', David Owen of the SDP and David Steel of the Liberals. 'David, David, what are we going to do? I'm half crazy trying to be like you . . .' She got away with it.

The result of the election on 11 June was a romp home for the Conservatives, with an overall majority of 102. The party took 376 seats, Labour 229, the Alliance 22 and other parties 24. For the victory crowd of party supporters chanting, 'Five more years,' she pulled out all the stops with a Churchillian reference to 'these islands':

It is wonderful to be entrusted with the government of this country – this great country – once again. And I want to say this to you: the greater the trust, the greater the duty upon us to be worthy of that trust. We will indeed endeavour to serve the people of these islands in the future as we have in the past.

After the election, she was asked if she were going to relax. She was – by painting and papering Carol's flat. She also had another home to redecorate. The Thatchers had sold Flood Street and had bought a house in Dulwich, London SE21, on an estate developed by Barratt Homes. The neo-Georgian house cost £400,000 and was supposedly a home for their retirement as well as an investment.

There she was, at sixty-one, Britain's first female prime minister, having won an historic third term of government. She was the longest-serving prime minister of her century. But old colleagues, notably Geoffrey Howe and Nigel Lawson, were becoming bitter or frustrated. How long before she would make room for one of them and shuffle off to Dulwich? With her tenth anniversary at Number 10 approaching, would anyone dare a discreet nod towards the door?

I I
The Road to Dulwich
(May 1987–November 1990)

The Americans very sensibly don't allow political leaders to go on for more than two terms in the White House. After eight years or so at the top, you start to come to the end of your shelf life. You've been surrounded on the whole by people who for years tell you what you want to hear and are reluctant to tell you what you don't want to hear. You begin to believe that you don't need bridges to cross rivers. That's inevitably what started to happen with Margaret.

Chris Patten, 2002

Douglas Hurd, Home Secretary from 1985 until made Foreign Secretary in late 1989, offered much the same observation as did Patten, when Environment Secretary in the final Thatcher cabinet. Hurd saw the prime minister misled by 'the ovations, the clapping, the courtiers who told her what she wanted to hear' so that she deceived herself as to her power and popularity. The now-iconic handbag was, in Hurd's view, a real weapon, whose actual form was the unguarded off-the-cuff remark, revealing 'a break between the brain and the tongue'. The prime minister's penchant for the sudden candid utterance, more extreme than – and often undercutting – what had been officially announced, delighted the press. To Hurd: 'This was the real Margaret Thatcher, this was the handbag and she rather enjoyed the effect she made.'

The Irish knew this form of assault well. In May 1984, after extensive amicable discussion with Ireland's Taoiseach, Garret FitzGerald, about a promising report by a think-tank called the New Ireland Forum, she sabotaged their efforts at a press conference. Brusquely listing three models for the future of Northern Ireland that the New Ireland Forum had proposed – unification, confederation or joint authority – she swatted each down with a curt 'That's out', 'That's out', 'That's out'. Her harsh words infuriated the mild-mannered FitzGerald for dismissing the political risks he had taken to endorse this tentative step towards Anglo-Irish cooperation in solving the intractable conflict.

She professed surprise at the hostile reaction she received. 'What did I *say*?' she implored FitzGerald next time they met.[1] She had meant, she thought, to say that their deliberations had progressed fruitfully beyond the three models with which they had begun. That she had been by no means implacably hostile to partnership was shown when, on 15 November 1985, both countries signed the Anglo-Irish Agreement, guaranteeing that there would be no change in the status of Northern Ireland except by agreement of the majority of the population living there.

Another memorable handbagging followed the October 1985 Commonwealth Conference in the Bahamas. After what Sir Geoffrey Howe, then Foreign Secretary, describes as 'a tremendously long discussion', Britain reluctantly agreed to go along with its Commonwealth partners' wish to increase sanctions against South Africa. At the press conference afterwards, however, the prime minister boasted how little Britain had actually yielded, pinching her fingers together to show how infinitesimal the concession had been. Howe shuddered. 'It was an undiplomatic thing to say. If you've won a victory, you don't proclaim it to the disadvantage of the people you've been negotiating with.'

Even in one-to-one encounters, she had become a terrifying female – a gorgon whose look could turn a man to stone. Max Hastings, editor of the *Daily Telegraph*, was invited to Sunday lunch at Chequers, but his chauffeur lost his way in the narrow lanes of Buckinghamshire. Knowing well the Thatcher fanatical insistence on punctuality, he trembled to think of the 'mad, frightening dominatrix of a premier, convinced of her own invincibility', waiting at his destination. When the car finally arrived an hour late, there indeed was the prime minister impatiently looking for him from the front steps.[2]

Irritation was not always her response to lateness. When Peregrine Worsthorne, editor of the *Sunday Telegraph*, and his wife Claudie were driving themselves to lunch at Chequers and their car broke down, the prime minister was most sympathetic and, when they did arrive, was solicitous to see that they were all right. But: 'Why don't you have a driver?' she demanded. 'I'll ring Conrad Black [later, Lord Black of Crosshaven, the owner of the *Telegraph* papers] in the morning.'[3] She did and Worsthorne soon did not have to drive for himself.

Overconfidence combined with suspicion brewed a deadly third ingredient: over-reliance on a small coterie. Chief among the people she trusted were (now Sir) Bernard Ingham, her press secretary, followed by Charles (now Lord) Powell, from 1984 her private secretary on foreign affairs. 'Courtiers' seems an inappropriate designation for two such strong-minded, sophisticated professionals, but her total trust in them reflected their unswerving loyalty to her. Each in his own way thought that the prime minister was right and her opponents wrong. To Kenneth Clarke, observing from the cabinet (he was Health Secretary), the pair grew 'steadily ever more adoring'. The new cabinet secretary, Sir Robin Butler (Sir Robert Armstrong having retired), who had worked with her earlier, saw that now, rather than sitting up all night polishing and repolishing her speeches, she would let Powell or Ingham write them.

Caught between courtiers and critics, she lost her buffer between the two. William Whitelaw suffered a stroke and resigned in January 1988. He was the man of whom she had told the Conservative Party, in the classic of her many unwitting double entendres, 'Every government needs a Willie'. She certainly needed hers. She consulted him on her myriad reshuffles.

She would take criticism from him as from none other. Her opponents found him useful too. Whitelaw was, Powell remembers, 'the man to whom cabinet ministers would go and tell how awful she was, how they couldn't bear working for her another moment'. He would pat them on the back and send them once more into the fray.

Whitelaw always spoke his mind. Early in the new parliament, the Conservative MP Robert Rhodes James asked him what he thought of the community charge promised in the 1987 election manifesto. Whitelaw stopped in his tracks and (according to Alan Clark's retelling) 'his face became empurpled ... He wrestled with some deep impediment of speech; finally burst, spluttering out the single word "TROUBLE". Then he turned on his heel.'[4]

What does it mean to win three elections? Monarchical delusions, perhaps. When Mark and Diane Thatcher produced a son, Michael, born in Dallas on 28 February 1989, the prime minister made the unforgettable announcement to the press: 'We have become a grandmother and Denis is delighted too.' Her apologists deny that she was assuming the royal 'we', but rather that she had so trained herself not to say 'I', as if she personified the government, that the unfortunate plural pronoun popped out by accident. Others were not so sure. Rumours abounded that the Queen disliked her weekly meetings with Mrs Thatcher.

Another consequence was that the tendency to preach – nurtured in the Finkin Street Chapel, Grantham – grew stronger. Believing that Scottishness was synonymous with thrift (and insensitive to the Scots' national feeling and sympathy for socialism), she offered the General Assembly of the Church of Scotland a sermon asserting the link between Thatcherite individualism and Christianity. Religious faith, she declared to her Edinburgh audience, ordained making and saving money.

Increasing reliance on her personal advisers sidelined her cabinet. Always peremptory at its meetings, she now seemed not to want any discussion at all. She was particularly curt with her quiet Foreign Secretary in a way that embarrassed onlookers. Chris Patten felt that 'the appalling way in which she treated Geoffrey Howe in cabinet – humiliating, belittling behaviour – didn't tell much decent about her'. Kenneth Clarke felt she treated him 'like an old boot'.

Howe was aware that he had the reputation of being her victim. He himself noticed the tremendous contrast between her manners in public and private:

I've never seen anyone more courteous, more deferential, than Margaret was in respect of Ronald Reagan and Mikhail Gorbachev and King Hussein of Jordan. On the other hand, dealing with her colleagues, she never seemed to have learned the lesson that those of us who've been in the Army had learned: you shouldn't be ticking off your middle-rank officers in front of the other ranks, so to speak.

Howe knew he irritated her. He talked pretty quietly and had the habit, after being interrupted, of going back to what he had been saying and continuing the same line of argument.

Kenneth Clarke saw the trouble as more general. Seeing his fellow cabinet members cowed into silence and inaction, he did not like hearing the prime minister declare, 'Why do I have to do everything in this government?' Nobody had the nerve to utter the unspoken thought – 'You *can't* do everything in this government. The problem is you've got to stop trying to do everything.'

Questions of Europe brought out her greatest vigilance. The Foreign Office, she feared, was beginning to compromise with its new European friends. She made a personal crusade of resisting efforts towards greater union – always in full command of the facts. Her worst critics could never deny her mastery of the intricate documents in Euro-speak that were placed before her. By no means was she an out-and-out anti-European. Under Edward Heath, she had canvassed for Britain's entry into the

European Economic Community in 1972. She had accepted the Single European Act of 1986 creating a genuine single market, but she wanted to go no further – certainly not towards European political integration, nor a common currency. As prime minister, however, she had been bruised by her long, justified and successful fight to reduce Britain's disproportionate contribution to the Community budget. And she had two new fears: that a strong EC would reintroduce socialism into Britain and that a bigger Germany would undermine her friend Gorbachev whom, she believed, she personally had brought to the attention of the West.

On the personal level, relations with her fellow European leaders were difficult. During her first years as prime minister, she irritated the French President Valéry Giscard d'Estaing and the West German Chancellor Helmut Schmidt with her stridency. The patrician Giscard was well known to have referred to her as 'la fille d'épicier' – the grocer's daughter.[5]

Her suppressed anger burst out in September 1988. When the European Commission President Jacques Delors came to Britain to address the Trades Union Congress in Bournemouth, he outlined his vision of a Europe far more encompassing than an economic single market. There would be social dialogue between bosses and unions, and collective bargaining at the European level. For the unions in every country, he promised that Europe would provide a tool to fight attempts to reduce their influence.

The trade unionists liked what they heard so much that they sang 'Frère Jacques' (albeit badly, Delors said later). His words were hardly music to the Thatcher ears. She had heard 'as much about the European "ideal" as I could take', she says in *The Downing Street Years*.[6]

Thirteen days later, in the Belgian university city of Bruges, she delivered her counterblast. No European superstate was going to come and threaten Britain's sovereignty. 'We haven't worked all these years to free Britain from the paralysis of socialism only to see it creep in through the back door of central control and bureaucracy from Brussels.'

Her bluntness stunned the pro-Europeans in her cabinet. Sir Geoffrey Howe in particular was outraged to hear her voice anti-European sentiments that he would find difficult to defend. The Bruges speech marked the beginning of virtual open warfare between the prime minister and her Foreign Secretary.

Temperamentally, she was inept at concealing her Little Englander reactions. She would introduce Charles Powell's wife Carla with the aside, 'She's Italian, you know.' ('As if', Powell felt, 'this would explain any subsequent attempt by my wife to climb on the table, or turn cartwheels or something.' To Powell, she seemed completely unembarrassable, saying in public things that no other head of government would dare to say. 'Only a Frenchman could have done that.'

Among her European counterparts, she got on least well with the bulky, charmless West German Chancellor, Helmut Kohl. Kohl was genuinely sad about the lack of rapport. In 1989 he invited her to his home in Deidesheim, a picturesque town in south-west Germany near the French border. He escorted her to Speyer Cathedral nearby where four Holy Roman Emperors were buried, and he thoughtfully arranged for a Bach fugue to be played during her visit. Taking Powell aside, Kohl voiced his hope that the prime minister could now appreciate that 'I'm not just a German, I'm a European,' adding, 'You've got to convince her.'

That would be difficult. As soon as she was back on the plane, she threw herself into her seat, kicked off her shoes and said, 'My God, that man is so German!' She had not much enjoyed the lunch, either – country fare of pig's stomach and liver dumplings.

'On the whole,' Powell concluded, 'foreigners were not Margaret Thatcher's cup of tea.'

*

May 1989 marked Margaret Thatcher's tenth year in power – the longest continuous tenure of a prime minister since Lord Liverpool 160 years earlier. However, she had become so detached from her colleagues and so unwilling to consult that some of them were beginning to feel it was time for her to think of stepping down. Denis Thatcher himself thought his wife perhaps ought to call it quits. Approaching her image-makers Tim Bell and Gordon Reece, he tackled Reece: 'Tell her it's time to go. You're her best friend.'

But Reece answered, 'I couldn't, Denis. I love her.'

'Steady, Gordon,' Denis replied. 'She's my wife.'

Mrs Thatcher's own intentions were quite clear. She had spelled them out to the *Sunday Times* the previous year: 'I hang on until I believe there are people who can take the banner forward with the same commitment, belief, vision, strength and singleness of purpose.'[7] By that standard, none of her prominent contemporaries measured up. She hoped to go on to win a fourth general election; then, perhaps halfway into her next term, one of the younger men she was bringing along might be ready. Her memoirs are unrepentantly ageist: 'I saw no reason to hand over to anyone of roughly my age while I was fit and active.'[8]

Into her third term, however, the economy was showing signs of overheating. Inflation and unemployment were rising steadily. Mrs Thatcher's new focus of distrust was her Chancellor of the Exchequer. She and Nigel Lawson met every week but they were not entirely open with each other. She believed that he had been surreptitiously shadowing the deutschmark – that is, intervening in the foreign exchange markets to keep the pound at a level of about three deutschmarks.

The immediate bone of contention was the exchange rate mechanism, locking the pound to a fixed rate based on a basket of European currencies. Lawson believed that only the ERM would protect the pound sterling against wild speculation. The prime minister was totally opposed to Britain's joining.

It was not easy to govern when her two highest-ranking

ministers, her Foreign Secretary and her Chancellor, were in complete disagreement with her on fundamental issues. As a counterbalance to Geoffrey Howe, she had, in Charles Powell, her personal foreign affairs adviser. Now she appointed – or reappointed (as he had served her from 1981 to 1983 in the Centre for Policy Studies) – Sir Alan Walters as her personal economic adviser. Walters, back in Britain after a time in Washington working at the free-market American Enterprise Institute and the World Bank, became her personal Chancellor. For those concerned with the theology of money, it was like living in the Kingdom of the Two Sicilies.

Her split with Lawson came out into the open just after her tenth anniversary celebration. On his way to an international conference in Spain, he learned that the prime minister had given a broadcast interview in which she blamed the rise in inflation on her Chancellor's intervention in foreign markets in order to shadow the deutschmark. Although they had long disagreed in private, this was her first public attack. Word of Lawson's fury swiftly reached London and soon Margaret Thatcher was on the telephone with a fulsome apology. She had been provoked, she said, by the idiocy of the BBC World Service interviewer. Lawson interpreted her call as a move to forestall his resignation.[9]

Watching the scene, the Conservative Party chairman, Norman Tebbit, thought that no government could withstand such a split at the top. Ingham, too, suspected that it would all end in tears.

The dangerous duo – alienated Foreign Secretary and Chancellor – presented themselves together at Downing Street on a Sunday morning in June just as she was about to depart for a meeting of the European Council in Madrid, where economic and monetary union were on the agenda. They delivered an ultimatum: either she would agree a date by the end of 1992 for Britain's entry into the exchange rate mechanism or they would resign. Both of them. There and then. Powell, who was going to Madrid with the prime minister, saw that this threat of dual resignation was far more serious than the two resignations in the Westland crisis of 1986: it was was 'a moment of pure poison'. Powell then realised that the prime minister was isolated in her own cabinet.

On the flight to Spain, she remained closeted with Powell and Ingham and did not speak to Howe, who was on the same plane. In Madrid she declined to come to the British ambassador's reception. Her Foreign Secretary had no idea, therefore, of what she was going to say on the exchange rate mechanism until she said it. It was not as bad as he and Lawson had feared: the neat, fudging statement drafted by Powell and Ingham said that Britain would indeed join the exchange rate mechanism – but only under certain highly detailed conditions, which effectively pushed the issue into the future.

No speech-writers were on hand a few weeks later in Paris when the prime minister gave an interview to *Le Monde*. The occasion was a meeting of the G7 or Group of Seven – the seven principal Western industrial powers – timed to coincide with the pageantry celebrating the bicentenary of the French Revolution. As a gift for President Mitterrand, she had made an excellent choice – a first edition of Dickens's *A Tale of Two Cities*. In her interview she was less sensitive. Asked what she thought of the momentous events of July 1789, she pronounced them terrible, disgraceful, full of terrible bloodshed: the complete opposite of democracy. If the French wanted a revolution to admire, they should study Britain's peaceful and democratic revolution of 1688.

Returning to London, she lowered her own guillotine on Geoffrey Howe. Called to Number 10, he was deposed as Foreign Secretary and demoted to Leader of the House of Commons and, as a sop, made deputy prime minister as well. For her new Foreign Secretary, she reached down to the next generation: the scarcely known John Major, born in 1943.

Nigel Lawson lasted as Chancellor a mere three months longer. He resigned on 26 October 1989. He felt he couldn't carry on, constantly undermined by the 'semi-public sniping'. Her retort was that if she let Alan Walters go, her own authority would be undermined. Lawson's replacement was none other than the Foreign Secretary, John Major, after only three months in his new post. Major, far more qualified to serve in the Treasury than at the Foreign Office, was replaced by Douglas Hurd. Hurd, four years at the Home Office, had been the logical choice for Foreign Secretary three months earlier but the prime minister tended to shy away from Etonian toffs.

Was she up to her own job? The party rules required that a vote be held if a challenger appeared. In December 1989 Sir Anthony Meyer, Conservative MP for Flint West in North Wales, a man with nothing to lose and no hope of winning, put himself forward as leader of the Conservatives. Naturally, the prime minister won the ballot. But the stalking horse had done his work. That sixty members of the Conservatives in Parliament either abstained or voted for Meyer sent a clear message of discontent with her leadership style and her unpopular poll tax, which had caused rage in Scotland long before it was launched.

In a faint attempt to rebuild her popularity with the parliamentary party, she held a series of meetings with groups of Tory backbenchers, but old habits die hard. 'When they'd each had their chance,' recalls John Whittingdale MP, then her political secretary, 'she would just then demolish them all, one by one.'

Relying more and more on her own instincts and prejudices, she had to weigh the prospect of a reunited Germany against her belief that Germany was a destabilising force in Europe. On 9 November 1989, the East German border had reopened; the following day the Berlin Wall came down. Should Britain support Germany's aspirations to reincorporate the eastern regions that had been under communist rule since partition in 1945? Hurd, her new Foreign Secretary, could see that she 'didn't make enough distinction between the Germany of Hitler and the Nazis, and the Germany she had been dealing with in the 1980s which was entirely different. She was very anxious that Germany, already the most successful economic power in Europe, with 15 million extra Germans, [might] begin to dominate even brutally.'

Her fears were tempered by Helmut Kohl's firm commitment to NATO and his determination that a new united Germany would be fully part of the military alliance. Even so, after the fall of the Wall, she carried in her bag a map of Europe with a black line drawn around a unified Germany and another around the even larger area encompassing the German-speaking peoples of Europe. 'I do not believe in collective guilt,' she states in her memoirs. 'But I do believe in national character.'[10] The German national persona, she thought (tracing it back to Bismarck), 'veered unpredictably between aggression and self-doubt'.[11]

To discuss this proposition, she invited a roster of experts on European affairs – historians, dons, interested politicians – to a weekend seminar at Chequers. The academics were, in Kenneth Clarke's recollection, 'utterly amazed to find themselves taking part in this eccentric exercise'. The seminar acquired some notoriety when Charles Powell's memo of the event was leaked to the *Independent* newspaper. It recorded, Clarke says, 'all this slightly barking stuff about the German national character, and she believed it'. Looking back, Douglas Hurd believes that Margaret Thatcher hoped the experts would rally behind her and say that German unification should be resisted because there was something innate and dangerous in the German character. 'But they refused to play along.'

Alan Clark, who was pleased to be included in the distinguished group, argued for accepting and exploiting German reunification but found the prime minister dead set against it. He recreated the scene for his diary:

'You're wrong,' I said. 'You're just wrong.'

Everyone at the table smirked at each other. Now he's really torn it; fucking little show-off, etc. During the coffee-break I cornered her.

'These are just a re-run of the old Appeasement arguments of
1938.'

'Yes,' she said, eyes flashing (she's in incredible form at the
moment), 'and I'm not an appeaser.'

John Major, whom I like more and more, said to me *sotto voce*,
'You're a military strategist. Oughtn't you to be sending your tanks
round the flank, rather than attacking head on?'[12]

Obviously the new Chancellor knew the tactics of manoeuvring
round the prime minister.

Her rigid views about Germany brought her into conflict with
her closest international ally, President George Bush. The United
States had invested a great deal in the rebuilding of West Germany and was pleased with its progress. Bush tried to argue
Margaret Thatcher out of her views and presented his case:
Germany had earned its place in the family of nations; it was a
democracy. But he knew he had not persuaded her.

As the 1980s gave way to the 1990s, in Bucharest the Ceauşescus
were executed at two hours' notice and in South Africa Nelson
Mandela was released after twenty-seven years' imprisonment
on Robbin Island.

In Britain the unease about the introduction of the community
charge, or poll tax, coincided with an increasingly gloomy economic forecast and a mounting restlessness within the Conservative Party. 'The Lady', wrote Alan Clark, 'is under deep pressure
now . . . practically every member of the Cabinet is quietly and
unattributably briefing different Editors or members of the
Lobby about how awful she is.'[13] Clark (accurately) related the
anger about the poll tax to the feeling that 'the Lady' had stayed
on too long.

The Community Charge has got on everyone's nerves of course, and
generated the most oppressive volume of correspondence . . . But I
am inclined to think that the Party in the House has just got sick of
her . . . When's the Revolution? In the meantime, all the wets and

Blue Chips and general Heathite wankers . . . stew around and pine for her to drop dead.[14]

The first of April was the unfortunate date chosen for the introduction of the community charge in England and Wales. Advertisements tried to show the bright side:

The Government is about to tear up the present system of domestic rates. And replace it with a fairer one. And high time too.

If your local council wastes money through sheer inefficiency, then it will have to ask for a bigger community charge.[15]

But there was near-universal condemnation despite the promise of ridding the country of high-spending, left-wing councils. All the prime minister's closest advisers warned her against it but such was her overconfidence that she believed her own determination could see anything through. She felt the old system of rates was particularly unfair to what she regarded as 'her' people – small businesses, widows living in their own homes, who paid rates while families in council accommodation paid virtually nothing. There was no arguing with her, according to Chris Patten:

Margaret didn't really want to listen to the argument. She wanted to believe that she could do anything, that this flagship would actually float merely because of her political will.

She was simply losing that magical touch she'd had for knowing just how far with the British public – and in particular the English public – she could stretch the elastic band of acceptability in policy terms.

Riots exploded in Trafalgar Square and Charing Cross Road as protesters battled police in scenes that had not been seen in the capital for a decade. The rioters included people declaring that they would not pay and others protesting against the years of Thatcherism, which – they felt – had not only left them behind but had also, through tax cuts, simply made the rich richer.

In response the prime minister used the same words as she had with the Falklands invaders and the Brighton bombers: 'These people are totally against democracy.'

Yet critics felt that her poll tax had struck a crippling blow *against* local democracy. Removing the power to set the rates from local councils was another step towards putting control in the hands of central government. The same shift had already happened with education, with responsibility transferred from the local level to the Department of Education in Whitehall.

Increasingly isolated in Europe, with an economy tipping into recession, and now anarchy on the streets, Margaret Thatcher, once seen as the Conservatives' greatest vote winner, was now an electoral liability. How could they get rid of the poll tax without getting rid of Thatcher? Lord Carrington, who was still her friend and who lived near Chequers, delicately put into words what was on everybody's mind: 'I said to her, if there was an election now, you might lose it. And to lose to Mr Kinnock would be really rather humiliating for you. Don't you think you ought to step down and allow somebody else to take over?' There was no answer.

The world stage can offer welcome relief to a beleaguered leader. At the Aspen Institute in Colorado in early August 1990 Margaret Thatcher spelled out what the requirements of democracy are: 'limitation of the powers of government, a market economy, private property and a sense of personal responsibility'.[16] While the meeting was in progress in a beauty spot high in the Rocky Mountains, Iraq invaded Kuwait. She was thus able to stand beside President George Bush to pronounce the invasion illegal. On her way back to Britain, she made an unscheduled stop in Washington in order to see Bush again. She assured the President that if he went to war she would commit British troops as well. At that meeting, she delivered her now-famous advice: 'George, this is no time to go wobbly,' exhibiting once more her flair for the unthinking sexual innuendo and also her Boadicean pity for the weaker sex. (Presenting her with the Presidential Medal of Freedom at the White House in March 1991, Bush told the joke against himself.)[17] The President was in fact in no danger of wobbling; he was committed to using force to resist the Iraqi advance into Kuwait.

The American trip was made under the stress of another terrible personal loss. Ian Gow, her good friend, former parliamentary private secretary and a strong pro-Unionist, the MP for Eastbourne and former Northern Ireland minister, was murdered by the IRA, blown up by a bomb placed under his car at his home. Injury was piled on injury when in the by-election at Eastbourne to succeed Gow, the ultra-safe Tory seat went to the Liberal Democrats by a 20 per cent swing.

That autumn, flanked by a new Foreign Secretary (Hurd) and a new Chancellor (Major) whom she could hardly sack, on 5 October 1990 she had to approve what she had fought so hard against: Britain joining the dreaded exchange rate mechanism. A woman under siege, her demeanour altered. Her fashion adviser Margaret King noticed that she would switch off and pull into herself: 'You could be speaking to her and you could see her click off. You knew immediately that you didn't have to say anything more for a while because she wouldn't hear a word.'

At the Rome summit meeting of the European Council at the end of October 1990, Jacques Delors could see that she was rattled, her emotions intensified. 'She became more and more brittle, making nervous gestures,' he recalls. In retrospect, he acknowledges: 'This is not something that only happens to women; other heads of government, sensing the last days of their power approaching – have acted in the same way.'

The prime minister went to Rome with her prejudices about national character undiminished (and, in her memoirs, undisguised): 'as always with the Italians it was difficult throughout to distinguish confusion from guile.'[18] She was implacably hostile to what was discussed, seeing in the various subjects such as trade or defence further institutional steps in the direction of federalism.

Her summary report to the House of Commons of what had transpired in Rome marked the final chapter in her calamitous dealings over Europe. She told them that the President of the European Commission, Jacques Delors, said at a press conference that he wanted the European Parliament to be the democratic body of the Community. He wanted the Commission to be the Executive. And he wanted the Council of Ministers to be the Senate. The handbag swung three times. 'No! No! No!' she declaimed.[19]

Geoffrey Howe was sitting next to her. He could not believe his ears: 'Our entire attitude towards Europe was being torn apart.' Neil Kinnock, watching, saw Howe's face grow dark, 'like a thunderous fiddle. He really was upset.' Howe resigned two days later – a day after the xenophobic tabloid, the *Sun*, summed up her treble defiance with one of its most famous headlines: 'Up Yours Delors.'

One of the privileges of resignation is the resignation speech. In his, on 13 November, Howe had his revenge for years of humiliation. He knew what its effect would be and asked his fellow mutineer, Nigel Lawson, to sit beside him while he gave it. There was no havering, no quiet meandering on this occasion. 'The language was lethal,' says Kinnock, still in admiration. 'There wasn't a single phrase that was wasted. It took Mrs T's head right off.'

Howe used a cricketing metaphor to describe what it was like going out to play only to find that 'their bats have been broken before the game by the team captain'. He himself had left the team, and he invited others to walk out with him, or, in parliamentary language, 'to consider their own response to the tragic conflict of loyalties with which I have myself wrestled for perhaps too long'.

Michael Heseltine had had four years since Westland to consider his position. On 14 November he informed the head of the 1922 Committee and the chief whip of his intention of standing for the leadership. A ballot was scheduled for Tuesday, 20 November, and Heseltine began campaigning aggressively.

The strategy for the prime minister was not so clear. She was scheduled to go to Paris on 18 November for a three-day international conference marking the formal end of the Cold War. Presidents Bush and Mitterrand, Premier Gorbachev and other leaders would be there. It would be demeaning to stay at home to court votes in the House tea room. Besides, the whips had canvassed the House Tories and told her things would be all right.

After a weekend at Chequers surrounded by her closest friends and advisers, she left for Paris. All knew the arithmetic. An overall victory on the first ballot required a margin of 15 per cent of the total vote. Denis, who was remaining behind, had done his own calculations. Cynthia Crawford, about to accompany the prime minister, said to him, 'Let's hope we will come back with the right vote from Paris.' Denis replied (holding, according to his daughter's biography, a large gin), 'Crawfie, she's done for.'[20]

For two days in Paris, Margaret Thatcher played her part of world leader at the conference on Security and Cooperation in Europe, the final summit of the Cold War. She gave a speech; she accepted congratulations from the President of Bulgaria for delivering (with President Reagan) freedom to Eastern Europe. Only at the end of the busy day of Tuesday, 20 November, did she return to the British embassy where she was staying.

With her advisers, plus the British ambassador, Sir Ewen Fergusson, she prepared to await the results of the first ballot in London. Positioned in a bedroom in the embassy residence's attic, the prime minister sat at a dressing table and next to her sat Peter Morrison, her parliamentary private secretary, in front of an open line. When the call came, he answered.

His words: 'It's not as good as we hoped.' Hers: 'Oh dear.' Denis Thatcher's, when his wife rang with the news, were: 'Congratulations, Sweetie Pie. You've won; it's just the rules.'[21] But a friend who was with him saw the tears roll down his face.

Instinct now took over. Margaret Thatcher was not an appeaser. Leading her entourage, she went out into the grounds of the residency where John Sergeant, the BBC's chief political reporter, was doing a live broadcast for the home audience on Mrs Thatcher's failure to win the first ballot. She approached the microphone to announce that she was very pleased that she had got the votes of more than half the parliamentary party; she would let her name go forward for the second ballot. The scene remains a celebrated television moment. Sergeant said afterwards that he could almost feel the unseen television audience of millions shouting at him, as if in a pantomime: 'She's right behind you!'[22]

Back at the residence, she went to change out of a black and brown patterned wool suit into an evening dress for the formal banquet at Versailles. President Mitterrand courteously held up the dinner until her arrival. All had heard the news. 'It must hurt, it must hurt a lot,' George Bush said in words she probably did not wish to hear. He was impressed by her composure. 'There wasn't a lot of self-pity that we saw. It was just this strong woman taking a tremendous blow and conducting herself in an admirable way.'

At the end of the momentous day, when she had returned to her room, Crawfie looked in to see if she was all right. She was more than awake; she wanted company. Just as in the long nights of the Falklands war, the two women had a drink and talked. Crawfie listened while the prime minister ran through scenes from her past life – Grantham, school, Oxford, Denis, the twins – 'and we didn't go to bed at all'.

After the following morning's signing of the summit document, the Charter of Paris, Margaret Thatcher returned to London where she consulted her closest political colleagues. They told her they thought she could win on the second ballot. Denis, in contrast, counselled, 'Don't go on, love.'[23] However, on leaving for the House of Commons, she spoke to the waiting press, back on her old form: 'I fight on, I fight to win.' Alan Clark came into her rooms and found her looking 'calm, almost beautiful'.[24] When she said she was determined to fight on, he warned her that the party would let her down. 'There was quite a little pause. "It'd be so terrible if Michael won. He would undo everything I have fought for."'[25]

She then summoned members of her cabinet in to see her, one by one. It was a decision she probably later regretted. Had she assembled them, they might have feared to break ranks. Individually, they were frank.

Cecil Parkinson and Douglas Hurd pledged their support, Hurd particularly because he didn't think it a good idea that the prime minister of Britain should be changed in that way. As she talked to the others, however, it became clear that her support had ebbed away to an extent she had not realised. Kenneth Clarke told her that standing against Heseltine would be like the Charge of the Light Brigade; she had no chance of winning. Chris Patten told her to step down and not to risk the humiliation of a second ballot. Others were blunter; the word 'humiliation' was often heard. After a succession of rebuffs, she saw that she had lost her cabinet, without whose approval she lacked the authority to govern.

Norman Tebbit, who had resigned from the cabinet in 1987 yet remained a close and active supporter from the backbenches, persuaded her to postpone a decision until she had talked to Denis. Returning home, she found his opinion unaltered: it was time to go. (Powell interprets Denis's advice as the reaction of a man enraged by the attacks on his wife; Denis felt that the party didn't deserve her if that was the way they behaved when the going got tough.)

Her decision was now made. She called her closest personal adviser, Bernard Ingham, who could tell she was in tears, and told him she had decided to resign. Then she called Crawfie and asked her to come round immediately because she was going to resign the next morning. Crawfie complied and found 'she already looked smaller'.

At nine o'clock next morning a red-eyed Margaret Thatcher held her last cabinet meeting. With a box of tissues at her right hand, she said she had an announcement to make. Everybody knew what it was. No one could look her in the eye. 'It was one of the most traumatic and embarrassing events I've ever been present at,' Powell remembers. Chris Patten recalls 'a very woeful miserable scene, because, inevitably, people around the table felt that she was going in a pretty shabby way. But I don't think that exit was our fault. She was part of the reason for her own exit.' In other words, around the table sat a silent male chorus thinking the unsayable: 'She asked for it.'

She felt (and continued to feel for long after) that she had been stabbed in the back. In retrospect, Hurd disagrees. 'She ran out of time. But in the end she asked people their views and they gave them. That's not a stab in the back.' Lord Carrington, another sympathiser, holds the same view: 'I suppose she thought it was a conspiracy because things were going very badly . . . but she was totally wrong. There wasn't.'

The news, released at 9.30 a.m. by the Press Association, was electric. People remember where they were when they heard it. City trading rooms came to a halt for the formal announcement. Passengers on the London Underground heard it over the trains' loudspeakers. Neil Kinnock told a cheering crowd of Labourites, 'Our greatest single asset is gone.'

The machinery now swung into action for others to enter the contest. Douglas Hurd and John Major put themselves forward. Bernard Ingham, however, was more worried about how the prime minister was going to perform in the House of Commons that afternoon in response to Kinnock's motion 'That this House has no confidence in Her Majesty's Government'. 'I was dreading, dreading, that speech,' he says. 'She was very, very upset.'

It was foreboding misplaced. Margaret Thatcher not only rose to the occasion of her last speech as prime minister, on 22 November 1990, but she triumphed – so witty and relaxed that many judged it her best parliamentary performance ever. Proud and confident, she delivered a resounding summary of the achievements of the Thatcher years: Britain's restored standing in the world, the retention of the Falklands, the broken monopoly of the trade unions, the sale of 1.25 million council houses to private owners, the privatisation of nationalised industry and lowered income tax. Very unusually, she had the House roaring with laughter. At one point, carried away, she stopped herself and asked, 'Where was I? I am *enjoying* this.'[26]

To one another, MPs were saying, 'If only she could've done that two or three weeks ago, she'd still be prime minister.' Alan Clark had to concede that 'the Lady . . . was brilliant. Humorous, self-deprecating, swift and deadly in her argument and in her riposte.'[27] Gratifyingly, Paddy Ashdown, leader of the Liberal Democrats, rose to say that her pre-eminent achievement, for which she would be most remembered, was the democratisation of the trade union movement. 'The Right Hon. Lady has also given us some sense of the value of sound money. She has also highlighted the importance of the market in our economy.'[28]

None who applauded this bravura performance knew that before the speech a doctor had been called to Number 10 to administer a shot of what Crawfie believed was Vitamin B_{12}. It was needed, Crawford said, 'because she was very, very low, and very tired by this time'.[29]

Throwing her personal support to John Major, she addressed the task of moving out of the two homes she and Denis had occupied for nearly a dozen years. At every general election, it had been her custom to have all her things packed, ready to move out in case she lost. This time the packing was not symbolic.

The Thatchers gave drinks parties for the staffs at both houses. At Number 10, welcoming their employees in the state dining room, the prime minister thanked everyone for a wonderful eleven and a half years; Denis stood up and said he hoped he hadn't been rude to anybody.

Heseltine was expected to win the leadership. As the day for the ballot drew near, however, the MORI poll showed Major drawn level with Heseltine. Alan Clark told Bob Worcester, head of MORI, 'Christ, Bob, these have to be rogue figures . . .' Worcester was equally incredulous: 'Look, Alan, we're MORI. We don't have "rogue" figures.'[30]

On the evening of Tuesday, 27 November, one week after the small group had hovered in the attic of the Paris embassy, waiting for results, the new ballot was counted. John Major had run far ahead of Hurd and Heseltine on the first ballot. According to the rules, with 185 votes, Major was two votes short of an outright win. However, both runners-up – Heseltine, with 131, and Hurd, with 56 – withdrew for the sake of party unity and pledged loyalty to the new leader.

After the result, three Thatchers – Margaret, Denis and Mark – went through the connecting door between Numbers 10 and 11 Downing Street (the official residence of the Chancellor of the Exchequer) and tendered their congratulations. As Major moved to go out and speak to the press, she offered to come with him. Major hesitated, to be rescued by Norman Lamont, chief secretary to the Treasury. 'Please let him have his moment,' Lamont told her, holding her back.[31] The papers next day carried photographs of the Oedipal scene: the anxious maternal face watching from an upstairs window while her protégé assumed her role.

She left Number 10 the next morning. Coming down from the flat with Denis and Mark, she walked the whole length of the corridor, past all the waiting staff, many clapping, some weeping. The staff's grief was genuine. Rarely before (or since, by some accounts) had they had an employer so appreciative of their efforts. The prime minister herself, fighting back tears of injustice and betrayal, couldn't speak. Her mascara had run down her cheek; Crawfie wetted a Kleenex and removed it. When Ingham gave the cue, 'This is it,' followed by Denis and Mark, she stepped out, made a brief statement and got into the car, waving with tear-filled eyes as she was driven to the Palace to give her formal resignation to the Queen, and from there to the house in Dulwich.

Waking up jobless in an unlived-in house on a featureless private estate in an unfamiliar part of London must have been like being propelled on to a new planet – clean, silent and uninhabited (except for the security police who had taken up station in the garage). Her impulse was to ring Crawfie. But how? Eleven and a half years in power had taken their toll; someone accustomed to saying, 'Get me Gorbachev,' didn't have the numbers of the people closest to her nor of the Downing Street switchboard. There was no alternative but to ask the police for help. Thus the first words that Crawfie heard from the former prime minister were a cry of the dispossessed: 'This is Margaret. From the garage.'

12
Life After Work

The shock of re-entry coincided with Christmas-time. Non-prime ministerial Christmas cards had to be ordered and a place found for the Christmas party planned for Number 10. Countless letters poured in; some apparently written in despair: 'I myself', Margaret Thatcher says in *The Path to Power*, 'was merely depressed.'[1]

She *was* depressed: a workless workaholic. Bernard Ingham compared the predicament to coming off heroin: 'You've devoted twenty-four hours of every day of your life for eleven and a half years to running the country and suddenly you have absolutely nothing to do.' Her driver, Denis Oliver, noticed how she had to keep going all the time: 'After Downing Street, she used to busy herself cleaning things. The apron would go on. I think she found some sort of therapy in dusting bookshelves – taking all the books off, all of them – and hoovering them. She preferred dusting the books to reading them.'

One thing she could do was reward Denis. Among the resignation honours that she was entitled to bestow, she made him a baronet: Sir Denis Thatcher, Baronet of Scotney. This recognition of the nation's favourite consort was widely applauded. There was, however, acid comment on the fact that the title, being hereditary, would pass in time to the unadmired, Dallas-based son and heir.

It was soon clear how Margaret Thatcher might keep busy. Within a week of departure from Number 10, she was, according to biographer Mark Hollingsworth, offered a contract by the Washington Speakers Bureau, the agency that had made Ronald Reagan reputedly the highest-paid speaker in the world.[2] Over tea with the Reagans during that bleak December, she discussed the contract and they advised acceptance.

Early in the New Year of 1991, she went to Los Angeles to celebrate Reagan's eightieth birthday. A dinner was given in her honour at the Beverly Hills Hotel; the guests included the media magnate Rupert Murdoch. In July, Murdoch's book-publishing company, HarperCollins, offered £3.5 million for her memoirs.

The deals were energising. Before long the Thatchers sold the hardly lived-in Dulwich house for £195,000 more than they had paid for it and moved back to the heart of London. At first they lived in flats loaned by friends; then, for £700,000, they bought a forty-year lease on a five-storey house at 73 Chester Square, Belgravia.[3] The deal was arranged with the millionaire brothers David and Frederick Barclay, through (now Lord) Tim Bell, still a friend and adviser. An office nearby at 35 Chesham Place provided a base for working on her memoirs and running the recently created Thatcher Foundation. The ever-loyal Cynthia Crawford remained an organiser and companion.

Disillusion with her chosen successor swiftly set in. In March 1991, hardly three months in office, Prime Minister John Major declared that Britain's place was 'at the very heart of Europe'.[4] In Washington at the time, Margaret Thatcher ignored the convention of not criticising one's country when abroad and lashed out against the danger of turning the European Community into a United States of Europe.

Gone was the old friendliness between her and her young protégé. From her body language when they met, he could see that she felt he held 'what she regarded as *her* job'.[5] In his professed desire to soften the hard edges of Thatcherism – 'to build a nation at ease with itself', in his later words, he began the dismantling of the despised poll tax.[6] By 1992 it was gone. She interpreted his changes as moves to undo her own achievements.

The real trouble was as much psychological as political. The outgoing prime minister had meant it when she said, 'I shan't be pulling the levers there, but I shall be a very good back-seat driver.'[7] Chris Patten was among many who were surprised by 'the extent to which she wanted to get her hands on the wheel from time to time'. Major felt he could drive by himself.

After an uncomfortable period on the Conservative back-benches (where another former prime minister Edward Heath glowered), she saw that she would be freer to speak her mind if she left the House of Commons and the Conservative whip there. In 1992 she gave up the Finchley constituency she had held for over three decades and accepted elevation to the House of Lords. She styled herself Baroness Thatcher of Kesteven – honouring her Grantham associations, including the Kesteven and Grantham Girls' School.

The time came to leave the Commons for the last time. Observing the scene from the press gallery was her former Central Office correspondence secretary, Matthew Parris:

The chamber was empty. Somebody's papers were strewn all over the dispatch box. She got all the papers into a neat little pile. Got them right this way. Got them right that way. Put them back in a neat pile, then walked out behind the Speaker's chair with one last glance behind her – just tidying up.

In 1992 the Maastricht Treaty, laying the foundations for a single European currency, was opened for signature by various European governments. The Danes turned it down. Britain ought to do the same, Margaret Thatcher believed. Writing in the *European* newspaper in October 1992, in an article timed to coincide with the Conservatives' annual party conference, she warned the British public about the Euro-trap lying in wait: 'Maastricht will hand over more power to unelected bureaucrats and erode the freedoms of ordinary men and women.'[8] But John Major toiled on and secured Britain a double opt-out from provisions in the treaty: from the Social Chapter, which protected many of the trade union special privileges that Britain had abolished, and from the commitment to join a European single currency. After a tough fight he got the treaty ratified by the House of Commons in May 1993, confident that he had secured Britain's place and influence in Europe.

From then on, the new baroness set herself to try to bring Major down, although he had won a general election in 1992 and had his own mandate. She began telling friends that she hoped the young Conservative MP Michael Portillo would oust Major in a leadership contest. According to Kenneth Clarke, it was a continuous, organised revolt: 'Backbench rebels were being sent to see her and she would stiffen them all up and tell them to go back and get this man out.'

Not a few asked her outright why she had become so hostile to John Major, who had inherited difficult problems with Europe and splits within the party. To Douglas Hurd, she answered, 'Oh well, I thought he was like me.' Hurd thought, Anybody less like her could be very difficult to find. She gave the same answer to Lord Carrington, whose private view was the same as Hurd's.

On her foreign lecture tours, preaching to the converted (conservative businessmen in the United States, Japan and the Middle East), for a fee reported to be $50,000 plus expenses for a half-hour lecture followed by questions, she found the adulation she lacked at home. As she travelled, Crawfie, who occasionally went with her, was pleased to see that 'everybody gave her such a huge welcome, particularly in the Saudi and that area of the world. That lifted her again.' The baroness quite liked donning headdress and long robes for her appearances in Muslim countries. However, in her travels she never overcame her dislike for anything but plain English fare. When she went to China and was treated to a thirteen-course banquet in the Great Hall of the People, she just pushed the food round the plate and ate nothing. The British embassy in Beijing greeted her upon her return with a big plate of smoked-salmon sandwiches.

Publication in 1993 of the first volume of her memoirs, *The Downing Street Years*, increased her invitations to travel abroad. The book, well written with the assistance of Robin Harris and John O'Sullivan, was a surprisingly good read, full of frank observations and insights even if self-justifying and selective as most memoirs are. It was followed two years later by *The Path to Power*, dedicated to the memory of Keith Joseph, which not only traced her life from Grantham to Number 10 but also, in its second half, presented a strong defence of her anti-European and anti-Major crusade.

In 1995, actively working to undermine John Major's leadership of the Conservative Party, she gave a television interview in which she openly accused the prime minister: 'a thousand years of history wrecked by a single currency'.[9] Major was mystified by her campaign against him, for he had gone no farther towards monetary union than refusing to rule out Britain's joining at some time in the future. He could not see why she so blatantly flouted party discipline by speaking out publicly rather than picking up the telephone and telling him what was on her mind. Her next move was to call for a renegotiation of the Maastricht Treaty.

Her old cabinet colleague Kenneth Clarke thought she behaved towards Major worse than Edward Heath had ever behaved towards her. Douglas Hurd, reopening the question many years later, asked outright: why had she pressed everyone to vote for Major in the leadership contest in 1990? 'And she said, "I'll tell you something I wouldn't tell to everybody. He was the best of a very poor bunch."' Apparently she had forgotten that Hurd had been one of that bunch.

In 1995 Major moved to put an end to the sniping from within his own party. He resigned as leader of the party, submitted himself for re-election and, in the resulting ballot, resoundingly defeated his challenger, John Redwood.

She got her wish to see him replaced a year and a half later when the Conservatives lost the general election of 1 May 1997 and Tony Blair became prime minister. Labour's win was hardly surprising, as the Tories had won the four previous elections in a row. Indeed, they probably would have lost the 1992 election had not the Labour leader Neil Kinnock snatched defeat from the jaws of victory by outrageous and premature triumphalism at an election-eve rally in Sheffield. In any event, Major stood down as party leader in June 1997. For his replacement, Lady Thatcher endorsed William Hague – with embarrassing fervour. She told a group of Conservatives: 'I am supporting William Hague. Now, have you got the name? William Hague. Vote for William Hague. For principled government, following the same type of government which I led, vote for him on Thursday. Got the message?'[10]

Her habit of talking to certain people as if they were slow children once sounded condescending; now it seemed senescent.

In early 1994, at the age of sixty-eight, while in South America publicising her book, she travelled for the first time to Chile. In Santiago, where she was sponsored by the Chilean Manufacturers' Association, a right-wing think-tank, and a millionaire builder with personal links to the deposed leader, General Augusto Pinochet, she gave a forty-five-minute address.[11] She had reached the final page of her talk when she gasped quite loudly and crumpled, striking her face on the microphone. Helped to her feet, she apologised and, to applause, walked out of the room.

It was the first sign that the Iron Lady was rusting. The British embassy statement blamed a stomach infection, seafood and the heat, but a television viewer might feel free to diagnose a minor stroke.

She was well enough two days later to attend a reception where she met General Pinochet for the first time. The parallels were striking – displaced leaders in enforced retirement, seeking abroad rewards denied at home – and they became friends.

In subsequent years, when Pinochet came to London, a city he loved, he saw her about ten times. In October 1998 at the age of eighty-two he was recovering from a spinal operation at the London Clinic when, at the request of the Spanish authorities, British police arrested him for crimes against humanity committed in the years following the overthrow of the Marxist President Salvador Allende. Outraged, Lady Thatcher wrote to *The Times*: 'He was a good friend to this country during the Falklands War. By his actions the war was shortened and many British lives were saved.' Her letter acknowledged that there had been violence and abuses of human rights in Chile but claimed that they had been 'on both sides of the political divide'. It was 'not for Spain, Britain or any other country to interfere in what is an internal matter'.[12]

Over the ensuing months, when Pinochet was held under house arrest at his home in Surrey, Lady Thatcher defended him in the House of Lords and at the Conservative Party conference. In the Lords she described how the general had 'saved Chile' at a time when 'communism was advancing through the hemispheres' so that now it was a place of 'thriving free enterprise'.[13] At the party conference in Blackpool, she sang the praises of the social and economic advances that Chile had achieved after Pinochet had routed Marxism. She went on to deride the left-wing student politics of Jack Straw, Labour's Home Secretary, and Prime Minister Tony Blair, which she now saw behind the persecution of Pinochet: 'What they couldn't and wouldn't abandon was the poisonous prejudices they harboured in their youth. And this, of course, was the situation when a trusting, elderly, former Chilean ruler chose to pay one too many visits to his beloved Britain last autumn.'[14]

The saga ended when the Law Lords ruled that the ailing Pinochet would not be extradited to Spain but allowed to return to Chile. It was arranged that the general would leave Britain from the Royal Air Force station at Waddington in Lincolnshire. The engines of the Chilean Air Force jet were already turning when there was a delay while a parcel from a well-wisher was carried out to the aircraft. It was a silver plate, a reproduction of plates cast in 1588 to commemorate Sir Francis Drake's victory over the Spanish Armada.[15]

Lady Thatcher had not lost her touch for the small personal gift.

She aged visibly, the nose became more pointed, the eyes narrower and clouded, the cheekbones sharper, the hair bigger. At an election rally in Plymouth in May 2001, she joked that her appearance had been advertised on a local cinema's billboard, 'The Mummy Returns'. The joke was painfully true: she seemed to be a fossil of her former self. But not in her clothes; the cut, fabric and colour remained uncompromisingly *à la mode*.

Her life appeared sad. The traditional consolations of old age were in short supply. Mark and his wife Diane shifted from Texas to South Africa; their two children, Michael and Amanda, rarely saw their grandmother. Carol, who never married, spends much of her time in Switzerland – the scene of her girlhood's happiest hours.

The friendship with Cynthia Crawford endured. They see each other every other week and have taken, with their husbands, 'little holidays together' to Provence and Monte Carlo:

We are great chums. I tell her things I wouldn't tell anyone else and she tells me things she wouldn't tell anyone else and at the end of the day we always sit down and kick off our shoes and have a chat and a drink. To some women she is a bit intimidating but we have always got on like a house on fire. I really love her to bits. She's my hero.

Woodrow (long since Lord) Wyatt also remained a friend. However, he worried on occasion whether 'she'd gone slightly off balance in some way'.

She'd made a recording of the Gettysburg address. She asked me to sit next to her, and she put her hand on my knee, and said, 'Loyalty,

loyalty. That is what life is all about.' And repeated it over and over again. The whole thing became an obsession. There are reports that she was drinking more – she certainly likes a good drink. So does Denis, but for different reasons. But she likes her drink and I don't think she ever adjusted to what happened.

Over the years she suffered a series of small strokes. In March 2002 her doctors advised her to stop making public speeches in order to reduce the stress that such occasions caused her. It is a stricture she found hard to obey.

As Britain's first woman prime minister, what did Margaret Thatcher do for women? Directly, almost nothing. Indirectly, everything. Baroness (Shirley) Williams, hardly a political admirer, maintains that the fact that Mrs Thatcher was able to be prime minister of a major Western country – and to do so from very humble beginnings – is doubly impressive. 'When men have daughters now, they don't any longer assume that their daughter can't really be anything very much. They know that she could be a prime minister.'

But does a woman have to manifest the bristling aggression that made Mrs Thatcher widely unloved?

In retrospect, Jacques Delors, President of the European Commission during the Thatcher prime ministership, is forgiving towards her stridency, her tendency to interrupt and talk for too long. 'She suffered from being a woman. This inequality of the sexes still exists, so she sometimes, as do many women, had to express herself more forcefully in her arguments and in her tone of voice in order to be heard.'

Looking back, Geoffrey (Lord) Howe concedes that it was unnerving dealing with a prime minister who was a woman. 'I don't think one liked shouting, savaging a woman – rhetorically, so to speak, particularly if the woman was inclined to answer back.'

For her part, Shirley Williams attributes Margaret Thatcher's rise and durability to being 'very courageous, and extremely ruthless':

It took a lot of guts. If there had not been an unwillingness of most of the senior figures in the party to challenge Ted Heath, who was very unpopular in the party and the country, she would not ever have become leader.

Her self-confidence had somehow survived a period in the cabinet between 1970 and 1974 when she was treated by Ted as a lesser being. He gave her little opportunity to speak except on her subject, and not long on that either. I never got treatment like that from Wilson or Callaghan when I was a member of the Cabinet.

The negative effect of Thatcher's femininity, in Williams's view, was that no one had the courage to defy her on the folly of the poll tax. 'Because she was a woman, they were not challenging her in a way they would have done if she'd been a male politician.'

There is another ingredient in the Thatcher rise which, Lady Williams believes, has been seriously underestimated: Denis.

Denis is seen as a joke figure, the amiable saloon bar chap who swills away gin and tonics and talks about golf. That's badly to underestimate him. He's the absolutely crucial factor in her later life, the way her father was in her early life, and she made in a way a switch from Alderman Roberts to Denis Thatcher. The same role was carried by both men.

The important thing about Denis is he was that bit older; he'd built up a fortune in the oil business. Therefore, by the time he married Margaret . . . he's already somebody who's sitting on top of his own success; who can therefore be relaxed about it and used to say he vastly enjoyed watching her climb up the greasy pole of politics because he wasn't competing with her.

An unanswered question concerns the extent to which Denis Thatcher influenced her policies. As the civil servants noticed in her days as Minister of Education, Denis's opinions could be detected in the strong, previously unvoiced views with which she would arrive back at the office on Monday morning after a weekend at home. Crawfie, an observer of the Thatcher domestic scene, also believed that the prime minister listened to her husband: 'They would always talk when they had what they called their "nightcap" and he would tell her if he thought she was absolutely wrong.'

Lord Hurd allows that Denis Thatcher possibly had something to do with the prime minister's dislike of the BBC, 'but she did dislike it':

She really thought the basis of the BBC was wrong and the compulsory licence fee. I had endless arguments with her about that. Her objection to the BBC was fundamental and philosophical but she was also irritated by what she thought was its bias against the government. She used to say, 'I never listen to the *Today* programme now, it's hopelessly biased, hopelessly biased.' And then, she'd say, 'particularly bad this morning'. And if you sort of giggled slightly and said, 'How did you come to know that, Prime Minister? You don't listen to it.' – 'Oh well, Denis told me.'

In her approach to broadcasting, Prime Minister Thatcher's preference for free-market solutions seemed to reflect a businessman's respect for a balance sheet. She was disappointed in 1986 when the Peacock Committee, headed by an economist, Professor Alan Peacock, failed to recommend that the BBC should get its income from selling advertising. Thwarted, she then tried to make independent television (ITV) more commercial, by introducing legislation to have the ITV franchises awarded, subject to quality controls, to the highest bidder. To her dismay, when the first franchise auction was held in 1991, TV-am, a station she admired for its tough stand against the unions, lost its franchise to a challenger that made an extravagantly high bid. She wrote to TV-am's chief executive, Bruce Gyngell, apologising for the unintended consequences of her reform:

I am only too painfully aware that *I* was responsible for the legislation. When I see how some of the other licences have been awarded
I am *mystified* that you do not receive yours and heartbroken. You
of all people have done so much for the whole of television – there
seems no attention to that.[16]

It is hard to believe that her views in general did not reflect
Denis's own. As they grew old together, her dependence on him
grew greater, and he continued to play his part well. During a
speech in which she told the same story three times, Denis was
seen mouthing 'repeat' at her.[17] In the autumn of 2000 she was
at the high table at a Lincoln's Inn dinner for former US Senator
George Mitchell. Taking her leave, she mistook Warwick Gould,
a Professor of English, for the head of the University of London,
and said, 'Goodnight, Vice-Chancellor!' Denis, right behind her,
said, 'Come on, Margaret. This is not a bloody constituency
meeting.' In 2001 she was sighted at Winfield House, the American ambassador's residence in Regent's Park, in a pink shantung
suit, bent with age and looking lost. 'Where's Denis?' she kept
asking.[18] Her reliance on him was touching.

With the twentieth anniversary of the Falklands invasion
approaching in 2002, she turned down an official invitation to
visit because she felt Denis was not strong enough to make the
trip.

The political figures whose interviews lie behind this book
include both admirers and antagonists. From their different per-
spectives, however, all accept that she was a powerful force for
change.

Kenneth Clarke: 'There never was such a thing as Thatcherism.
Margaret was not an ideologue. She was essentially pragmatic –
a right-wing populist with great intelligence, very good political
instincts. Margaret was actually at her best a very good right-of-
centre, instinctive solver of problems. Although she is one of
our greatest leaders of the twentieth century, she has also turned

out to be one of the most destructive forces we've had within the party.'

Geoffrey (Lord) Howe: 'If one looks back, we would never have achieved what we did achieve under her leadership had it not been for this intolerable quality of determination. Her achievement in foreign policy, in recognising Gorbachev's talent and effecting the introduction between Gorbachev and Reagan, was probably the most important action in the foreign field.'

Douglas (Lord) Hurd: 'Her main quality as British prime minister was drive. She pushed and pushed and pushed again, and the result was that she was able to do things that some of us had despaired of.' He lists curbing trade union power, bringing down inflation, and dismantling the ownership of the state: 'three things that Britain badly needed in the 1980s and got only because of Margaret Thatcher's conviction and drive'.

Neil Kinnock: 'What Mrs Thatcher did was to say there is in most human personalities a degree of selfishness – it is a great motive force, a source of energy for society; she legitimised it. She almost legitimised poverty to give evidence to the fact that the poor were to blame for their poverty, the unemployed for their unemployment. She conveyed the impression that this wasn't a matter of great concern – that to make a concession in the direction of generosity would impede competitiveness and be a dreadful burden on the economy.'

Nigel (Lord) Lawson: 'There is some truth in her belief that she was a lineal successor of Churchill – although his challenges were infinitely greater. The United Kingdom during the 1970s was regarded with pity and derision, the sick man of Europe, the country with the most marvellous past and marvellous history but no future: a kind of museum economy – quaint and charming.

'The trade union law had to be changed so that they could do their proper job and not become an estate of the land, part of the government, wielding political power. We had to give people incentives, which meant bringing income tax down.'

Cecil (Lord) Parkinson: 'In retrospect, I think she will be seen as the person who rooted socialism out of the economy, put the unions into a proper perspective and set the economy firmly on the right lines.'

Matthew Parris: 'She will be seen as an important late-20th-century Prime Minister. My guess is that she will be seen as the most important.'

Sir Chris Patten: 'I certainly believe that Margaret Thatcher will be regarded as one of the most successful prime ministers of Britain. She made Britain governable again. She laid the foundations for a modern market economy in Britain. The terrible paradox is that she helped to save the country but helped to throw the Conservative Party into turmoil for years.'

Sir Charles Powell cites the end of the Cold War, getting 'our money' back in Europe and the Falklands. 'What counts for me was that she made Britain count again, first in its own eyes, then in the eyes of the rest of the world.'

James (Lord) Prior: 'Strangely enough her legacy to the country will be more important and a greater asset than her legacy to the Conservative Party – she damaged it quite a bit, but I think the things she did for the country desperately needed doing . . . She left Mr Blair a pretty good legacy. She was tiresome to work with for someone with my own point of view but I think that history will speak highly of her.'

On the legacy of this determined woman, the verdict is in, and unanimous. She saved her country but ruined her party; the unhealing division within the party over Europe is proving almost fatal. She was incontestably one of the most important British prime ministers of the second half of the twentieth century, and arguably the most influential.

She has never recovered from the blow she suffered at the hands of her own party. Former President George Bush remembers her telling him sadly, 'I miss it, I wish I were there!' To Charles Powell, she is as strong in her belief now as she was in

1990 that she was betrayed by her colleagues and that she would have won the 1992 election. He dismisses the conspiracy theory: 'It was three hundred Conservative MPs in a state of extreme dither who got rid of Margaret Thatcher.'

To remind her of happier times past, every year at Christmastime, Powell and Bernard Ingham take her out to lunch: 'And we have a very jolly time. Traditionally, towards the end of lunch, she announces that it's time we link arms, march back up Whitehall, through the gates of Number 10, take the place over and run the country properly.' Powell's sorry conclusion: 'I don't believe Margaret Thatcher's had a happy day since she ceased being prime minister.'

For a great many, it was a happy day when she stepped down. Yet love her or hate her – and her bifurcated persona validates both views – few could deny that the Grantham roots bore fruit. By changing national attitudes towards property, work and money, she made Methodists of us all.

Notes

CHAPTER 1

'Methodist means method'

1. Quoted in Patricia Murray,
   Margaret Thatcher: A Profile,
   p. 13.
2. *The Times*, 21 January 1936.
3. Murray, p. 15.
4. *Grantham Journal*, 2 June 1917.
5. Murray, p. 11.
6. Brook Lapping, archive footage,
   Maggie: The First Lady,
   Programme I.
7. Murray, p. 13.
8. Margaret Thatcher (hereafter
   referred to as MT), *The Path
   to Power*, p. 17.
9. Ibid.
10. Murray, p. 13.
11. John Campbell, *Margaret
    Thatcher*: vol. 1: *The Grocer's
    Daughter*, p. 15.
12. Muriel Cullen, interview in
    Daily Telegraph, 13 February
    1975.
13. Quoted in Campbell, p. 5.
14. MT, *Path to Power*, p. 12.
15. Murray, p. 11.

16. MT interview with Miriam
    Stoppard, *Woman to Woman*,
    Yorkshire Television, 19
    November 1985.
17. Ibid.
18. *Grantham Journal*, 6 February
    1937, quoted in Campbell,
    p. 37.

CHAPTER 2

Getting out of Grantham

1. MT, *Path to Power*, p. 17.
2. Rudyard Kipling, 'Recessional'.
3. *The Times*, 18 January 1936.
4. *The Times*, 20 January 1936.
5. MT, *Path to Power*, p. 18.
6. MT interview with Miriam
   Stoppard, *Woman to Woman*,
   Yorkshire Television, 19
   November 1985.
7. Brook Lapping, archive footage,
   Maggie: The First Lady,
   Programme I.
8. MT, *Path to Power*, p. 19.
9. MT, *Path to Power*, p. 13.
10. MT, *Path to Power*, p. 10.
11. Murray, p. 22.

12. Ibid.
13. Diana Honeybone, conversation with Brenda Maddox (hereafter referred to as BM), 18 July 2002.
14. Hilary Hillier, conversation with BM, 11 June 2002.
15. Ibid..
16. D. H. Lawrence to Louise Burrows, 7 October 1908, *Letters of D. H. Lawrence*, vol. 1, pp. 78–9.
17. MT, *Path to Power*, p. 11.
18. Brook Lapping, archive footage, *Maggie: The First Lady*, Programme I.

CHAPTER 3
Crystal-clear Conservative

1. Ruth Clayton, conversation with BM, 7 October 2002.
2. Pauline Cowan Harrison, conversation with BM, 20 September 2002.
3. Ibid.
4. Nicholas Wapshott and George Brock, *Thatcher*, p. 46.
5. Nina Bawden, *My Oxford*, p. 76.
6. Bawden, pp. 76–7.
7. Hazel Bishop Hofman, conversation with BM, 9 October 2002.
8. MT, *Path to Power*, p. 41.
9. Jane Howard, *Margaret Mead: A Life*, p. 239.

10. MT, *Path to Power*, p. 38.
11. MT, *Path to Power*, p. 13.
12. Peter Conradi, *Life of Iris Murdoch*, p. 211.
13. Roy Jenkins, *Churchill*, pp. 841–2.
14. Penny Junor, *Margaret Thatcher*, p. 20.
15. Quoted in Campbell, p. 58.
16. Ibid.
17. MT, *Path to Power*, p. 48.
18. MT, *Path to Power*, pp. 50–1.
19. Quoted in MT, *Path to Power*, p. 52.
20. MT, *Path to Power*, p. 39.
21. Georgina Ferry, *Dorothy Hodgkin*, pp. 228–9.
22. Ferry, p. 320.
23. Hugo Young and Anne Slocum, *The Thatcher Phenomenon*, p. 17.
24. Ibid.
25. Pauline Cowan Harrison, conversation with BM, 20 September 2002.

CHAPTER 4
The Joy of Kent

1. Carol Thatcher, *Below the Parapet: The Biography of Denis Thatcher*, p. 58.
2. *Erith Observer*, 17 February 1950, quoted in Campbell, p. 80.
3. MT, *Path to Power*, pp. 74–5.

4. Carol Thatcher, p. 63.
5. Quoted in Campbell, p. 84.
6. MT, *Path to Power*, p. 75.
7. Carol Thatcher, p. 64.
8. Carol Thatcher, p. 54.
9. Carol Thatcher, p. 60.

CHAPTER 5
Having It All

1. Carol Thatcher, p. 64.
2. MT, *Path to Power*, p. 76.
3. Carol Thatcher, p. 66.
4. George Gardiner, *Margaret Thatcher: From Childhood to Leadership*, p. 51.
5. MT, *Path to Power*, p. 77.
6. Carol Thatcher, p. 76.
7. MT, *Path to Power*, p. 21.
8. MT, *Path to Power*, p. 78.
9. Carol Thatcher, p. 69.
10. MT, *Path to Power*, p. 81.
11. 'Wake Up, Women!', *Sunday Graphic*, 17 February 1952.
12. Ann Dally, *A Doctor's Story*, London, Macmillan, 1990, pp. 9–10.
13. Carol Thatcher, p. 70.
14. MT, *Path to Power*, p. 85.
15. Carol Thatcher, p. 71.
16. Ibid.
17. Campbell, p. 22.
18. MT, *Path to Power*, p. 88.
19. MT, *Path to Power*, p. 82.
20. Carol Thatcher, p. 78.

21. MT, *Path to Power*, p. 82.
22. *Evening News*, 9 October 1959, quoted in Campbell, p. 124.

CHAPTER 6
A *Woman*? The *Tories*?

1. MT, *Path to Power*, p. 111.
2. Campbell, pp. 128–9.
3. Quoted in Campbell, p. 134.
4. MT, *Path to Power*, p. 113.
5. MT, *Path to Power*, pp. 106–7.
6. MT interview with Miriam Stoppard, *Woman to Woman*, Yorkshire Television, 19 November 1985.
7. Carol Thatcher, p. 91.
8. Ibid.
9. Campbell, p. 158.
10. Carol Thatcher, p. 2.
11. MT, *Path to Power*, p. 138.
12. Wapshott and Brock, p. 63.
13. *Sunday Times*, 5 March 1967, quoted in Campbell, p. 175.
14. Campbell, p. 162.
15. Ibid.
16. Carol Thatcher, p. 53.
17. Young and Slocum, p. 22.
18. Mark Hollingsworth, conversation with BM, 25 January 2003.
19. *Times Higher Education Supplement*, 22 February 1974.
20. David McKittrick, *The Nervous Peace*, p. 76.

21. Andy Beckett, *Pinochet in Piccadilly: Britain and Chile's Hidden History*, p. 198.
22. MT, *Path to Power*, p. 266.
23. Ibid.
24. Edward du Cann, *Two Lives: The Political and Business Careers of Edward du Cann*, p. 163.
25. Campbell, p. 291, n. 114.
26. Campbell, p. 299.
27. Brook Lapping, archive footage, 4 February 1975.
28. Callaghan's quote repeated by Cecil Parkinson in Brook Lapping, archive footage, *Maggie: The First Lady*, Programme II.

CHAPTER 7
Stepping to the Right

1. Brook Lapping, archive footage, *Maggie: The First Lady*, Programme II.
2. MT, *Path to Power*, p. 251.
3. Ronald Higgins, conversation with BM, 2002.
4. Quoted in Hugo Young, *One of Us: A Biography of Margaret Thatcher*, p. 169.
5. MT, *Path to Power*, p. 372.
6. MT, *Path to Power*, p. 308.
7. Ronald Millar, *A View from the Wings*, p. 240.

8. Campbell, p. 124n.
9. Obituary of Sir George Gardiner, *The Times*, 18 November 2002.
10. Garret FitzGerald, *All in a Life*, p. 38.
11. Millar, p. 219.
12. MT in conversation with Michael Aspel, LWT, July 1984.
13. *Daily Telegraph*, 5 February 1975.
14. Jane Reed, conversation with BM, 2 August 2002.
15. Terry Keane, in her Irish *Sunday Independent* column, frequently made this gibe about Irish President Mary Robinson in the 1990s.
16. MT, *Path to Power*, p. 361; Beckett, p. 188.
17. MT, *Path to Power*, p. 362.
18. Campbell, p. 354, quoting a speech given in Finchley, 31 January 1976.
19. Carol Thatcher, p. 236.
20. Sue MacGregor, *Woman of Today*, p. 177.
21. MacGregor, p. 181.
22. Matthew Parris, *Chance Witness: An Outsider's Life in Politics*, excerpted in *The Times*, 23 September 2002.
23. Young, p. 113.
24. 'No experience needed',

Anthony Harris, *Financial Times*, 29 August 1975.

25. Quoted in Campbell, p. 393.
26. Quoted in Young, p. 147.
27. *World in Action*, 27 January 1978.
28. John Cole, *As It Seemed to Me*, p. 189.
29. Millar, p. 261.

CHAPTER 8
No Gain without Pain

1. MT, *The Downing Street Years*, p. 21.
2. MT in conversation with Michael Aspel, 21 July 1984; Brook Lapping, archive footage.
3. Bernard Ingham, *Kill the Messenger*, p. 168.
4. Ingham, p. 170.
5. Carol Thatcher, p. 133.
6. Quoted in Young, p. 7.
7. MT, *The Downing Street Years*, p. 90.
8. Ibid.
9. Brook Lapping, archive footage, *Maggie: The First Lady*, Programme III.
10. Andrew Thomson, *Margaret Thatcher: The Woman Within*, pp. 68–9.
11. Thomson, p. 70.
12. MT, *The Downing Street Years*, p. 385.

13. Young, p. 239.
14. *Independent on Sunday*, 23 September 2002, p. 16.
15. John Hoskyns, *Just in Time: Inside the Thatcher Revolution*, pp. 315–16.
16. Ibid.
17. Hoskyns, p. 303.
18. Ibid.
19. Quoted in Carol Thatcher, p. 173.
20. Young, p. 242.
21. Carol Thatcher, p. 146.
22. Bruce Arnold, *Margaret Thatcher: A Study in Leadership*, p. 239.
23. Paul Halloran and Mark Hollingsworth, *Thatcher's Gold: The Life and Times of Mark Thatcher*, p. 67.
24. Thomas, p. 24.

CHAPTER 9
Finest Hours

1. Lord Carrington, *Reflections on Things Past: The Memoirs of Lord Carrington*, p. 370.
2. Young, p. 266.
3. MT, *The Downing Street Years*, p. 208.
4. Brook Lapping, archive footage, *Maggie: The First Lady*, Programme III.
5. Ibid.
6. Ibid.

7. Ibid.
8. Cole, *As It Seemed to Me*, p. 190.
9. Barnett and Curry, *The Battle for the BBC*, p. 39.
10. Cecil Parkinson's comment to a journalist, reported in Young, p. 343.
11. MT, *The Downing Street Years*, p. 307.
12. Brook Lapping, archive footage, *Maggie: The First Lady*, Programme III.
13. MT, *The Downing Street Years*, p. 382.
14. Brook Lapping, archive footage, *Maggie: The First Lady*, Programme III.

CHAPTER 10

Not a Hair out of Place

1. Lisa Armstrong, 'Hirsute you, Mr President', *The Times*, T2, 19 July 2002, p. 8.
2. Ingham, p. 310.
3. MT, *The Downing Street Years*, p. 435.
4. Alan Clark, *Diaries*, p. 135.
5. Ibid.
6. Cole, p. 282.
7. Clark, p. 150.
8. *Spectator*, 24 November 1984.
9. Leo Abse, *Margaret, Daughter of Beatrice: A Politician's Psycho-Biography of Margaret Thatcher*, p. 210.
10. MT, *Downing Street Years*, p. 419.
11. Ibid.
12. Junor, p. 151.
13. Thomson, p. 22.
14. Carol Thatcher, p. 130.
15. Carol Thatcher, p. 131.
16. Brook Lapping, archive footage, *Maggie: The First-Lady*, Programme III.
17. Ferry, p. 375.
18. Ibid., p. 358.
19. Ibid.
20. Millar, p. 314.

CHAPTER 11

The Road to Dulwich

1. Garret FitzGerald, conversation with BM, 11 February 2003.
2. Max Hastings, *Editor: An Inside Story of Newspapers*, pp. 59–60.
3. Sir Peregrine Worsthorne, conversation with BM, 6 January 2003.
4. Clark, p. 195.
5. Quoted in Young, p. 187.
6. MT, *Downing Street Years*, p. 743.
7. *Sunday Times*, 8 May 1988.
8. MT, *Downing Street Years*, p. 755.

9. Nigel Lawson, *The View from No. 11: Memoirs of a Tory Radical*, p. 921.
10. MT, *Downing Street Years*, p. 791.
11. Ibid.
12. Clark, *Diaries*, pp. 276–7.
13. Clark, p. 288.
14. Clark, p. 289.
15. Brook Lapping, archive footage, *Maggie: The First Lady*, Programme IV.
16. MT, *Downing Street Years*, p. 800.
17. Halloran and Hollingsworth, p. 250.
18. MT, *Downing Street Years*, p. 765.
19. MT, *Downing Street Years*, p. 833; House of Commons television coverage.
20. Carol Thatcher, p. 263.
21. Ibid.
22. John Sergeant, speech to the Broadcasting Press Guild, accepting an award for the best outside broadcast of 1990, 12 April 1991.
23. MT, *Downing Street Years*, p. 846.
24. Clark, p. 366.
25. Ibid.
26. Hansard, 22 November 1990, vol. 181, col. 451.
27. Clark, p. 368.
28. Hansard, 22 November 1990, vol. 181, cols. 454–5.
29. Brook Lapping, interview with Crawford and others, gives no information about the actual content of the injection.
30. Clark, p. 369.
31. John Major, *John Major: The Autobiography*, p. 200.

CHAPTER 12

Life After Work

1. MT, *The Path to Power*, p. 466.
2. Halloran and Hollingsworth, p. 249.
3. Halloran and Hollingsworth, p. 246.
4. MT, *Path to Power*, p. 475.
5. Major, p. 215.
6. Major, p. 214.
7. Major, p. 200.
8. Major, p. 361.
9. Major, p. 613.
10. Brook Lapping, archive footage, 18 June 1997.
11. The event is well described in Andy Beckett, *Pinochet in Piccadilly*, p. 221.
12. MT, letter to *The Times*, 22 October 1998.
13. Beckett, p. 235.
14. Beckett, p. 239.

15. 'Lady Thatcher Gives Armada Plate', *The Times*, 5 March 2000.

16. Paul Bonner and Lesley Aston, *Independent Television in Britain*, vol. 6: *New Developments in Independent Television, 1981–92: Channel 4, TV-am, Cable and Satellite*, p. 379.

17. Matthew Parris, *The Times*, 23 September 2002.

18. Warwick Gould to BM, 17 November 2002.

Bibliography

The place of publication is London unless stated otherwise.

Abse, Leo, *Margaret, Daughter of Beatrice: A Politician's Psycho-Biography of Margaret Thatcher*, Jonathan Cape, 1989.

Anderson, Oliver, *Rotten Borough: The Real Story of Mrs Thatcher's Grantham*, Fourth Estate, 1989, reprint of Ivor Nicholson & Watson, 1937 edition, with subtitle.

Arnold, Bruce, *Margaret Thatcher: A Study in Leadership*, Hamish Hamilton, 1984.

Atkinson, Max, *Our Masters' Voices*, 1984, p. 113.

Barnett, Steven and Curry, Andrew, *The Battle for the BBC*, Aurum Press, 1994.

Bawden, Nina, *In My Own Time*, Virago, 1994.

Beckett, Andy, *Pinochet in Piccadilly: Britain and Chile's Hidden History*, Faber & Faber, 2002.

Bonner, Paul and Aston, Lesley, *Independent Television in Britain*, vol. 6: *New Developments in Independent Television, 1981–92: Channel 4, TV-am, Cable and Satellite*, Palgrave Macmillan, 2003.

Campbell, John, *Margaret Thatcher*, vol. 1: *The Grocer's Daughter*, Pimlico paperback 2001; first published Jonathan Cape, 2000.

Carrington, Lord, *Reflections on Things Past: The Memoirs of Lord Carrington*, Fontana/Collins, 1989.

Clark, Alan, *Diaries*, Weidenfeld & Nicolson, 1993.

Cole, John, *As It Seemed to Me*, Weidenfeld & Nicolson, 1995.

Conradi, Peter, *Life of Iris Murdoch*, HarperCollins, 2001.

Currie, Edwina, *The Edwina Currie Diaries 1987–1992*, Little, Brown, 2002.

du Cann, Edward, *Two Lives: The Political and Business Careers of Edward du Cann*, Upton upon Severn, Images Publishing, 1995.

Ferry, Georgina, *Dorothy Hodgkin: A Life*, Granta Books, 1998.

——, *A Computer Called LEO*, Fourth Estate, 2003.

FitzGerald, Garret, *All in a Life*, Macmillan, 1991.

——, *Reflections on the Irish State*, Dublin, Irish Academic Press, 2003.

Gardiner, George, *Margaret Thatcher: From Childhood to Leadership*, William Kimber, 1975.

Halloran, Paul and Hollingsworth, Mark, *Thatcher's Gold: The Life and Times of Mark Thatcher*, Simon & Schuster, 1995.

Hastings, Max, *Editor: An Inside Story of Newspapers*, Macmillan, 2002.

Healey, Denis, *The Times of My Life*, Penguin, 1990; first published Michael Joseph, 1989.

Hollingsworth, Mark, *The Ultimate Spin Doctor: The Life and Fast Times of Tim Bell*, Coronet paperback, 1997; first published Hodder & Stoughton, 1997.

Honeybone, Michael, *The Book of Grantham 1980*, Buckingham, Barracuda, 1980.

Hoskyns, John, *Just in Time: Inside the Thatcher Revolution*, Aurum Press, 2000.

Howard, Jane, *Margaret Mead: A Life*, Harvill Press, 1984.

Ingham, Bernard, *Kill the Messenger*, HarperCollins, 1991.

Jenkins, Peter, *Mrs Thatcher's Revolution: The Ending of the Socialist Era*, Jonathan Cape, 1987.

Jenkins, Roy, *Churchill*, Macmillan, 2001.

Junor, Penny, *Margaret Thatcher: Wife, Mother, Politician*, Sidgwick & Jackson, 1983.

Keegan, William, *Mrs Thatcher's Economic Experiment*, Allen Lane, 1984; Penguin paperback 1984 (reprinted twice with a second postscript) 1985.

Lawson, Nigel, *The View from No. 11: Memoirs of a Tory Radical*, Corgi paperback, 1993; first published Bantam Press, 1992.

MacGregor, Sue, *Woman of Today*, Headline, 2002.

Bibliography

McKittrick, David, *The Nervous Peace*, Belfast, The Blackstaff Press, 1996.

Major, John, *John Major: The Autobiography*, HarperCollins, 1999.

Millar, Ronald, *A View from the Wings*, Weidenfeld & Nicolson, 1993.

Murray, Patricia, *Margaret Thatcher: A Profile*, W. H. Allen, 1980 (new and revised edition).

Ogden, Chris, *Maggie*, New York, Simon & Schuster, 1990.

Parris, Matthew, *Chance Witness: An Outsider's Life in Politics*, Penguin Viking, 2002.

Pevsner, Nikolaus, *Lincolnshire (Buildings of England)*, Penguin, 1964.

Sampson, Anthony, *The Essential Anatomy of Britain: Democracy in Crisis*, Hodder & Stoughton, 1992.

Sheppard, David, *Steps Along Hope Street: My Life in Liverpool and London*, Hodder & Stoughton, 2002.

St John Stevas, Norman, *The Two Cities*, Faber & Faber, 1984.

Taylor, Andrew, 'The "Stepping Stones" Programme: Conservative Party Thinking on Trade Unions, 1975–9', Keele University Centre for Industrial Relations, *Historical Studies in Industrial Relations*, no. 11, Spring 2001, 109–33.

Thatcher, Carol, *Below the Parapet: The Biography of Denis Thatcher*, HarperCollins, 1996.

Thatcher, Margaret, *The Downing Street Years*, HarperCollins, 1993.

——, *The Path to Power*, HarperCollins, 1995.

Thomson, Andrew, *Margaret Thatcher: The Woman Within*, W. H. Allen, 1989.

Tyler, Rodney, *Campaign: The Selling of the Prime Minister*, Grafton Books, 1987.

Wapshott, Nicholas and Brock, George, *Thatcher*, Futura, 1983; first published Macmillan, 1983.

Young, Hugo, *One of Us: A Biography of Margaret Thatcher*, Macmillan, 1989.

Young, Hugo and Slocum, Anne, *The Thatcher Phenomenon*, BBC Books, 1986.

Index

MT refers to Margaret Thatcher; D refers to Denis Thatcher
Generally, titles have not been given

Kipling, Rudyard 15, 21, 135,
174
Kohl, Helmut 202, 207
Kuwait: invasion by Iraq 210–11

Labour Club, Oxford 29–30
Labour Party 34, 40, 80, 82, 84,
91–3, 195; Kinnock purges
hard left 183; Sheffield rally
(1992) 225; Blair wins
general election (1997) 225
Lady's Not for Burning, The
(Fry) 132
Laing, Hector 143
Lamb, Larry 118
Lamont, Norman 218
Land-Rover 184
Lapping, Anne xvi–xvii
Lapping, Brook: *Maggie: The
First Lady* (TV) xv, xviii;
MT and Tory old guard
125; MT as host 129; Howe
Budget (1981) 134; MT as
honorary man 140;
Falklands war 152; miners'
strike (1984) 159–60, 166;
Brighton bomb 162; MT's
simplistic convictions 174;
MT's dress sense 191;
general election (1987) 194
Larkin, Philip 80
Lawrence, D. H.: birthplace
xviii, 22
Lawson, Nigel xv, 133, 138, 169,
212: becomes Chancellor of

Exchequer 158; Westland
affair 176–80, 187; MT and
ERM split 181, 203–4, 205;
opposition to community
charge (poll tax) 183;
Walters's unwelcome
involvement 204; meets MT
with Howe 204; resigns
(1989) 205–6; comment on
MT's premiership 232; *see
also* economic affairs
Lawton, Frederick 61
Leach, Henry 147
Lenzerheide (Switzerland):
Thatcher family holidays
78–9
Lewes Police College: Brighton
bomb (1984) 164
Lewin, Terence 153
Liberal Party 69, 70, 72, 157,
195
Liberty 189
Lib–Lab pact (1977) 116, 117
Libya, bombing of (1986) 184
Liverpool, Lord 203
Lloyds Bank 176–7
Lonrho (company) 95–6

Maastricht Treaty (1992/3)
222–3, 224
MacGregor, Sue 113–14
Macleod, Iain 83
Macmillan, Harold 64, 70–1, 74,
99, 149, 191
Maddox, Brenda xv–xix